RENEWALS 45
DATE DUE

GAYLORD			PRINTED IN U.S.A.

BEYOND THE
FINAL SCORE

· · · · · · · · · · · · · · · ·

CONTEMPORARY ASIA IN THE WORLD

CONTEMPORARY ASIA IN THE WORLD

David C. Kang and Victor D. Cha, Editors

This series aims to address a gap in the public-policy and scholarly discussion of Asia. It seeks to promote books and studies that are on the cutting edge of their respective disciplines or in the promotion of multidisciplinary or inter-disciplinary research but that are also accessible to a wider readership. The editors seek to showcase the best scholarly and public-policy arguments on Asia from any field, including politics, history, economics, and cultural studies.

BEYOND THE FINAL SCORE

THE POLITICS OF SPORT
• • • IN ASIA • • •

VICTOR D. CHA

COLUMBIA UNIVERSITY PRESS   NEW YORK

Columbia University Press

Publishers Since 1893

New York   Chichester, West Sussex

Copyright © 2009 Columbia University Press

All rights reserved

A Caravan book. For more information, visit www.caravanbooks.org.

Library of Congress Cataloging-in-Publication Data

Cha, Victor D., 1961–

Beyond the final score : the politics of sport in Asia / Victor D. Cha

p.   cm. — (Contemporary asia in the world)

Includes bibliographical references and index.

ISBN 978-0-231-15490-1 (cloth : alk. paper) — ISBN 978-0-231-51929-8 (e-book)

1. Sports—Asia—History. 2. Sports—Political aspects—Asia.

3. Olympics—Political aspects—Asia. 4. Olympic Games (29th : 2008 : Beijing, China)

I. Title. II. Series.

GV649.C43   2009

796.095—dc22

2008023579

Columbia University Press books are printed on permanent and durable acid-free paper.

This book is printed on paper with recycled content.

Printed in the United States of America

c 10 9 8 7 6 5 4 3 2 1

References to Internet Web sites (URLs) were accurate at the time of writing. Neither the author nor Columbia University Press is responsible for URLs that may have expired or changed since the manuscript was prepared.

To the memory of my father, Moon Young Cha
1934–2005
An eternal Columbian (GS '59, MBA '61)

● ● ●

CONTENTS

FIGURES AND TABLES

FIGURES

TABLES

PREFACE

This is a book that I have wanted to write for the past ten years or so. It was one of those projects where one keeps a folder as one comes across different articles, citations, and stories with the intention one day to write it all up.

The inspiration for the book came from a trip I took to Indonesia and Australia as part of the delegation of a former Stanford colleague, Secretary of State Condoleezza Rice. Over one of the informal dinners with the traveling press corps, the conversation turned to sport, and she completely floored me with her encyclopedic knowledge of professional sports (particularly the Cleveland Browns). If someone this important knew that much about sport, I thought, then it has to matter in politics in some fashion.

So when I left the White House in May 2007 after serving since 2004 on the National Security Council as a director of Asian affairs, I believed this would be the perfect time to take up the task. It would also be a good way to deal with "policy withdrawal"—that is, when the adrenalin rush of fifteen-to-sixteen hour days and seven-day weeks at the NSC is replaced by the sinking feeling that you no longer know tomorrow's news today.

I began reading up on the topic from the day after I left the White House compound and planned a course, "Cultural Diplomacy in Asia," for the fall 2007 semester at Georgetown, around the readings. In part, time pressures were severe because I left government about eight months later than I had originally planned and also because I wanted to get the book out around the time of the Beijing Olympics.

I am indebted to many people and institutions for their help in bringing this project to completion. My students in the Cultural Diplomacy class were wonderful sounding boards for the readings and for their different observations and stories. Portions of the project were presented at the Institute for International and Strategic Studies in London, the School for Oriental and

African Studies, Harvard University's Asia Center, Stanford University, the Center for Strategic and International Studies, and Georgetown University's Mortara Center for International Studies.

My longtime friend and colleague Dave Kang at Dartmouth has heard me talk of this project over the years and read chapters, offering his usual good advice and critical comments in his California-style good humor. Bob Jervis read earlier chapters, and his encouragement and opinions continue to matter to me more today than any other international relations scholar I know of. I continue to benefit from advice and discussions with Mike Green, my colleague in government and now at Georgetown, who understands the "theory-policy" nexus in Asia better than most. I am grateful to Dana Allin, Bob Gallucci, Fred Hiatt, Chris Hill, Jim Kelly, Abraham Kim, Christine Kim, Kate McNamara, Derek Mitchell, Andy Nathan, Tae-Gyun Park, Gary Quinlan, Leslie Vinjamuri, Erik Voeten, Ezra Vogel, Dennis Wilder, and two anonymous reviewers for their comments on the project.

Anne Routon is my editor at Columbia, and she is, quite simply, an author's dream. She kept me focused on the topic and on the timeline and encouraged me to write in a manner that was still scholarly but with resonance for a larger readership. Because of unexpected demands on my time for personal reasons, Anne took on an even larger role in shepherding the manuscript for which I am extremely grateful. Michael Haskell cleared his desk of many important projects in order to supervise both the manuscript and production editing for the book. The application of his skills to this work has made it infinitely better substantively and a much easier read.

My departure from government was not well timed in terms of the grant-giving calendar. Thus, I received no foundation support or research grants for this book. I worked with one part-time undergraduate research assistant, Taylor Fincher, who did a fantastic job in all aspects, from collecting press clippings to creating charts to doing outreach for interviews. He deserves much credit for the work.

My beloved wife, Hyun Jung, or "Honey," has been so very supportive of all of my work. My mother, Soon Ock Leem, and brother, Michael, have always been there for me with love and understanding. I dearly miss my father, Moon Young Cha, to whom this book is dedicated. This work would have benefited greatly from many interesting conversations with him, and without them, it is not nearly as good a piece of work.

In this book, there are many stories about the Olympics and the athletes that perform in them. My favorite athletes, however, are my sons Patrick (eleven) and Andrew (seven). Andrew is a sports buff, nicknamed the "vacuum cleaner" for his baseball fielding—so he was quite excited that Dad was writing a book about the topic.

Patrick plays in the Bethesda–Chevy Chase baseball, football, and basketball leagues. He has been sidelined as I write this book because of illness, but I look forward to seeing him back on the fields, contributing to his team's victories.

CHRONOLOGY OF THE MODERN OLYMPICS

VENUES OF THE SUMMER OLYMPICS

Year	Host City, Country, Notes
1896	Athens, Greece
1900	Paris, France
1904	St. Louis, Missouri, United States: Chicago original host, but Games relocated to St. Louis for World's Fair
1906	Athens, Greece: Intermediate games proposed to be held in Athens at two-year intervals; not counted as one of the Olympiads
1908	London, United Kingdom
1912	Stockholm, Sweden
1916	Berlin, Germany: Cancelled (World War I)
1920	Antwerp, Belgium
1924	Paris, France: Winter Games start this year in Chamonix, France
1928	Amsterdam, Netherlands
1932	Los Angeles, California, United States
1936	Berlin, Germany: Sailing events held in Kiel-Schilksee
1940	Helsinki, Finland: Original host was Tokyo; Games moved to Helsinki; cancelled (World War II)
1944	London, United Kingdom: Cancelled (World War II)
1948	London, United Kingdom
1952	Helsinki, Finland
1956	Melbourne, Victoria, Australia: Equestrian events held in Stockholm, Sweden
1960	Rome, Italy
1964	Tokyo, Japan
1968	Mexico City, Mexico
1972	Munich, Germany: Sailing events held in Kiel-Schilksee

1976	Montreal, Quebec, Canada
1980	Moscow, Soviet Union
1984	Los Angeles, California, United States
1988	Seoul, Republic of Korea
1992	Barcelona, Spain
1996	Atlanta, Georgia, United States
2000	Sydney, New South Wales, Australia
2004	Athens, Greece
2008	Beijing, China
2012	London, United Kingdom

VENUES OF THE WINTER OLYMPICS

Year	Host City, Country, Notes
1924	Chamonix, France
1928	St. Moritz, Switzerland
1932	Lake Placid, New York, United States
1936	Garmisch-Partenkirchen, Germany
1940	Garmisch-Partenkirchen, Germany: Sapporo, Japan original host; moved to St. Moritz; moved to Germany; cancelled (World War II)
1944	Cortina d'Ampezzo, Italy: Cancelled (World War II)
1948	St. Moritz, Switzerland
1952	Oslo, Norway
1956	Cortina d'Ampezzo, Italy
1960	Squaw Valley, California, United States
1964	Innsbruck, Austria
1968	Grenoble, France
1972	Sapporo, Japan
1976	Innsbruck, Austria
1980	Lake Placid, New York, United States
1984	Sarajevo, Yugoslavia
1988	Calgary, Alberta, Canada
1992	Albertville, France
1994	Lillehammer, Norway
1998	Nagano, Japan
2002	Salt Lake City, Utah, United States
2006	Turin, Italy
2010	Vancouver, British Columbia, Canada
2014	Sochi, Russia

BEYOND THE
FINAL SCORE

· · · · · · · · · · · · · · · · ·

1

PURISM VERSUS POLITICS

We've all done it with varying degrees of skill. It is a universal language and one of the world's oldest pastimes, one that in its perfect execution approximates an art form. No, this is not a book about sex. It is a book about sports, and in particular the politics of sports and world affairs.

Political science refers to sports as "an institutionalized competitive activity that involves vigorous physical exertion or the use of relatively complex physical skills by individuals whose participation is motivated by a combination of intrinsic and extrinsic factors . . . it is played under standardized conditions with strict limits of time and space. It has rules and stresses fair play, discipline and organization and professionalism."[1] We all know it in a simpler form as something that we started to play as kids and that many of us continue to play today. But how do we think about sports and its role in the world? This is a timely and relevant question given that in August 2008, the biggest country in the world hosted one of the world's biggest sporting events—the Beijing Olympics.

A trip to Beijing starts at the airport, where you taxi on the tarmac past a dragonlike structure recognized as the single largest terminal building in the world; it was constructed in preparation for the 2008 Olympic Games. On the expressway to Beijing, you whiz past thousands of saplings planted as part of a "million-tree" city-beautification and environment project. Cruising the city thoroughfares, one quickly loses count of the number of high-rise construction cranes amid gleaming new spires rising out of the rubble of demolished old "hutong" neighborhoods.

The pace and scale of Beijing's facelift is an awesome testament to how much the Olympics transforms the host city, but does this transformation go beyond concrete and glass to spurring changes in politics and society? More generally, how is sport related to a country's political development and its sense of nationhood? How has China sought to portray itself to the world with these Games? Do gleaming new buildings represent a new China, or are they merely a façade for old China? Do the Games mark China's rise as a responsible global power? Or might the Games be remembered as the "Smoglympics" for Beijing's suffocating air quality, or, as Mia Farrow termed it, the "genocide Olympics" for China's irresponsible policies in Darfur, or the "Saffron Olympics" for Beijing's coddling of the corrupt leadership in Burma?

These questions and others about the significance of sports in international affairs will be the topic of this book. Its arguments do not represent new breakthroughs in political science; rather, I attempt merely to offer a systematic way of thinking about how sports and the Olympics matter in world politics. There has been surprisingly little written about this even though countries have gone to war over sport and fought for sovereign recognition through sport, and it is a daily part of the lives of citizens around the world. Indeed it is astounding that a phenomenon that matters so much has been so little studied by a field that purports to explain relations among states and human beings around the world.

THE ARGUMENT

The study of international relations purports to understand why states go to war, how nations negotiate, how economies become interdependent through trade, and other phenomena, including the effects of nationalism, nongovernmental actors, and terrorism on states. In this regard, I make three basic arguments about sport. First, sport matters in world politics because it can create diplomatic breakthroughs (or breakdowns) in ways unanticipated by regular diplomacy. Just as a small white ping-pong ball promoted a thaw in relations between the United States and China, sport helped to end the Cold War in Asia and remains a unique instrument of diplomacy, building goodwill in a region of the world that lacks this commodity.

Second, sport is an unmistakable prism through which nation-states project their image to the world and to their own people. Sport creates emotion on a broader scale that is not replicated by any other form, such as music, art, or even politics. There is little else that can inspire as much emotion and pride among countrymen as the victory of an athlete or team garbed in national colors. In some instances, sport is critical to the process of independence and nation building. Conversely, poor performance in sport can render negative images of national identity and self-worth beyond anything imagined by politics.

Third, sport can be a facilitator of change within a country. This change is certainly physical in the sense that cities, particularly in Asia, that have hosted major sporting events like the Olympics have experienced a rapid transformation, with everything from new airports, to highway networks, to city skylines, to even a "toilet revolution" (adopting Western-style versions). But the change can also be political in some cases, playing a critical role in the democratization of a country, as occurred in South Korea with the 1988 Seoul Olympics.

Each of these arguments is extremely relevant to the 2008 Beijing Games. Beijing authorities portrayed these Games as China's "coming-out party" with two weeks of stellar athletic competition in iconic state-of-the-art facilities that showcased China's economic boom, all against the backdrop of her ancient and storied civilization. The medal performance of strong, fast, and tall Chinese athletes constituted a source of pride for 1.5 billion countrymen and marked the end of China's place as the "sick man" of Asia. The Games provided about as high-profile an international stage as possible for Beijing's crash course in environmental cleanup. But all the Chinese gold won at Beijing risks losing its luster without responsible Chinese behavior in policies related to human rights, Burma, Darfur, and Tibet. This is because Olympism is, in its purest form, a classical liberal ideal emphasizing freedom, effort, merit, and individual spirit and dignity. The world watches to see whether the vast change brought to China by its hosting the 2008 Games can have an impact on Beijing's domestic and foreign policies.

A conversation about sport necessarily begins with a general look at ways in which the worlds of sport and politics have collided either by design or by chance, much to the consternation of sports "purists." I look at why sport might matter more in Asian politics than in other parts of the world. In chapter 2, I then offer three arguments about the political effects of sport in terms of promoting diplomacy, amplifying national identities, and facilitating domestic and foreign policy change. In the remaining chapters, I illustrate these arguments with historical cases and with reference to the Beijing Olympics. Some of the cases are well known, such as Nixon and Kissinger's ping-pong diplomacy to open relations with China. Some are less well known, such as South Korea's quiet but successful use of sports diplomacy in conjunction with the 1988 Seoul Olympics and the 1990 Asian Olympiad to forge ties with China and the former Soviet Union at the end of the Cold War. And some are bizarre, such as Beijing's attempts before the Olympics to ban one million cars in three days from city streets to reduce pollution and to standardize the minimum number of smiling teeth that should be visible when Chinese ushers greeted their guests at the Games. I also include some anecdotes and personal observations regarding sports and diplomacy from my service at the White House on the National Security Council. The worlds of political science and policymaking tell us that sport cannot drive international relations on its own, and this is not what the book claims. But sport is a unique factor in world politics that can create opportunities that might not otherwise exist for policymakers. It can influence a government's behavior in ways that theories of political science might completely overlook. And it can create politically relevant cathartic experiences on a world scale that few other events can approximate. After reading this book, you will still love sports for its own sake, but you will hopefully gain an appreciation of how sport matters beyond the final score.

SPORT PURISM VERSUS POLITICS

Many would take umbrage at the political discussion of sport. For such "purists," sport may be many things, but it should not be political. As the former U.N. secretary-general Kofi Annan once described, sport is a global force acting as a common language extending across racial, religious, and social boundaries. The notion of sport as apolitical in the twentieth century is often associated with the Cold War era and, in particular, the liberalist backlash against the communist state's use of sport to demonstrate superiority over the West.[2] But the roots of sport purism go much deeper. Dating back to the ancient Greek Olympics in 776 b.c., sporting competitions offered a temporary reprieve from daily life for the purpose of developing and nourishing strong bodies and minds. Purists see sport as animating dreams and inspiring youth and cite the five Olympic rings, designed by Baron Pierre de Coubertin (founder of the modern Olympic movement) and adopted in 1913, as the single most widely known image, recognized by over 90 percent of the world's population today. The original Olympic Charter cautions strongly against the use of sport for political purposes and decries such use as dangerous to Olympic ideals. "Rule 51" of the modern charter is the core principle of sport purism, forbidding any form of political, racial, and political demonstration in any of the sites, events, venues or related areas by the athletes. After the first and second World Wars, the "Olympic Movement" symbolized the use of sport as an occasion for cultural exchange and promotion of international understanding. For purists, therefore, politics is anathema to sport, which should be valued intrinsically as a normative good. "Sports is too important," said Milan Zver, the Slovenian minister of sport and president of the European Union, "It is too

FIGURE 1. CLOSING CEREMONIES, ATHENS, 2004

SOURCE: © GEORGE TIEDEMANN / CORBIS.

important to use it as a political instrument."[3] In the words of former International Olympic Committee president Avery Brundage, politics is a "savage monster" always ready to ravage the Olympic movement.

Businessmen would argue that sport is not about politics but about making money. Sporting "mega-events" like the Olympics, Super Bowl, or World Cup have become multimedia global entertainment bonanzas financed by huge corporate-sponsorship deals. Just a taste of the numbers makes this aspect abundantly self-evident. Some 30 billion people viewed the 1994 World Cup, played in the United States, and corporations paid US$400 million to gain "official product" status. In preparation for the 2002 World Cup, cohosts Japan and Korea had public- and private-sector contributions in the range of $4 billion to build seventeen new stadiums and related facilities. FIFA sold the broadcast rights for $800 million.[4] The Olympic numbers are staggering. In 1960, the Rome Games cost about $50 million, and the Moscow Games two decades later cost about $2 billion. The 2004 Athens Games cost a record $11 billion. The budget for the 2008 Beijing Games is estimated at $40 billion, and that's before cost overruns. ABC paid only $25 million to broadcast the Montreal Olympics in 1976, and NBC paid $87 million for the

Moscow Games in 1980. More recently, NBC paid $456 million for rights to the 1996 Atlanta Games and, in one of the largest deals in television history, paid $3.5 billion for televised rights to the Summer Olympics through 2008 (Sydney, Athens, and Beijing).[5] Once Beijing was given the Games, Fortune 500 companies like General Electric, Nortel, Boeing, Kodak, Walmart, and others flocked to Beijing. Visa, McDonalds, Coca-Cola, General Electric, and others paid some $19 billion to Beijing organizers and the IOC to be partners, sponsors, and licensees.[6] Adidas reportedly paid $80 million to be an official Olympic sponsor, which only appears small when compared to the company's aspirations to hit the $1 billion annual sales mark in 2008. Its competitor Nike opened on average two new stores a day in China in the run-up to the Olympics.[7] Many major American companies landed deals associated with the Olympics that establish a foothold in the world's largest market. Otis Elevator Company did $100 million worth of deals installing elevators in Beijing's new subway stations. Johnson and Johnson augmented its position in China by sponsoring a triage and medical-training center for Chinese medical personnel to treat athletes and spectators during the Games. United Parcel Service, another corporate sponsor for the Games, marshaled the huge logistics center for the Games. ITT won $10 million in contracts for water pumps and water-treatment systems for the Olympic stadium and kayaking course and expected its annual $500 million in revenue in China to grow by 20 percent. General Electric provided the ultrasound equipment, power, lighting, and security systems for the Olympic sites, Beijing airport, and the subways and expects to double its $5 billion revenue in China by 2010. Morrison and Foerster, a San Francisco law firm with experience from the Winter Games in Salt Lake City, succeeded over 120 other competing firms to become the legal counsel for the Beijing Olympic Organizing Committee.[8] American corporations estimate that the emerging consumer middle class in China is basically the size of the entire U.S. population. That's a demographic that's hard to ignore. Gaining a foothold through the Olympics ensures incredible revenues for the next quarter-century, at least. Sport is undeniably about business, and some would even argue that the latter drives the former. It's no wonder that some surmise that the strong desire of large corporations to gain entry to the Chinese market influenced the IOC's decision to give the Games to Beijing.[9]

Corporate receptivity to the notion of boycotting the Games was unsurprisingly low. The Olympics is probably the single biggest advertising opportunity on the planet. Ninety percent of the world population with access to a television will watch part of the Games. The discussion at Warren Buffett's annual shareholder meeting in Omaha, Nebraska, in 2008 summed up the situation. When asked about the Beijing Games, Buffett and his associate Charlie Munger made clear that corporations do not see the Olympics as an opportunity to render punitive political judgments. In China's case, especially, the overall direction of the country over the past two decades has been positive; thus the Games should engender more encouragement, not sanctioning.

In spite of the purists' view, there is no denying that sport, particularly international sport, is political. The irony of Brundage's remark about keeping politics out of sport is that it was hardly apolitical. He made it, as IOC vice president, in the context of defending the decision to allow the Nazi regime to host the 1936 Olympic Games. Even in defense of purism, statements about sport are political.

TRUCES

There are many ways to think about the link between sport and politics, and undoubtedly numerous examples spring to mind. But let us narrow these down to a few initial observations. One example is the link between sport and political truces. The historical practice of sport can have a pacific effect among peoples. At the first Olympic festival of the ancient games in the ninth century b.c., the "Olympic truce" or "ekecheiria" was established by signature treaty of three kings, Iphistos of Elis, Cleosthenes of Pisa, and Lycurgus of Sparta, in which all hostilities would stop and the civilized world would come together while the games were played.[10] During the truce periods, athletes and citizens could travel in safety to participate or to view the Games. In medieval Europe as well as in ancient Chinese civilizations, sport was used as a means to subdue conflict even temporarily.[11] The modern version of this is the temporary reprieve from ongoing domestic or international tensions that sport sometimes offers. The French national football team's performance in the 1998 World Cup, for example, came at a time of deep ethnic difficulties and offered a welcome, though brief, moment of unity for the country. In 2000, the two Koreas entering the Olympic Stadium in Sydney, Australia, together as one team was arguably the highlight of the opening ceremony as it gave the world a moment to imagine through sport an end to the Cold War in Korea and a unified country. The victory of the Iraqi football team, composed of Sunni and Shiite players, at the July 2007 Asian World Cup offered a moment of unity for all sects to enjoy amid a deteriorating civil order at home. In Africa, where state failure and warfare are common, football offers a momentary bridge between populations.[12] Playing together creates a temporary truce at a minimum and, at best, a richness of possibilities that people can entertain on the field but not in the political arena.

CONDUIT FOR CONFLICT

Sport can also be a prism through which political conflict is refracted. Rather than creating a truce, sport's pacifying effects can be manipulated by elites to divert the attention of the masses away from political or socioeconomic problems. Sport has been used by elites to captivate their political subjects, ensure acquiescence, and subvert rebellions.[13] Similarly, Marxism interprets the role of sport in capitalist societies to be the diversion of workers' attention away from forming class consciousness.

George Orwell in a famous essay in 1945 described sport as "war minus the shooting."[14] While this is a bit of an exaggeration, sport often can become a conduit for conflict and a release valve for simmering historical animosities. For example, when the Soviet Union and Hungary met in the semifinals of men's water polo at 1956 Melbourne Olympics, they did so in the wake of the Soviet invasion of Hungary. The match, which became known as the "Blood in the Water" match, was about more than goals. Though Hungary won decisively 4 to 0, a brawl ensued when a Soviet player head-butted a Hungarian opponent, and both teams and their fans emptied the benches and bleachers in the melee. In 2004, Japan and China met in the finals of the Asian Football Cup. For the Chinese, a victory over Japan, their former colonizer, was not just a matter of sport, but a matter of historical redemption. When the Japanese team won 3 to 1, angry Chinese crowds threw soda bottles at the Japanese players as they tried to leave the pitch and broke the car windows of Japanese diplomats and VIPs. Japanese fans in the stands escaped the angry mob by running on to the field, where they had to be protected by security police. The Chinese authorities provided additional protection to the Japanese embassy after the match as crowds gathered demanding that Japan "apologize" (presumably for past historical transgressions, not for winning the football match). All this from a football match? As one observer noted, this was more than just hooliganism; it was politics and sport mixing in the worst way.[15]

Perhaps the most well known case of sport and interstate conflict is the "soccer war" between El Salvador and Honduras in 1969. Relations between the two neighbors had been far from ideal as Salvadorans chafed at attempts by the Honduran government to enact land-reform legislation that would discriminate against Salvadoran immigrants escaping their government and seeking better employment opportunities in the relatively richer Honduran economy. Against this political backdrop, the two countries competed in the qualifying rounds for the FIFA World Cup. The first qualifying game took place in Honduras with the home team victorious. The second qualifying match took place in San Salvador with a Salvadoran victory, but after the match riots broke out with home-team fans attacking the visiting Hondurans as they retreated from the stadium. The rioting was reported back in Honduras where Hondurans retaliated by attacking Salvadoran immigrants, eliciting protests that Honduras was engaging in anti-Salvadoran pogroms. Amid these high emotions, the third and tie-breaking match took place in June 1969, which El Salvador won in a gripping 3 to 2 shootout. In the same month, the government of San Salvador broke diplomatic ties with Honduras in protest over the "pogroms." Border clashes ensued, and on July 14 the Salvadoran military launched an armed attack into Honduras complete with air strikes against targets well inside its neighbor. Six days of war ensued until a truce was negotiated by the Organization for American States, but only after 4,000 deaths on both sides. As much as Hondurans and Salvadorans love soccer, this conflict was obviously about more than the final score, but the soccer war illustrates how sport can be a powerful conduit for the expression of political conflict.

BOYCOTTS AND BANS

Sport has also been subjected to instrumental use as a tool of statecraft. Governments will use sport to convey political messages of protest. Sport's high profile is often deemed an effective medium for getting a message out to a wide audience. It also symbolically conveys one's political intentions. Furthermore, sport is relatively costless to the government relative to other means of statecraft such as war or economic sanctions.

The most common forms of this instrumental use of sports have been either boycotts or bans from sporting events. The most well known cases, of course, were the U.S. decision to lead a boycott of the 1980 Moscow Olympics in protest over the Soviet Union's invasion of Afghanistan in 1979 and the Soviet-led boycott of the 1984 Los Angeles Olympiad in retaliation. These were arguably the darkest years of the Olympics, as the use of sport as a Cold War instrument of statecraft reached its most extreme. But they were far from the only instances. At the 1956 Melbourne Games, for example, Egypt, Iraq, and Lebanon boycotted in protest over the Suez crisis. In 1976,

FIGURE 2. ANTI-SOVIET BUMPER STICKER AT THE 1984 OLYMPIC GAMES

SOURCE: © DOUGLAS KIRKLAND / CORBIS.

twenty-two African nations protested New Zealand's continued competition with South Africa's all-white "Springboks" rugby team, threatening to boycott the Montreal Olympics in protest over New Zealand's participation in the Games. China boycotted the Olympics for over two decades in protest over the IOC's decision at the time to adopt a two-China formula to allow the participation of Taiwan. And in 1988, North Korea boycotted the Seoul Olympics when their far-fetched proposals to cohost half of the games was turned down by the IOC.

Banning a nation from sporting events is another method of conveying strong political messages. The most well known are the Olympic bans on the defeated powers after the two World Wars. In 1920, Austria, Bulgaria, Germany, Hungary, and Turkey were not permitted to participate in the Games, and in the 1948 "Games of Renewal," bans were imposed on Germany and Japan. The most effective sport bans, however, arguably were the ones imposed on South Africa for its apartheid policies. In 1964, the IOC, citing Olympic ideals of nondiscrimination and meritorious competition, banned South Africa from participation in the 1964 Tokyo Games because of their refusal to allow for a mixed-race national team. This ban was maintained through the 1968 Mexico City Games, and in 1976 the South African national Olympic organizing committee was banned from the IOC. The following year, Commonwealth nations agreed on banning all sports competition with South Africa, and this was followed by the expulsion of South Africa from the International Rugby Board. The latter action constituted a huge blow to South Africa. The Olympics ban was bad, but South Africans took their rugby extremely seriously. They took extreme pride in the all-white Springboks national team and refused to allow a mixed-race team. New Zealand was the only country that continued regular rugby competitions with the Springboks, until pressure mounted on New Zealand to comply with the Commonwealth sport ban, which they eventually did after rugby matches in 1981 with the Springboks resulted in massive protests and arrests. Many argue that the sport ban on rugby was a critical factor in South African government's decision to end apartheid.[16]

The use of sport bans and boycotts by governments is relatively free of cost for the implementing party yet gives the impression of action and political conviction. This is one reason discussions of boycotts swirled around the 2008 Beijing Olympics. On the first anniversary countdown of the Games on August 8, 2007, and in the aftermath of the demonstrations in Lhasa, Tibet, in March 2008, American congressmen made a series of statements calling for a boycott of the games in protest of China's policies in Darfur, its crackdown in Tibet, and product-safety problems with lead paint on children's toys made in China. In many ways, the calls for a boycott were predictable as it was relatively costless (i.e., cheaper than trade sanctions) to the politicians (not to the athletes) yet showed their constituencies that they were "doing something." At the same time, it is very costly to Beijing and might effect a change in behavior.

Finally, the converse of a sport ban—recognition and invitation—has also been used as a powerful diplomatic instrument. In contrast to the boycott-blighted years of South African sport during apartheid, FIFA's awarding of the 2010 World Cup to the country offers a powerful symbol of international recognition of South Africa's place in the world, closing the door on its difficult past. Particularly for newly formed nations, recognition by an international sports body is considered extremely important in terms of overall diplomatic recognition and acceptance in the world community. As Christopher Hill has noted, participation in international sporting events often connotes legitimate statehood and hence has been a principle fiercely fought over at length by the two Chinas, the two Germanies, the two Koreas, Southern Rhodesia, and others.[17]

STAGING

Sporting events like the Olympics can act as a stage from which individuals send the globe wider political messages. The display of black-fisted gloves by John Carlos and Tommie Smith on the medal stand at the 1968 Mexico City Games effectively conveyed to the world the state of racial tensions in the United States. American tennis star and 1989 French Open men's champion Michael Chang used his trophy presentation to express empathy with the democracy activists in Tiananmen Square. While the host country of every large sporting event seeks to put the country's best foot forward as it occupies the spotlight, fascist and communist regimes in particular have utilized the stage to demonstrate to domestic and international audiences the supposed superiority of their flawed domestic systems. The 1936 Berlin Games were arguably the best example of this dynamic. The IOC gave the games to the Weimar Republic in 1931. After the rise of the Nazi regime two years later, and despite international pressure, the IOC chose not to take the Games out of Hitler's grasp. The result was a grandly orchestrated event staged solely for the purpose of demonstrating Nazi superiority. These were the first live-televised Olympics, and by all accounts, the Germans put on an incredible show. Indeed, some of the theatric innovations were later adopted as standard fare in subsequent games (for example, the torch-lighting ceremony originated in the Berlin games). Hitler became personally involved in the details of the preparations, making decisions on ceremonies and displays of Nazi uniforms and insignia. He even constructed myths about the links between Germanic and ancient Greek peoples—physically displayed in the Dietrich Eckart Amphitheater and other pieces of monumental architecture celebrating Aryan youth—in an attempt to have the Games permanently staged in the country. The hosts dominated in the medal count, besting the United States by winning eighty-nine medals, including thirty-three gold. The four gold medals that an "inferior" African American athlete, Jesse Owens, won in track-and-field events (100 meters, 200 meters, 4X100 meters, and long jump), however, undermined Hitler's attempts to stage games featuring Aryan superiority.[18]

TERRORISM

The world has discovered tragically that sporting events make attractive targets for terrorists. They offer a high-profile, widely watched, and widely attended venue in which disaffected groups can make statements through violence against the innocent. Until recently, sporting events were also relatively lax in security, most of which was focused on crowd control rather than defending against a terrorist act. For terrorists, the symbolism of athletes clad in the colors of their countries represents an easy target to demonstrate dissatisfaction with government policies. The two most well known cases of sport's victimization by terrorism occurred in Europe in 1972 and in Asia in 1987. A day before the start of the 1972 Munich Olympiad, eight Palestinian terrorists entered the Olympic village, killing two members of the Israeli team and taking nine others hostage. A tense crisis ensued that was broadcast over the entire world as the Palestinians demanded the release of 234 prisoners held by Israel. The Israeli government refused to negotiate, and all nine athletes died in a failed rescue attempt at the airport as the terrorists and their hostages attempted to board a plane for Cairo. The Games began after a one-day delay in the start of the opening ceremony, but athletes like American gold medal swimmer Mark Spitz and others left early after completing their events. The Germans spent only $2 million on security (versus $600 million in Athens in 2004), and the terrorists later testified that they simply hid their weapons in lockers inside the village and walked in without any scrutiny. Ironically, Germany's perceived lax security was intentional—the organizers sought to make the Games accessible and free in order to erase any memories of the militarist Nazi Olympics. As observers recalled, "There was no barbed wire, no cameras, no motion detectors, no barricades. At the entrance, unarmed guards in powder blue shirts looked more like ushers at Disneyland."[19] The Olympics would never be the same after this tragic event; international athletes had become political targets.

Terrorism would touch sport in Asia as well. North Korea expressed outrage that the 1988 Olympic Games were given to their archrival in the south. Despite having never submitted a bid to host the Games, the Pyongyang regime demanded after the fact that they be given the right to cohost, and the IOC, with Seoul's consent, engaged in negotiations to stage some portion of the events in North Korea. When the negotiations broke down in 1987 over the North's obstinate demand that they be given half of all the events, including the opening and closing ceremonies, Pyongyang responded by calling for a communist boycott of the games, which the Soviet Union summarily rejected. In an effort to undermine Seoul's successful hosting of the Games, the current leader of North Korea, Kim Jong-il, orchestrated one of Asia's worst terrorist acts, blowing up a Korean civilian airliner in November 1987 over Burma and killing more than a hundred passengers. The impact of terrorism on sport has since been evident in the inordinate money and

FIGURE 3. "MURDER IN MUNICH": *TIME* COVER, SEPTEMBER 18, 1972

preparation that must now go into staging every event. The reason is clear, as the Palestinian spokesman during the 1972 Munich ordeal explained: "Sport is the modern religion of the Western world. So we decided to use the Olympics, the most sacred ceremony of this religion, to make the world pay attention to us."[20]

STUFF HAPPENS

Sport is also linked to politics by the fact that "stuff happens." What this means is that sport events can spontaneously create political phenomena. Here, we are not talking so much about sports hooliganism, which is a risk that comes with most large sporting events and is associated with a combination of mob mentalities, socio-economic dynamics, and copious amounts of alcohol. Rather, what may start out as a match can without warning turn into a political event. Afghanistan under the Taliban regime, for example, banned all forms of entertainment, including music, art, dancing, and television. A person could be pulled out of her car, and whipped and beaten for playing music on the car radio. But football was permitted. In 2000, a BBC correspondent observed a football match along with 20,000 spectators. As she described it, the quality of the game left a lot to be desired, but the sight of Afghans cheering and enjoying themselves was rare. The audience started to clap, which was another practice banned by the Taliban. But as she described it, clapping was just the beginning:

> But more daring resistance was to come.
> Half way through the first half, it was time for the late afternoon prayers.
> Pick-ups full of police from Vice and Virtue drove into the stadium and circled round. Using loud speakers, they ordered everyone to come onto the pitch and pray. . . .
> A few thousand people straggled onto the grass, but most remained resolutely standing. Policemen leapt into the stands, whips in hand.
> But the crowds just melted away before them, only to reform a little further up the stands. . . .
> It was a show of resistance. That is unheard of in Kabul.[21]

Two years later, Afghanistan sent an underperforming forty-four-member national soccer team to the fourteenth Asian Games in Busan, Korea. Their performance was dreadful, losing 10 to 0 to Iran and 11 to 0 to Qatar. But simply playing on the pitch generated a huge response from the crowds as this was the first time the country had participated in an international sporting event since 1994. Just showing up was a statement of immense political significance; the country liberated from Taliban rule by the U.S.-led invasion was again playing soccer in stadiums that had been used by the Taliban as execution arenas.

In 2007, an Iran-born player on the German national soccer team requested of his coach that he not be played in a European Championship qualifier match against Israel. This rapidly spiraled into an international diplomatic dispute. Pro-Israeli groups condemned the allegedly anti-Semitic nature of the player's actions and demanded that the German soccer league take disciplinary action. Always sensitive to Nazi Germany's history and eager to maintain good relations with Israel, German politicians spoke out against the player's action and demanded that the league ban him from the national team. The German soccer federation responded by instituting an education program about Germany's history for all players in the soccer league. Meanwhile, the player, Ashkan Dejagah, who holds duel citizenship in Iran and Germany, said he only asked not to play for fear that family members still living in Iran would be in danger (since the 1979 revolution, Iran does not recognize Israel's right to exist and bans its citizens from visiting the country).

In 1966, the North Korean men's soccer team qualified for the FIFA World Cup tournament and made it to the quarterfinal round, the furthest of any Asian team (until 2002). This, in itself, was a monumental feat for the unknown team that oddsmakers had as 1,000-to-1 underdogs, but the political repercussions were most interesting. After beating Australia, the team went to England to play its matches in the small, sleepy town of Middlesborough. For the British foreign ministry, the North's unexpected entry to the tournament raised all sorts of political issues. FIFA regulations allowed for the flying of the national flags of the competing teams, but the U.K. did not formally recognize the DPRK diplomatically. At the height of the Cold War, U.K. officials were concerned about what sort of precedents would be set by flying the DPRK flag. As the foreign ministry was mulling its way forward, the mayor of Middlesborough, seeking simply to be a gracious host and sportsman, welcomed the players and coaches to his town, hoisted the DPRK national flag, and had them over for sherry. The city became infatuated with the team and cheered for them loudly as the underdogs in their first round loss to a very physical Soviet team. Soon, English schoolboys were asking for the autographs of the players and wearing makeshift soccer jerseys with the hand-drawn pictures of the DPRK flag and the names and numbers of the DPRK players. When the DPRK team advanced to the next round, 3,000 fans from Middlesborough followed the team to Liverpool, where the DPRK miraculously defeated Italy in front of crowds who cheered them as though they were the hometown favorites. When they took the lead in the quarterfinals against powerhouse Portugal, there was bedlam in the stands, and even after their loss, this team from the communist North at the height of Cold War tensions still received incredible adulation.

SUPERPOWER OLYMPICS

At no time has sport been more political than during the battle between the superpowers during the Cold War. Victories in sport became synonymous with statements of superiority of one domestic system over the other as states vicariously fought the Cold War through their athletes. This competition reached its height, ironically, in decisions not to compete—when the United States boycotted the 1980 Moscow Olympics and the Soviets boycotted the 1984 Los Angeles Games. The impetus for the political use of sport came from the Soviet Union's decision to abandon the Marxist notion of sport as a bourgeois enterprise designed to divert attention away from the class struggle; instead they would use sport as part of the larger ideological struggle with the West. The Soviet Union made this decision in 1947 and joined the IOC in 1951 with the express purpose of attaining world supremacy in international sport. It subsequently exploded on the international scene at the 1952 Helsinki Summer Games, amassing a medal count rivaling that of the United States, and it dominated the ensuing winter games in Italy. Soviet performances demonstrated the degree to which sport had become a state project. Two of the top three medal and total point winners thereafter in every summer and winter Olympic Games were Soviet bloc countries.[22] Their athletes and coaches were treated like national heroes, receiving the Order of Lenin for providing "irrefutable proof of the superiority of socialist culture over the moribund culture of capitalist states."[23]

The political importance attached to sport by communist states was motivated not only by superpower competition with the West but also by the desire to gain international prestige. Strong sport performance was deeply connected with national identity. For East Germany, a small country of under 17 million and strongly desirous of international acceptance as a legitimate nation-state like its larger western neighbor, sport took on enormous political significance. When East Germany was finally able to compete in the 1972 Munich Games, they performed astoundingly well, beating West Germany in the medal count at every subsequent summer games. Indeed,

TABLE 1   OLYMPIC MEDAL COUNTS, 1896–2004 SUMMER OLYMPICS

YEAR	FIRST PLACE (TOTAL MEDALS)	GOLD/ SILVER/ BRONZE	SECOND PLACE	G/S/B	THIRD PLACE	G/S/B
1896	Greece (45)	10/18/17	United States (18)	11/6/1	Germany (13)	6/5/2
1900	France (105)	30/41/34	United States (47)	19/14/14	United Kingdom (33)	16/7/10
1904	United States (235)	75/82/78	Germany (12)	4/4/4	Canada (6)	4/1/1
1906	France (42)	15/9/18	Greece (34)	8/13/13	United Kingdom (24)	8/11/5
1908	United Kingdom (143)	56/49/38	United States (46)	22/12/12	Sweden (25)	8/6/11
1912	Sweden (63)	23/24/16	United States (63)	26/17/20	United Kingdom (41)	10/15/16
1920	United States (96)	41/27/28	Sweden (64)	19/21/24	United Kingdom (43)	14/16/13
1924	United States (99)	45/27/27	France (40)	14/14/12	Finland (37)	14/13/10
1928	United States (56)	22/18/16	Germany (39)	11/19/9	Finland (25)	8/8/9
1932	United States (110)	44/36/30	Italy (36)	12/12/12	Finland (25)	5/8/12
1936	Germany (101)	38/31/32	United States (57)	24/21/12	Italy (27)	9/13/5
1948	United States (84)	38/27/19	Sweden (46)	17/11/18	France (32)	11/6/15
1952	United States (76)	40/19/17	Soviet Union (70)	22/29/19	Hungary (42)	16/10/16

TABLE 1   OLYMPIC MEDAL COUNTS, 1896–2004 SUMMER OLYMPICS *(continued)*

YEAR	FIRST PLACE (TOTAL MEDALS)	GOLD/ SILVER/ BRONZE	SECOND PLACE	G/S/B	THIRD PLACE	G/S/B
1956	Soviet Union (97)	37/28/32	United States (74)	32/25/17	Australia (35)	13/8/14
1960	Soviet Union (103)	43/29/31	United States	34/21/16	Germany (41)	12/18/11
1964	Soviet Union (93)	30/30/33	United States (90)	36/26/28	Germany (50)	10/22/18
1968	United States (107)	45/28/34	Soviet Union (91)	29/32/30	Hungary (32)	10/10/12
1972	Soviet Union (99)	50/27/22	United States (94)	33/31/30	East Germany (66)	20/23/23
1976	Soviet Union (124)	49/41/34	United States (94)	34/35/25	East Germany (89)	40/25/24
1980	Soviet Union (195)	80/69/46	East Germany (126)	47/37/42	Bulgaria (41)	8/16/17
1984	United States (173)	83/60/30	West Germany (58)	17/18/23	Romania (52)	19/16/17
1988	Soviet Union (134)	54/31/49	East Germany (102)	37/35/30	United States (94)	36/31/27
1992	Soviet Union (111)	45/38/28	United States (106)	37/34/35	Germany (82)	33/21/28
1996	United States (101)	44/32/25	Germany (65)	20/18/27	Russia (62)	26/21/15
2000	United States (95)	39/24/32	Russia (87)	32/28/27	Australia (58)	16/25/17
2004	United States (103)	36/39/28	Russia (92)	27/27/38	China (63)	32/17/14

SOURCE: COMPILED FROM HTTP://WWW.DATADASEOLYMPICS.COM.

TABLE 2 OLYMPIC MEDAL COUNTS, 1924-2006 WINTER OLYMPICS

YEAR	FIRST PLACE (TOTAL MEDALS)	GOLD/ SILVER/ BRONZE	SECOND PLACE	G/S/B	THIRD PLACE	G/S/B
1924	Norway (17)	4/7/6	Finland (10)	4/3/3	United States (4)	1/2/1
1928	Norway (14)	6/4/4	Sweden, (5) United States (5)	2/2/1, 2/2/1	Austria (4)	0/3/1
1932	United States (12)	6/4/2	Norway (10)	3/4/3	Canada (7)	1/1/5
1936	Norway (15)	7/5/3	Sweden (7)	2/2/3	Finland (6), Germany (6)	1/2/3, 3/3/0
1948	Norway (10) Sweden (10)	4/3/3, 4/3/3	Switzerland (9)	3/4/2	Austria (8), United States (8)	1/3/4, 3/3/2
1952	Norway (16)	7/3/6	United States (11)	4/6/1	Finland (9)	3/4/2
1956	Soviet Union (15)	6/3/6	Austria (11)	4/3/4	Sweden (10)	2/4/4
1960	Soviet Union (21)	7/5/9	United States (10)	3/4/3	Finland (8), Germany (8)	2/3/3, 4/3/1
1964	Soviet Union (24)	11/7/6	Norway (15)	3/6/6	Austria (12)	4/5/3
1968	Norway (14)	6/6/2	Soviet Union (13)	5/5/3	Austria (11)	3/4/4
1972	Soviet Union (16)	8/5/3	East Germany (14)	4/3/7	Norway (12)	2/5/5
1976	Soviet Union (27)	13/6/8	East Germany (19)	7/5/7	West, Germany (10), United States (10)	2/5/3, 3/3/4
1980	East Germany (23)	9/7/7	Soviet Union (22)	10/6/6	United States (12)	6/4/2
1984	Soviet Union (25)	6/10/9	East Germany (24)	9/9/6	Finland (13)	4/3/6
1988	Soviet Union (29)	11/18/10	East Germany (25)	9/10/6	Switzerland (15)	5/5/5

TABLE 2   OLYMPIC MEDAL COUNTS, 1924–2006 WINTER OLYMPICS *(continued)*

YEAR	FIRST PLACE (TOTAL MEDALS)	GOLD/ SILVER/ BRONZE	SECOND PLACE	G/S/B	THIRD PLACE	G/S/B
1992	Germany (26)	10/10/6	Soviet Union (23)	9/6/8	Austria (21)	6/7/8
1994	Norway (26)	10/11/5	Germany (24)	9/7/8	Russia (23)	11/8/4
1998	Germany (29)	12/9/8	Norway (25)	10/10/5	Russia (19)	9/6/4
2002	Germany (35)	12/16/7	United States (34)	10/13/11	Norway (24)	11/7/6
2006	Germany (29)	11/13/5	United States (25)	9/9/7	Austria, (24) Canada (24)	10/7/7, 8/9/7

SOURCE: COMPILED FROM HTTP://WWW.DATABASEOLYMPICS.COM

the East Germans won one gold medal for every 425,000 citizens (versus the United States at one gold per 6.5 million citizens). Although the world would later learn about the role of performance-enhancing substances in East Germany's rise to prominence, these revelations only underline the degree to which sport had political significance. Performing well was a statement designed to gain international respect, recognition, and acceptance as a sovereign nation.

For Moscow, sport was also important in terms of maintaining unity within the communist bloc of countries. Sport provided a way of organizing the satellite countries to focus on a common objective. Indeed, a division of labor was established in which countries had different tasks. The Hungarians, for example, were specialists in sports medicine; the Bulgarians, in sports psychology; the Czechs, in physical training; and the East Germans focused on scouting young talent. Sport assistance in the form of training facilities, scouting, and other help also provided a means for the Eastern bloc to reach out to friendly or nonaligned countries in Asia, Africa, and Latin America. As one observer correctly noted, "This enabled the Soviet leaders to use sport to integrate the various socialist societies, bind them to Soviet institutions and policies, and to maintain and reinforce the USSR's 'vanguard' position within the bloc."[24] Precisely because sport was a political and ideological battleground with the West, defections by Eastern European athletes were extremely controversial as they shattered the myth in graphic and personal terms. Moscow's chance to host the Games in 1980 was seen as a huge accomplishment, if not the crowning achievement of the state's dedication to sport. The Carter administration's decision to boycott the Games in protest of the Soviet invasion of Afghanistan, in this regard, was ironic. Unlike the Soviet's state-run and subsidized sport machine, the majority of American athletes preparing for the Games were amateurs who received little help from the U.S. government. Yet the government prohibited its athletes from fulfilling their dreams for political reasons. The boycott not only was an unprecedented step in linking sport to politics but also ensured that the Soviets would retaliate four years later. These two boycotts achieved little in terms of political objectives while devastating the dreams of many athletes.

DOES SPORT MATTER MORE IN ASIA?

In May 2008, in the run-up to the Beijing Olympics, Japan Airlines repainted the exteriors of its aircraft with larger-than-life photographs of Japan's past Olympic medalists, from marathoners to synchronized swimmers, to drum up support for Japan's athletes at the Games. The faces, set against the snow-white hulls of the planes, were mildly frightening and only a bit strange (Japan Airlines also used to put Pokemon images on their planes), but the act also raises questions: Would American or European air carriers have imagined doing this? What motivates Asia to this extreme when it comes to sport?

FIGURE 4. SUMMER OLYMPIC GAMES VENUES: 1896–2012

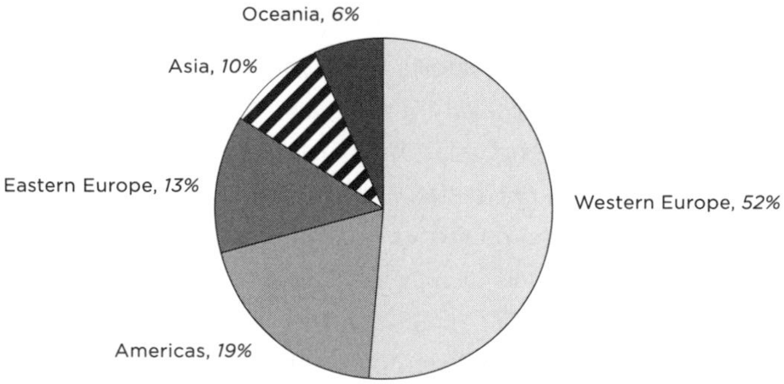

Oceania, *6%*
Asia, *10%*
Eastern Europe, *13%*
Western Europe, *52%*
Americas, *19%*

SOURCE: DATA FROM WWW.DATABASEOLYMPICS.COM.

FIGURE 5. WINTER OLYMPIC GAMES VENUES: 1924–2014

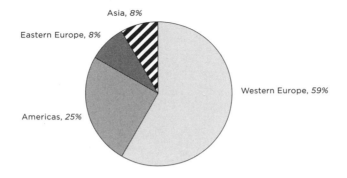

SOURCE: DATA FROM WWW.DATABASEOLYMPICS.COM.

Not only is sport political, but it is arguably more political in Asia than elsewhere in the world. Why is this so? Undeniably, international sport is political everywhere it is staged and played, but there are a couple of factors that might make it especially so in Asia. First, the political significance of an event like the Olympic Games is greater in this region simply because the Games come to Asia so infrequently. For the first sixty years of the modern Olympics, the Games were solely located in Europe and America (only in 1956 did they go as far as Australia). Between 1896 and 2004, the Summer Games traveled to Asia only twice, and the Winter Games have also come to Asia only twice since their inception in 1924, both times in Japan (see the "Chronology of the Modern Olympics" and figures 4 and 5). The Summer Games did not come to Asia until 1964 (Tokyo) and then only once after that in 1988 (Seoul). By contrast, London and Paris will have hosted the Summer Games a total of five times by 2012. Amazingly, the 2008 Beijing Games constituted only the third time that the Summer Olympics came to Asia. This rarity is not for lack of trying. Tokyo sought to host the 1940 and 1960 Games; Nagoya, the 1988 Games; Beijing, the 2000 Games; and three other Asian cities vied for the 2008 Games (Bangkok, Kuala Lampur, and Osaka).[25] This effort is also reflected in Asian membership in the IOC, which has increased over the years (see figure 6). So a sporting event like the Olympics, when staged in Asia, truly constitutes a "mega-event." And it naturally has more political meaning than it would in Europe or America.

Sport also matters more in Asia because of the turbulent histories that still afflict the nations there. Historical animosities translate readily into political disputes in Asia. There is no denying that historical memories

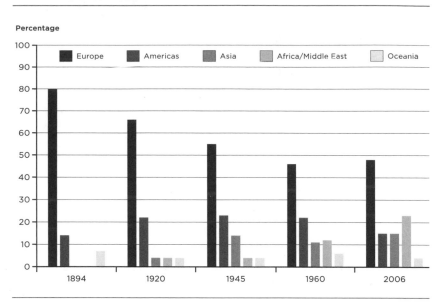

Percentage

Legend: Europe, Americas, Asia, Africa/Middle East, Oceania

SOURCE: DATA FROM WWW.DATABASEOLYMPICS.COM.

linger among Europeans, but any resentments and anxieties arguably may not sit as close to the surface as they do in Asia. Take territorial disputes, for example. Europe has seen its fair share of these, as has Asia, but they do not resonate as strongly politically in Europe as they do in Asia. Germany today, for example, cares less whether Alsace and Lorraine belong to the French. In Asia, however, Japan and Russia still care very deeply about ownership of the Northern Territories, so much so that the dispute has impeded their ability to sign a peace treaty after World War II to this day.[26] Japan and China still scuffle over the disputed sovereignty of the Daoyutai or Senkaku Islands. And Korea and Japan—who are about the closest thing to allies among the countries of Asia—still nearly come to blows over rights to the Takeshima or Tokdo Islands. In Asia today, moreover, the leaders of nations will refuse to meet with one another because of controversial historical actions or statements. Both China's and South Korea's presidents refused to meet with Prime Minister Junichiro Koizumi of Japan as late as 2006 because Koizumi paid respects at Yasukuni Shrine, which is a memorial commemorating imperial Japan's war dead. A long string of diplomatic disputes over insensitive statements by politicians or because of controversial history textbooks have afflicted Japan-Korea and Japan-China and

REGION	1894	1920	1945	1960	2006
Western Europe	10 (67%)	27 (51%)	23 (41%)	24 (37%)	38 (33%)
Eastern Europe	2 (13)	8 (15)	8 (14)	6 (9)	10 (9)
Asia	0	2 (4)	8 (14)	7 (11)	17 (15)
Africa	0	1 (2)	0	2 (3)	20 (18)
Middle East	0	1 (2)	2 (4)	6 (9)	6 (5)
South/Central America	1 (7)	6 (11)	9 (16)	11 (16)	13 (11)
North America	1 (7)	6 (11)	4 (7)	4 (6)	5 (4)
Oceania	1 (7)	2 (4)	2 (4)	4 (6)	5 (4)

SOURCE: SUSAN BROWNELL, *BEIJING'S GAMES* (LANHAM, MD.: ROWMAN AND LITTLEFIELD, 2008), 179.

Korea-China relations. Westerners are often astounded by how much history remains alive in Asia.

Sport acts as an outlet for pent-up historical resentments in ways that cannot be expressed through regular diplomacy. To put it bluntly, Japan's imperial past in Asia causes most former colonies to view every contest with Japan as a historical grudge match. In 1920, Koreans under Japanese occupation formed the Chosun Sports Association. Meant as an amateur athletic club, it was still strongly associated with an underground independence movement because sport was one of the only ways Koreans were permitted to congregate as a group. So when the association had the opportunity to play rugby against a Japanese team, the Koreans were told they were not playing to win but to fight for Korea's independence (they won the match).[27] Japan still ruled Korea sixteen years later when Sohn Kee Chung, a Korean, won the marathon at the 1936 Berlin Games. Sohn's victory was a cathartic event for the prideful but colonized Koreans, who felt humiliated by the medal stand ceremony where Sohn received the gold as a subject of the Japanese empire and stood stoically during the playing of the Japanese national anthem. Angry Korean newspapers carried photos the next day of Sohn's victory but with the Japanese flag airbrushed out of the picture replaced by the Korean flag. These journalists were promptly arrested by the colonial police.[28]

This cocktail of history, sport, and politics is very potent in Asia. As I noted in the case of the 2004 Japan-China Asian Cup football final, it can lead to angry Chinese mobs attacking Japanese players, forcing thousands of Japanese fans to flee onto the pitch to avoid being trapped in the stands. In the 2008 East

Asian football championships in Chongqing, China—a city heavily bombard-ed by imperial Japan during World War II—the Chinese team was fined more than 4,500 dollars after their loss to Japan for excessively rough and unsports-manlike play. "A flying kick from goalkeeper Zong Lei injured Japan's Michi-hiro Yasuda, while Li Weifeng grabbed winger Keita Suzuki by the throat and Yasuhito Endo was left writhing on the floor after a kick to the thigh."[29] Sports reports readily noted that the unusual physicality of these matches stemmed from historical antipathy. Japan also protested the fact that the referee for the match did not give a "red card" to any of the Chinese players, penalizing them with expulsion. The referee was from North Korea—another country with a lot of pent-up historical resentment toward its former colonizer.

This historical anger can also lead to bitter and sometimes petty actions meant to take political jabs at the other side. South Koreans, for example, found their winning the 1988 Olympic bid that much sweeter because they beat out Nagoya, Japan; furthermore, they chose a Korean judo athlete to read the Olympic oath as a way to thumb their noses at Japan. FIFA of-ficials were taken aback by the intensity of competition between Japan and South Korea as cohosts of the 2002 World Cup. Originally, Seoul had shown little interest in trying to bring the cup to Asia—until they learned of the seriousness of the Japanese bid. As one observer noted, the Korean bid was motivated by history first and soccer second:

> Seoul wanted to be in on the action, if not to spoil the party which seemed more and more to be on the cards. . . . The history of the 2002 World Cup cannot be separated from the history of imperialism in East Asia, albeit that imperialism has characterized not so much the relationship between the West and the East as the relationship between Japan and Korea. For South Korea, there was in the offing a clear opportunity to redress its hu-miliating past at the hands of Japan and the Japanese.[30]

The cohosts argued bitterly over everything from the venue for the open-ing ceremony and championship match to the order of the names on the official logo (i.e., Korea-Japan or Japan-Korea World Cup). FIFA officials grew so worried about the historical animosity that they dispensed with the convention that called for the Japanese emperor to attend the opening cer-emony in Korea.

A third reason sport is more political in Asia than elsewhere has to do with the dynamism of the region. The pace of political and economic devel-opment in Asia is unprecedented. Countries move from postcolonial status and agrarian economies to OECD advanced industrial economies in three to four decades. Similar changes took over two centuries in the West. Conversely, we have also witnessed economic collapses in Asia as recently as a decade ago with the Asian liquidity crisis. The compacted nature of change in Asia means that much nation building takes place, and the symbolism of sport as a part of this nation building is strong. As I will discuss, the most notable event in sport diplomacy was when Chairman Mao invited the U.S. ping-pong team to China on the occasion of the World Table Tennis Championships in Japan in 1971. But what was of equal significance was that these 1971 championships represented the emergence of China from the dark Cultural Revolution period through its first international engagement in years. Before this, the First National Worker's Games in 1955 marked the establishment and consolidation of the PRC. The 1964 Tokyo Olympics would have had much less political significance if Japan had not been a defeated fascist regime that returned after two decades to the international system as a democracy and Cold War ally of its former enemies. The 1988 Seoul Olympics might have had less political meaning if Korea had not made this meteoric rise from a postwar farm economy to the twelfth largest economy in the world over a period of only four decades. The 2002 World Cup might have had less significance if it did not mark South Korea's recovery after the 1998 Asian financial crisis. And the 2008 Beijing Games might have garnered less attention if they did not showcase China's incredible rates of 10-plus percent economic growth.

The combination of unresolved and still raw historical enmities, rapid social change, and the importance of reputation and "face" causes sport to be more politically explosive in Asia than elsewhere. Add to this the fact that sporting mega-events like the Olympics and World Cup come to Asia only about once every two decades, and there is a strong mixture of history, sport, and politics.

LIBERAL OLYMPICS, ILLIBERAL CHINA?

As I noted already, China's hosting of the Games constituted only the fifth time that the Olympics came to Asia (Tokyo, 1964; Sapporo [winter], 1966; Seoul, 1988; and Nagano [winter], 1996). Enormous effort went into Beijing's preparations for the Games, including the breakneck construction of facilities and Herculean attempts at improving air quality. The Beijing leadership strained hard to keep the international focus on the sporting aspect of the Games and chafed at all attempts to shine the Olympic spotlight on China's policies on human rights and foreign policy. The former American president George H. W. Bush at an October 2007 U.S.-China event in Washington, D.C., supported Beijing's effort at sport purism, saying he was "not keep[ing] scorecards on anything else."[31] His son maintained that he would attend the Games even amid the Chinese crackdown on Tibetan demonstrators in Lhasa in March 2008 because the Olympics are about the athletes and not about politics. To the extent that there was a wider message, Beijing sought to focus on the key themes of hosting "harmonious," "green," and "hi-tech" Games, showcasing the country's growth and development.

Olympics without politics, however, is an oxymoron. And the Beijing Olympics without expressions of political dissent was a pipe dream. A PRC official took me to lunch in Georgetown after the movie director Steven Spielberg resigned as artistic director from the Games to protest China's Darfur policies in February 2008. He knew I was writing about the Olympics, and he asked how China could stop the pressure and keep the focus on sports? I told him, "You can't stop it." The concept of Olympism and the modern Olympic movement dating back to 1896 have always been closely associated with classical liberal ideals. The original Olympic charter states that the Games reflect sport's appreciation of individual effort, fair play, rules and institution, and success based on merit—all consonant with quintessentially liberal political values. Indeed, Pierre De Coubertin, founder of the modern Olympic movement, tried actively after World War I to associate the spirit of the games with the political goals of the League of Nations with the hope that sport could operate as an international institution that could help to prevent another world war.[32] After World War II, as the world sought to form another liberal institution, the United Nations, that could govern sovereign nations and foster rules and cooperation to prevent war, Olympic organizers sought again to associate the spirit of the games with this liberal institution. As a reminder of these ties, the U.N. flag is flown at all Olympic competitions, and the IOC and U.N. have worked on joint projects in poverty alleviation, education, health promotion, gender equality, environment, and HIV treatment. The U.N. General Assembly passes a resolution before each games calling on all participating nations to "observe within the framework of the Charter of the United Nations, the Olympic Truce, individually and collectively."[33]

With the U.N. passage of a similar resolution for the Beijing Games, the key question becomes how does one address the obvious and yawning gap between the spirit of Olympism and the political character of the Chinese regime? This was a harder stretch for China that many might have thought. For China, sport since 1949 has been merely a reflection of the class ideology of the party-state. The Chinese had national games for each group the state favored—National Soldiers' Games (1952), National Minorities' Games (1953), and National Workers' Games (1955).[34] Against this historical backdrop, executing the logistics of hosting the 2008 Olympic Games could not obscure the fact that one of the world's most illiberal political systems must somehow cope with the liberal influence of Olympism. Beijing addressed this gap by simply denying it, and ruthlessly crushing all signs of free speech and dissent. The Chinese enacted changes in some areas, cosmetic and temporary in nature, but still significant in that these changes could create spillover effects that last past the end of the Games. As I will discuss in later chapters, Beijing had to handle the meeting of liberal ideals and illiberal reality in full view of the tens of thousands of media agents that descended on the country to cover the Games and the hundreds of millions of people around the world who viewed them on television.

Whether sport is political or not is ultimately a personal choice. Former Olympians such as Kenyan gold medalist Kip Keino (now an IOC member) choose purism, saying the Games bring together today's youth for "fair play and for sharing the Olympic spirit" and not for politics.[35] But others are like American speed skater and Turin Olympic gold medalist Joey Cheek, who founded Team Darfur (a collection of former Olympians protesting China's actions in Sudan), and who observes, "Countries stage the Games not just because they like sport but because they want to showcase their country, people, culture and political systems. It makes no sense to say it is not political."[36] By choice or not, it is nevertheless impossible to deny the link. Whether in the tradition of the Olympic truce, as an outlet for conflict, as a tool of politicians, or as a target of terrorism, the scorecard weighs favorably toward politics over purism.

2

THE ARGUMENT

Scholars of international politics do not pay much attention to sport. Sport does not occupy a week's lecture on the syllabi of most world politics classes at universities, and it barely receives mention in Western and Eastern course textbooks on international politics.[1] The link between sport and politics is so rarely made in academia that when I chose to teach a full course on it at Georgetown in the fall of 2007, it made the *Washington Post*. By contrast, those who study sport rather than world politics have not observed the former's impact on nation-states, instead largely working in fields like sport psychology and medicine and, in a social science context, in the fields of anthropology, sociology, and gender studies. Here, the interest has always been somewhat predictable and parochial. The Japanese, Germans, and Italians, for example, have looked at the role of sport in fascist systems; American and Soviet sociologists have looked at the role of sport in communist societies; and the Europeans have studied the pathology of soccer hooliganism.

MUMBO JUMBO

The "mutual neglect" of sport and politics, as one author termed it, started to dissipate in the 1980s after the boycotts of the 1980 Moscow Games and 1984 Los Angeles Games garnered worldwide attention.[2] The increased attention by these international relations experts, however, has done little to enlighten and probably more to obfuscate and confuse the picture. If the operative question is how sport "fits" into our understanding of world politics, then the bottom line is that the existing literature offers no clear or consistent answers.

There are three schools of thought in international relations, all of which would claim that sport reinforces its own distinctive principles. One school focuses on state power as the key to understanding international relations. For this worldview, events that we read about in the newspaper daily are largely generated by governments competing with one another based on their sovereign use of national militaries and economic resources. Sport in this regard is merely another playing field for interstate competition and cooperation. After all, international sport is organized around athletes and teams who represent their respective countries. "Team USA" is not just a collection of athletes but an embodiment of American sovereignty in the realist worldview. For this "power" perspective, moreover, outcomes in international sporting competitions reflect the relative strength and wealth of nations. It is no accident that the Americans and the Soviets competed so fiercely through sport during the Cold War as an extension of their geopolitical rivalry and that the Chinese garnered top medal tallies in the Olympics as a reflection of their rising power and status.

Another school of thought sees world politics not just in terms of powerful states but as supplemented by a multiplicity of nonstate actors, organizations, and businesses separate from their national governments. This school sees the mutually dependent ties that grow out of economic and political interaction and the rules set by international institutions as critical to world politics. This group would see sport as equally supportive of its own worldview. Sport is not merely an extension of national government policies but operates on an entirely separate field of play that reflects the rich interconnectedness of the world. Sport federations like the IOC and FIFA constitute real actors in international relations that are not affiliated with one state. Moreover, sport federations can even act upon states and compel changes in policies, just as the Commonwealth sport federation imposed a ban on South Africa for its apartheid policies in the 1980s. While some might point to the 1980 Moscow Olympics boycott by the West as an example of how the nation-state ultimately determines sport, this school of thought would point to the fact that governments like Great Britain could not stop their national Olympic committee from participating despite Cold War politics.

For a third school of thought, which emphasizes the role that nonmaterial factors like values, ideas, and national identity play in the world, sport would again be seen as reinforcing its distinctive worldview. Sport is not just a game but a mode of social interaction among citizens around the world that can create cooperation (or conflict) that transcends state boundaries. Because sport performance is a source of pride, one cannot underestimate the extent to which sport becomes interwoven with a nation's view of itself.

One cannot understand why small countries like Cuba or East Germany devoted such a large percentage of their national resources to sport or why governments undertake the economic risk to host sporting mega-events like the Olympics without understanding the importance that reputation, patriotism, and prestige play in world politics.

There is yet a fourth contrarian group of experts who believe that sport does not "fit" into any traditional ways of thinking about world politics. They believe that sport, in fact, alerts us to the inadequacies of all the current schools of thought that focus on either state power, institutions and interdependence, or social interaction. For these people, sport is exemplary of how transnational phenomena increasingly define the international system more than traditional views that focus on state-to-state relations. In their own words, sport helps us to understand the international system because it "provide[s] an access point, for it is an important *part of that* system, and, as such, is shaped by it while simultaneously influencing it."[3] In this regard, these authors see sport as: "A dialectic of nationalism and internationalism, the distant and the local, the immediate and the mediated, the personal and impersonal" in which they call for an "exploration of the international system via analysis of sport, whose specific processes and structures are related to a wider international social totality."[4] This is both confusing and uninteresting. Once you get past the social science jargon, this passage says that studying global sport enlightens us to the complexities of world politics beyond the three schools of thought. This is a completely agreeable observation. But the question becomes, what next? In other words, the diagnosis by these astute scholars may be correct, but what is the alternative model? The mumbo jumbo of international relations scholarship therefore leaves us with no clear answers about the link between sport and international relations. The three schools of thought all disagree on the political value of global sport. And a fourth group of experts, while pointing out the problems, offers no real framework for thinking about them.

HOW TO THINK ABOUT SPORT AND POLITICS

What we need is a simple and clear framework for how to think about sport and politics—not metatheory, but a practical and policy-oriented understanding derived from the history of sport. The link between sport and politics is not found in debates that try to validate or invalidate the three schools of thought in international relations. That debate may be useful to graduate students, but it is not useful to the educated and interested general reader.

Instead, a more useful line of inquiry starts with the simple premise that the study of international relations aims to explain war and peace, diplomacy and statecraft, foreign policy, and trade and commerce. The question to be answered, then, is: How does sport contribute to these outcomes?

SPORT AND IDENTITY

I preview here the three key areas where sport has mattered in politically significant ways for world politics. First, sport, national pride, and international prestige are inextricably intertwined. The desire to host major events like the Olympics and to perform well in them is intimately related to a nation's sense of its self-image and the pride of its citizens. Participation and performance in global sport is also related to a country's international prestige and the message that a government wants to send to the world about its country. This dynamic applies uniformly, whether we are talking about Beijing in 2008, Los Angeles in 1984, or even Berlin in 1936. Sport acts as a prism through which national identity gets refracted domestically and internationally.

Why is sport such a critical lens for identity? Because sport creates emotion. Winning or losing in international sport is a cathartic experience felt by the entire nation. Emotions of joy or anger emerge among countrymen that are not easily replicated in any other arena, be it art, music, politics, or business. This emotion causes countries to see their national image as affected by their performance in sport. The Margaret Thatcher and John Major governments took poor British performances in global sport so seriously in the 1980s that they ditched the minister of sport and put all decisions within the prime minister's office. They created a new Department of National Heritage with improved sport performance as a priority. The Australian government undertook similar measures after their subpar performance in the 1976 Montreal Olympics. This was not sport for sport's sake but equated directly with a country's heritage and self-worth. As I will show in later chapters, sport has been used as a critical instrument for building national identity and for nation building. In the 1956, 1960, and 1964 Olympics, for example, a unified German team represented the aspirations for creating a sense of unity between the two Germanies despite the Cold War conflict. In a spirit of compromise, Beethoven's *Ode to Joy* was played when West or East German athletes took the medal stand rather than national anthems. But as the division solidified and the Berlin Wall was erected, this symbol of unity disappeared with the 1968 Summer Games. After the Cold War, newly reunified Germany and Yemen used sport to help build a sense of national unity. The two Koreas have used sport to vicariously experience dreams of unification. By contrast, regimes like Nazi Germany and the Soviet Union used sport to demonstrate and assert the superiority of their system and politics to a domestic and international audience. Sport can also feed national image and identity in negative ways by reinforcing stereotypes. For example, the 1998 German team's FIFA World Cup performance was referred to by BBC sport commentators as "cold-hearted and efficient."[5] Japan's women's volleyball team toured Europe and went undefeated in all of its exhibition matches against the larger European women. Rather than praising the team's superior performance, which would eventually lead to the gold medal in the 1964 Olympics, European commentators nicknamed the team the "witches of the East" and commented on the small, nameless, faceless, black-haired industrious players. Moreover, what may start out as a sporting event with positive images could easily turn ugly. When Germany was excluded from the 1920 Olympic games in Antwerp and 1924 Paris Olympics because of its actions in World War I, two German sport leaders, Theodor Lewald and Carl Diem, lobbied to bring the games to Germany as a way of validating Germany's return to the community of nations. However, after the IOC awarded the 1936 Games to the Weimar Republic as a symbol of European postwar reconciliation, Hitler and the Nazis took over and turned the event into a stage to demonstrate Nazi supremacy. In Africa, Robert Mugabe sought to host the sixth African Games in Zimbabwe as a way of eventually being the first African host of the Olympics and cementing Zimbabwe as the leader of the continent. With Chinese support, Zimbabwe pulled together the infrastructure to host the games in 1995, and Mugabe made sure to invite international leaders and the IOC to the opening ceremony. But Mugabe was embarrassed to find an empty stadium for his guests to witness as organizers changed the time of the opening ceremony and no one informed the public adequately. Then the torch-lighting ceremony was delayed because the flame was stuck in traffic. As spectators filed into the stadium, the organizers tried to explain the reason for the confusion only to find that the public address system had broken down. When the torch finally arrived at the stadium, a beleaguered and perspiring audience and a livid Mugabe stood dumbfounded as the torch kept going out each time they tried to use it to ignite the stadium flame to signal the start of the games.[6]

SPORT AND DIPLOMACY

Second, sport has been successful at facilitating diplomacy in international relations. At certain times throughout history, sport has helped foster progress in difficult situations when normal diplomacy was ineffective. Sport can create public goodwill or provide the opportunities for high-level contacts that might help to spur forward a stagnant diplomatic process. While "ping-pong" diplomacy and Nixon's opening to China is the most well known case, there are other interesting cases in Asia that I shall discuss. Sport is usually not a sufficient condition on its own to create a breakthrough in diplomacy. Usually, it is combined with other trends, and its added value comes in its uniqueness and timing. In Iran, for example, wrestling was used in the mid-1990s to attempt to foster a temporary opening with the new Khatami regime. In my own dealings with the DPRK as deputy head of the U.S. delegation to the Six Party Talks, I raised the issue of using sport to create some diplomatic momentum at difficult times in the nuclear negotiations (discussed in chapter 4). Baseball has been used as a tool to improve relations between the United States and Cuba. As far back as 1975, Kissinger and Secretary of State William Rogers talked with baseball commissioner Bowie Kuhn about replicating with Cuba the "ping-pong" diplomacy with China. In 1999, the Baltimore Orioles and the Cuban national team played exhibition games in the United States and Havana, and the event was widely seen as a bilateral effort aimed at thawing relations.

SPORT AND CHANGE

Third, sport can act as an engine of change in world politics. This change can be both physical and political. Countries that host major sporting events like the Olympics undergo a massive facelift in which entire cities are virtually rebuilt and refitted with new infrastructure to meet the standards of modernity and user-friendliness for the globalized traveler. Tokyo in preparation for the 1964 Games, and Seoul in preparation for the 1988 Games underwent physical transformations at a breakneck pace, including the building of new state-of-the-art airport terminals and a national campaign to renovate restroom facilities (discussed in chapter 5). More significant, though, are the political changes that sport can effect in domestic or foreign policy. In South Korea, for example, the 1988 Olympics also helped to spur political change as the country dispensed with its military dictators and transitioned to a peoples' democracy. There is no denying the massive physical change in China as a result of the 2008 Games in terms of environmental cleanup and new roads, parks and trees, and buildings. But the more significant dynamic is the extent to which the small changes the government made in China's human rights and foreign policies to appease international pressure before the Games take root and blossom into more fundamental political change. Illiberal regimes like Beijing that host an event like the Olympics contend with a catch-22. They desperately seek to host flawlessly executed Games in order to demonstrate the country's power and prestige and to bolster its reputation to a domestic and international audience. At the same time, though, the international spotlight of the Olympics creates acute pressures on the regime to change flawed illiberal policies. As a Free Tibet activist observed, "If [effective] pressure is ever to be brought to bear on China, it is in the run-up to the Olympics."[7] Whether these policies pertain to human rights or to foreign policies, China faces pressure it had never conceived of before, involving not just NGOs but movie stars, Nobel laureates, and even athletes. Beijing's instinct might be to ignore all these pressures, but to do so would result in a public relations disaster at the Games and ultimately damage China's prestige rather than improve it. The result is that China is forced to respond and make changes in its policies.

THE 2014 WINTER OLYMPICS

The arguments for identity, diplomacy, and change previewed above will be used throughout the rest of this book. However, the recent bid for the 2014 Winter Olympics offers a good illustration of how sport quickly becomes political along these three lines. Russia, Austria, and South Korea competed intensely in the autumn of 2007 to be the IOC's choice to host the 2014 games. Each candidate had its appeal. Russia offered the beautiful resort of Sochi, located on the Black Sea coast and nestled at the base of the stupendous Caucasus Mountains. The Austrians offered up Salzburg, the home of Mozart and a mecca of European winter sport. Unlike Sochi, Salzburg already has world-class venues in place, and the Austrians were well practiced in playing host, having done so twice at Innsbruck, in 1964 and 1972. South Korea put forward a bid for the city of Pyeongchang. An unconventional choice, Pyeongchang lacked a strong tradition of winter sport like Salzburg, but it benefited from the IOC's memory of two well-run winter games in Sapporo and Nagano Japan in 1972 and 1998 (the only times the Winter Games have been to Asia). Moreover, this was Pyeongchang's second bid; it almost upset Vancouver in the competition for the 2010 winter games and was therefore seen as a serious contender for 2014.

The three countries campaigned hard to win the IOC's favor. The Russians, armed with the professional image consultants who had helped London win the 2012 Summer Games, argued that they had not hosted the

Olympics since the 1980 Moscow Games and that their time had come. President Vladimir Putin, an avid skier, came to Guatemala for the IOC vote and uncharacteristically conversed with attendees at the meeting in English, French, and Spanish in order to win their favor. Putin announced a $12 billion capital commitment by federal and regional governments to fund the Games and build the infrastructure should Sochi win the bid. Austria campaigned on its proven record of hosting 250 European world championships and two Olympics. Like the Koreans, this was Austria's second bid, having come in third in the competition for the 2010 Vancouver Games. Chancellor Alfred Gusenbauer went to Guatemala to court the IOC, but in the end, the Austrian bid was hampered by a blood-doping scandal at the 2006 Turin Games in which the IOC banned six Austrian athletes.[8] The Koreans felt confident going into the final IOC vote in Guatemala, having almost won the 2010 bid. They pressed the point that Asia had only hosted the winter games twice in the past hundred years. They substantially improved their bid package from 2010 to have, by all accounts, the best technical presentation of the lot for 2014. This gave them a leg up over Sochi which had little extant infrastructure or technical plans. President Roh Moo Hyun also traveled to Guatemala to lobby for the IOC vote and in particular opined about how winning the games would help foster unification of the two Koreas.

Much to the surprise of some, Sochi, Russia, was the IOC's choice in spite of Salzburg's and Pyeongchang's experience competing for the 2010 bid. The news was greeted with jubilation in Moscow and disappointment in the other capitals.

What is so interesting about the bid for the 2014 Winter Games is how the three themes of identity, diplomacy, and change resonate throughout the discussion. When news of the IOC choice reached Russia, it was immediately contextualized in terms of Russia's national identity and global image. Putin described the bid as the world's recognition of Russia's growing international status and prestige. Commentators referred to the 2014 bid as marking Russia's reemergence from a decade of economic malaise dating back to 1998 when the country suffered from an acute crisis because of a sharply devalued ruble and billions in debt defaults. Buoyed by economic growth and high energy prices, Russian commentators associated the Sochi bid with the country's "getting off its knees" and returning to the world as a global leader.[9] All this came with just winning the bid—they had not even hosted the games yet! Sport in this sense is a powerful prism through which national images get refracted. Success in sport is intimately tied to nationalism and is seen as validating self-identity and aspirational goals.

The Koreans justified their candidacy in terms of how sport could create breakthroughs in North-South reconciliation in ways that regular diplomacy could not. In addition to their strong technical report, the ROK bid committee expressly made the point that Pyeongchang was situated in Gangwon, which was the only province divided between North and South on the peninsula. The provincial governor melodramatically stated how it "pained him" to be chief bureaucrat for Korea's only divided province and that Pyeongchang's hosting the games would help to end the stigma of national division.[10] While in Guatemala President Roh continued to play up these appeals to the IOC. Roh declared that Pyeongchang's hosting would act as a diplomatic bridge toward Korean unification. He promised that the two Koreas would amaze the world by entering the opening ceremonies as a unified team as they had done in Sydney in 2000. Roh made clear his view on the causal role that sport can play even where regular diplomacy fails:

A formation of a unified team will have two meanings: it will be the result of accelerated and closer cooperative relations between the two Koreas and will be an important milestone at how far Korea has come, it will add impetus in bringing reconciliation to our relations. We believe the enhancement of sport [between the two Koreas] is among the most important national strategies.[11]

Hours before the IOC selection committee was to announce their decision, the North Korean national Olympic committee chair, Jang Ung, declared in dramatic fashion that his country would for the first time officially support the South Korean bid committee's proposal to host the games. Jang further stated that if Pyeongchang won, then the North would cooperate in jointly training and fielding a united Korean team, in participating in the torch relay (thus implying a single united peninsula), and in hosting the opening and closing ceremonies. These would have constituted significant new steps in inter-Korean cooperation, confirming how sport can create diplomatic opportunities that might not otherwise exist.[12] In the end, despite their having come in second for the 2010 Games, the Koreans did not win—probably because they overplayed the diplomatic card. The flip side of stressing so emphatically that sport can facilitate inter-Korean breakthroughs is to insinuate that a contrary decision by the IOC would render the international body guilty of undermining unification—not a good strategy.

The Olympic bidding process, with its technical presentations by candidate cities, provides an idea of the amount of physical change that sport can unleash on a country. Hosting a sporting event like the Olympics is akin to throwing a party for the world for two weeks. Cities go through a systematic process where they try to secure the bid seven years before the event; then they undertake a massive national preparation project entailing hugely expensive infrastructural changes that cost tens of billions of dollars for everything from new airports to highways to environmental cleanup. At about the five-year mark, the city will host a smaller-scale regional event as a dress rehearsal for the big event. The Koreans followed such a strategy in preparation for the 1988 Summer Games in Seoul and already had developed much of the infrastructure in preparation for the 2010 bid. What was surprising about the Sochi win for 2014 was the lack of physical preparation, other than a $12 billion capital commitment up front. What the Russians can be assured of now is a breakneck pace of development until 2014 and costs that are sure to surpass $12 billion. As I will discuss, countries that are on the cusp of emerging from developing-nation status often use sporting events like the Olympics as a rapid accelerator of development to globalize a city's infrastructure, telecommunications, and hotels. Each time this has happened, whether in Seoul 1988, Mexico City 1968, or Beijing 2008, the scale and pace of transformation is breathtaking.

The interesting question is whether the physical change translates into political change. In the cases of Sochi in 2014 and Beijing in 2008, regimes that are less than democratic are hosting a sporting event that is the embodiment of liberal values. The Olympic Charter prizes individualism, freedom, and fair and open competition, among other values, all of which could be considered anathema to illiberal political systems. In addition, the media attention that accompanies the Olympics Games has the effect of shining the international spotlight on flaws in a country's domestic system and foreign policies. How countries like China and Russia respond to this unintended political aspect of sport is a hugely important question with implications far beyond the final gold medal tally.

3

MORE THAN JUST NATIONAL PRIDE

Sport captures the national imagination. When an athlete representing her country competes and wins, she elicits a feeling of success and a patriotic identification among her countrymen that art, music, entertainment, and politics cannot replicate. Sport is a powerful prism through which national identity gets refracted; it affects how a nation sees itself and the image it wants to portray to the rest of the world. The key link between sport and identity is emotion. Victories represent the validation of one's place in the world, or they symbolize a national aspiration. Sport is a cathartic and emotional experience that lends to prideful self-identification (think "USA! USA!").

Sport can be manipulated by elites to create allegiance. The nationalistic identification with sport is a form of expression that does not challenge state stability; it often fosters unity and can distract from other problems. For this reason, political elites have actively intervened in staging big sporting events as an instrument for creating national identity and unity.[1] Colonizers used sport to "civilize" and subsume the traditional culture of the colony and create an allegiance to the colonizer (e.g., the introduction of cricket by the British). Sport also became a way to represent the birth or rebirth of a nation, just as the 1972 Munich Olympics represented West Germany's arrival on the world stage and, as I shall discuss in detail later in this chapter, the Olympic Games in Asia represented the arrival of Japan, Korea, and China.

NATION BUILDING

We know that sport can create national pride. That is fairly intuitive, but in what observable ways is this link between sport and national pride and identity manifested? Sport can be a powerful symbol of nation building because it promotes a sense of unity and identity in young nations or newly formed ones. In Yemen, for example, sport was used effectively to forge positive attitudes toward the unification of the country. The 1990 union of North Yemen (the capitalist Yemen Arab Republic) and South Yemen (People's Democratic Republic of Yemen) was bound to be dominated by the relatively better off North. In spite of North Yemen's larger population and richer economy, the guiding principle adopted by the political leadership for an initial three-year period of integration was unity based on strict equity. The government tried its best to faithfully administer this equity principle as it went about the enormous task of stitching together the country. Uniting the two governments' faceless bureaucracies, ministries, and postal systems equitably, however, did not capture the imagination of the Yemeni people like unification of the two football leagues.

Think about it. If, for argument's sake, the cities of New York and Boston were to unite (admittedly impossible), few people would pay much attention to the merging of city government bureaucracies like the Port Authority or the transit systems. But everyone would be intensely interested in a merger of the New York Yankees and Boston Red Sox. And the success of this merger would have significant impact on the citizens' identification with and support for the larger union. The symbolism of sport in this admittedly far-fetched example is clear.

In Yemen, the union of the two leagues had to be carefully considered. The initial step was to bring the two leagues and teams together to play in Yemen's first unified football season. The symbolic importance of this first season for fostering feelings of unity was not lost on the Yemeni leadership. They appropriately named the first championship tournament the "Yemen Cup." More important, they played the final match on the first anniversary of unification. A national team then had to be selected to compete in the 1990 Asian Games in China. Again, principles of unity and equity became very significant. Planners had to choose between fielding a team of the best players, regardless of whether they hailed from the north or south, or adhering to a strict quota system regardless of the players' relative talent. The former promised a better team, and that team's performance might foster positive feelings about unification. On the other hand, the team's strong performance might be offset by feelings of alienation and discrimination felt by some Yemenis.

In the end, the Yemenis chose the quota system, selecting thirty-two members for the national team equally from the north and south. Every last detail was meant to ensure a sense of equity. The team roster listed northern and southern players alternately. Captainship of the team rotated every four games between a northerner and southerner. The two assistant coaches were from the north and south (the head coach was Brazilian). Obviously, this did not make for the best team, but the organizers cared less about winning and more about a public display of equity that would help the nation-building process between the two peoples. Sport became a stage on which important ideational and political messages could be sent about how the political leadership wanted the united nation of Yemen to come together. As one observer correctly noted: "Competing as a truly unified team was the central concern; at best, winning the matches was a secondary matter. Symbols were clearly more important than substance."[2]

North and South Korea have also used sport to create a sense of unity. Through participating together at international sport events, the two halves of a nation have sought to live vicariously the dream of national unification. In June 2000, president Kim Dae Jung of the south and Kim Jong Il of the north held a breakthrough summit; it constituted the first meeting between peninsular leaders since Korea's division in 1950 and was the showpiece of South Korea's "sunshine" policy of engagement with the North. Shortly thereafter, the world watched with rapture as 180 North and South Korean athletes participated in the opening ceremonies at the Sydney Olympics as a single delegation flying a white "unification" flag with a U.N.-blue-colored peninsula emblazoned on it. Though the two Koreas did not field united teams for the actual Olympic competition, the symbolism of unity was not lost on the spectators, who gave the Koreans a standing ovation. Two years later at the Asian Games in Busan, South Korea, the two delegations again marched together in the opening ceremonies in an equally moving moment. The Busan games marked the first time the DPRK participated in an international sporting event hosted by the ROK, and they brought a large delegation of more than 600 athletes, cheerleaders, and officials, who were warmly welcomed in the South. At the 2003 Asian Winter Games in Aomori, Japan, the two Korean teams not only marched together in the opening ceremony but ate meals, sat in the bleachers, and, of course, rooted against the Japanese together.[3]

The aspirations of the ROK are eventually to field a united team of the best athletes to compete, not just march, at the Olympics. The inter-Korean negotiations for the Beijing Olympics and other international sporting events took place in Guangzhou in September 2005 between the two National Olympic Committees, and an agreement was reached in principle to field a united team. Negotiations continued in Kaesong, with the IOC sometimes participating as a third party and actively encouraging the talks in spite of real-world disruptions like the DPRK missile tests in July 2006 and nuclear test in October 2006. The IOC chair, Jacques Rogge, sent letters to both DPRK leader Kim Jong-il and ROK president Roh Moo-hyun urging a solution and even promising an increased number of spots for a united Korean team. The two sides reached agreement on the flag of a united team (the "Unification" flag) and the anthem to be played on the medal podium (a traditional Korean folk song, "Arirang"), and even the uniforms, but the negotiations ran into the same dilemma faced by the Yemenis. According to officials involved in the talks, the ROK held to the standard that a united team for Beijing should field only the best athletes and best talent from the two countries.[4] This merit-based approach did not work for the DPRK, however, which wanted to use a quota system of 50 percent for each country.[5] For a country like South Korea, with world-class athletes and one of the world's largest economies, this formula was hardly acceptable. In the end, the two countries agreed to field once again a unified delegation of supporters for the Beijing Games. The February 2008 agreement specified that they would send a total of 600 supporters to Beijing by train from the South, across the DMZ, and through North Korea on railways refurbished by the South.[6] Though not as substantive as the Yemen case, sport allowed the two countries to vicariously live out hopes and aspirations that diplomacy could not create. Sport created feelings of unity and accorded to the weaker North equality and respect.[7]

ASSERTING INDEPENDENCE

Another way that sport and identity are linked is through the assertion of national independence. Throughout history, sport has served as a channel for expression of political independence and a distinctive identity. In Europe, for example, Irish sport was intimately linked with opposition to English rule for over a century. The Gaelic Athletic Association was established in 1884 with the express purpose of promoting traditional Gaelic sports. The GAA mounted an aggressive campaign to revive traditional Irish sports such as hurling and Gaelic football. It also consciously resisted English sports like rugby, soccer, and cricket. Only the fourth Olympic Games of the modern era and the first to hold medal ceremonies with the national flags of the three winners, the 1906 Olympics in Athens offered another opportunity for the assertion of Irish identity. Peter O'Connor, an Irishman who was unable to register for the Games as an Irish athlete and could only do so under the British Olympic Council, won the silver medal in the triple jump. During the medal ceremonies, O'Connor shimmied up the flagpole to pull down the

British Union Jack and waved the Irish flag in protest. Sport became a potent symbol of Ireland's political independence and resistance at the beginning of the twentieth century.[8]

In Asia, the adoption and later rejection of baseball was intimately connected with Japanese assertions of national identity and independence. Today, Major League Baseball enjoys its largest overseas market in Japan, where some 60 percent or $100 million of its foreign revenues originate. With stars like Hideki Matsui of the New York Yankees, Ichiro Suzuki of the Seattle Mariners, Daisuke Matsuzaka of the Boston Red Sox, and fourteen others in the major leagues, Japan's love for baseball spans the national and international. Former Japanese prime minister Junichiro Koizumi was a big baseball fan and used to played catch with President Bush of the United States. Japan's longest-serving ambassador to the United States, Ryozo Kato, when asked which was his greater love, Mrs. Kato or baseball, reportedly responded sheepishly that he has been playing baseball long before he met his beloved spouse. Kato retired from the Japanese foreign ministry in 2008 and was rewarded for his service to the nation and the U.S.-Japan alliance with his greatest personal honor—becoming commissioner of Japan's professional baseball league. Japanese baseball teams are incredibly popular; hometown players who do well in the American major leagues make front page news; and an entire generation of Japanese youth have adopted the games as the national pastime.

Japan's interest in baseball was sparked by American missionaries from the 1850s through the 1870s, and baseball emerged as one of the first team sports in a country that engaged in individualistic pastimes like judo and kendo. As one author noted, baseball was appealing to the Japanese because the conduct of the game reflected values that were seen as consonant with those of Japan, including the emphasis on harmony, order, loyalty, and discipline.[9] American baseball teams toured Japan in the early twentieth century, bringing stars such as Babe Ruth, and they were wildly popular. The game even changed Japanese vocabulary as many baseball terms in English were adopted as loan words in Japanese. The adoption of baseball was linked to Japanese identity in two positive and complementary ways. First, it validated the notion of Japan as a modern nation. At this time in history, Asia was contending with the intrusion of Western powers and the question of whether Asia was capable of "modernization" along the lines of the West. The adoption of American baseball by the Japanese fit well with their own view that they were the only Asian power capable of modernization and internationalization. Second, while baseball reinforced Japan's view of its own modernity, it also showed that traditional Japanese values were compatible with Western modernization. Because baseball was seen as reflecting values that were traditionally Japanese, it symbolized the ability of Japan to modernize but still retain its cultural identity.

By the 1920s and 1930s Japan's identity and its views on baseball changed. After having established itself as the premier imperial power in Asia by defeating the Chinese in wars in 1895 and the Russians in 1904, Japan grew anxious after World War I when Tokyo came to feel that the postwar settlements did not accord Japan its rightful place in the international hierarchy of states. As relations with the United States deteriorated, baseball came to be seen by the ultranationalists in Japan as the sport of the adversary and as "un-Japanese." The first step at remediation was to "Japanize" the game by removing all American phrases. But eventually they banned the game entirely, and baseball did not return to Japan until after World War II, when occupation authorities reintroduced the game as a way to bring reconciliation between the two nations. America's pastime became a symbol for asserting an internationalized Japanese identity in the nineteenth century, only to be replaced by a nativist nationalism in the early twentieth.[10]

TOILETS AND "STEAMED CRAP"?

While sport can inspire nations to view themselves as distinct and special, it can also create the opposite effect, an impulse toward conformity. Sport and national identity have been woven together in terms of a country's global "standardization." The idea here is essentially that hosting global sporting events matters deeply for national pride and identity even as it pushes a nation toward international conformity. Hosting tens, if not hundreds of thousands of international spectators and media agents compels a country to do its best to depict itself as meeting a globalized, five-star, "blue-ribbon" standard and to promote its identity as a modern, advanced nation. Hosts do not want to be seen as "backward" and "underdeveloped" but as cosmopolitan and as "user-friendly" for any jetsetter from Los Angeles or Zurich. This impulse is strongest for countries just on the cusp of development, such as those Asian nations that are rapidly trying to meet the global standard but at the same time are painfully insecure that they will be viewed as anything but cosmopolitan.

A nation's desire to conform is manifest in the rapid development of infrastructure, hotels, and airports before big sporting events (as I will discuss later), when nothing less than "state-of-the-art" facilities is acceptable. But the intensity of this standardization impulse is demonstrated most vividly in the small details rather than the big, billion-dollar projects.

One example? Toilets.

In preparation for the 2002 FIFA World Cup, Korea spent billions of dollars to build seventeen new state-of-the-art stadiums in conjunction with its cohost, Japan. Hotels were renovated, and city landscapes were beautified. But the Koreans wanted to leave no stone unturned. They wanted to ensure that Europeans and North Americans that came to Korea for the World Cup would feel as though Seoul and surrounding cities were no different from Paris or Chicago. The football matches were to be played in different cities, and foreigners would be taking road trips around the country both to attend the matches and to take in the sights. For Koreans this raised concerns about highway rest stops and, in particular, the lavatory facilities. Planners thought it would reflect badly on Korea's international image as a globalized modern country if foreigners walked into a rest stop and saw only Asian-style squat toilets. This prompted a major campaign to renovate all the toilets in Korea. In October 2001, the Koreans hosted the three-day World Toilet Summit attended by hundreds from the industry and some curious tourists. The summit featured photo exhibitions of winning restrooms and percussionists playing music on toilets. In later symposia, "visitors were given the opportu-

FIGURE 7. SOUTH KOREAN TOILET-SHAPED HOUSE

SOURCE: © EPA/CORBIS

nity to create fecal-shaped sculptures from clay in random colors complete with eyes and polka-dotted bowties, for use as desk ornaments or refrigerator magnets."[11] The goal of the summit was to raise lavatory standards nationwide because clean and modern rest rooms were perceived to comport with the image of an advanced, cosmopolitan nation—hence the logo for the campaign: "Clean Toilet, Clean Korea."[12] The mayor of Suwon City in South Korea, Sim Jae-duck earned the nickname of "Mr. Toilet" for his leadership and gained international notoriety for building a toilet-shaped house (see figure 7); he was later elected to parliament. The Koreans gained the support of the World Health Organization, and became the engine of a global campaign to improve restroom facilities for the estimated 2.6 billion people around the world who lacked proper facilities.

Planners for the Beijing 2008 Olympics experienced similar impulses to conform and put forward the image of a modern, user-friendly nation. The tourism bureau knew that the tens of thousands of foreign spectators for the Games would be fanning out through the city and sampling Chinese cuisine. Only a fraction of these would be able to read Chinese characters, and most would have to navigate their way through the unsystematic English translations of items on the menu. Most of these translations were very rough, if not incorrect. Some were downright scary. Befuddled but famished tourists would sometimes find themselves puzzling over whether they should order "Steamed Crap" (steamed carp), "Bean Curd made by a Pock-Marked Woman" (stir-fried tofu in hot sauce), "chicken without sexual life" (spring chicken), "The temple explodes the chicken cube" (Kungpao Chicken), or "Burnt Lion's Head" (Chinese-style meatballs). So the Beijing Tourism Bureau released a list of some 2,753 items commonly found on Chinese restaurant menus and standardized their English translations. While the immediate purpose of the tourism bureau's actions was to make life easier for the foreigner and perhaps also to dissuade them from rather strange impressions of Chinese dietary habits, Olympics organizers were clearly focused on using sport to convey an image of a modern, clean, and globalized China to the world.

SPORT AS SOFT POWER

Sport can translate into "soft power" for some countries. Sport is not just a tool to express national identity or to convey an image of modernity; in some cases a positive reputation in sport can augment a country's global status and position on the world stage. In this sense, strong performance in sport becomes a power asset—albeit soft power—to the country's benefit. Perhaps the best example here is the case of Australia. Australia is a country that punches way above its weight on the global stage. It is respected as a serious global citizen and a contributor to numerous multination efforts by the United Nations and other organizations devoted to poverty alleviation, climate change, and peacekeeping. Australia was one of the four key members of the Tsunami Relief Core Group (including the United States, Japan, and India) established in December 2004 to respond to the tsunami that hit South and Southeast Asia. It has been a critical ally in the global war on terror, committing combat troops and special forces to operations in Iraq and Afghanistan. Australia was one of three countries in the Bush administration's second term to be given an Official Visit to the White House, which is the highest ceremonial visit that can be bestowed on a foreign leader. The other two countries were the world largest democracy (India) and one of the world's largest economies (Japan). How has Australia managed these accomplishments and attained a level of prestige and treatment in the international system when it is a middle-ranking (at best) power in terms of overall capabilities?

Some of Australia's gravitas in recent years stemmed from the close relationship shared between its former prime minister, John Howard, and President Bush. They became good friends with similar worldviews and domestic agendas. This closeness was reflected not only in the granting of a rare Official Visit to Howard when he came to the White House in May 2006 but also in personal touches like the donation of two saplings from the White House arboretum (descended from trees planted by Presidents John Adams and James Madison) to the Australian ambassador's residence in Washington.[13]

Australia's international prestige also stems from the way it has effectively used sport to bolster its reputation and image. Both its strong performance in and its hosting of major global sporting events have put Australia on the map as a country to be reckoned with. Australia has hosted the Olympics a disproportionate number of times since 1896 given its population, having had the games in Melbourne (1956) and in Sydney (2000). By contrast, all of Asia hosted the summer games only three times over the same period. At the 1956 games, Australia took thirty-five medals overall and thirteen gold, placing them third in the overall standings, and in 2000 they finished third overall with fifty-eight medals—remarkable achievements given the relative size of the population. Moreover, the Australians take their sport seriously. In 1976 when the Australian Olympic team performed poorly at the Montreal Games, winning only five medals (none gold), the government established a national sports institute and boosted public spending in order to improve performance.

Australia has developed a reputation as the gold-standard host of global sporting events. The 2000 Sydney Olympics was widely acclaimed as one of the most well managed Games in Olympic history. Coming after the 1996 Atlanta Games, in particular, which were not well managed, the Sydney Games stood out as exceptional. Both the regular Games and the Paralympics received acclaim from the IOC and sportswriters. Some commentators proclaimed that Sydney should become the permanent host city for the Summer Games, and they raved about the organization, hospitality, and beauty of the city. Others commented that Sydney made Paris look like a small town in Texas.

How does being a great host and having great athletes translate into soft power? First, sport draws the international spotlight to Australia. Second, once in the spotlight, Australia enjoys natural spillover effects. Its citizens are good hosts and good athletes, but the country itself is displayed as a model of liberal-democratic values, an open economy, and a global citizen in a region of the world where such values have not yet become universal. For Americans, sport has allowed Australia to tell its story as a country that shares a New World heritage with the United States and, moreover, has fought side-by-side with the United States in every modern war.

These were the very same messages that were broadcast to the world by Secretary of State Condoleezza Rice during her Australia trip in March 2006. Her three-day schedule was typically filled with meetings with Prime Minister Howard, Foreign Minister Alexander Downer, and the rest of the Australian cabinet. She met with veterans of the wars in Iraq and Afghanistan and gave a lecture to a university audience in addition to numerous other events. But the Australians and Rice's communications director, Jim Wilkinson, knew full well the secretary's love of sports, and they scheduled a day trip to Melbourne for Rice and her party (myself included) to attend the Commonwealth Games. At the swimming event, Rice watched the meets with Olympic gold medalist and world record holder Ian Thorpe, and she participated in gold-medal presentations for some of the participants. Her visit to the Commonwealth Games received significant media attention, and the spectators were wildly enthusiastic to see the American secretary of state in the stands.

While this is great public relations, it also demonstrates an important link between sport and soft power. Hosting Rice at the games garnered Australia worldwide attention on the global stage. While the visual message was a shared American-Australian love of sport, the deeper political message was of a strong partnership and alliance based on common values in both sport and society—open competition, the rule of law, transparency, and fair play.

This had the effect of elevating a remote country to the center stage as a model of liberal democracy and global citizenship.

It is interesting to note that Australia's global reputation cannot be explained in terms of material power as the country is not a top-tier military or economic power. Nowhere was this soft power more apparent than in the 1993 IOC decision on the host for the 2000 Summer Olympics. The two finalist cities were Sydney and Beijing. By most metrics, Beijing should have been favored. China had not yet had the Games while Australia had hosted once already. Bringing the Games to the world's largest population would have had untold benefits for the Olympics and its many corporate sponsors. But on ideational grounds, there was no contest. Australia was viewed as a society that fully embraced and embodied the values of the Olympic ideal. China, on the other hand, only four years removed from its brutal crackdown on the student demonstrators in Tiananmen Square, represented the antithesis of this ideal. Sport and soft power were mutually reinforcing for Australia. And for China, it would take another eight years before Beijing would win the bid for the Games.[14]

IDENTITY AND THE OLYMPIC GAMES IN ASIA

The history of the Olympic games in Asia is a brief but extremely interesting one. As noted already, in the hundred-plus years of the modern Olympic movement, the hallmark Summer Games have come to Asia only three times. All of these occasions, however, were "mega-events" in the truest sense of the term and marked critical watersheds for the national identities of the host countries, as well as in the images they sought to present to the world. For Japan in 1964, Korea in 1988, and China in 2008, there was arguably no single event in the post–World War II era that played a bigger role in shaping the nations' narratives of where they had come from and what they aspired to be in the future. The story begins with Tokyo.

THE TOKYO OLYMPICS OF 1964

The Tokyo Olympic Games of 1964 were an unprecedented experience for both Japan and Asia. Because this was the first time the Olympics were held in an Asian city, Japan was in many ways seen as the region's trailblazer and as the first Asian power on the world stage after the Second World War. Questions abounded about how well the Games would fare in an Asian culture. Would the infrastructure meet world-class standards? Would language barriers prove to be a problem for organizing the Games? The stakes were high. Each successive Olympics up to that point had promised to be the largest yet, and Tokyo was no exception. The 1964 Games were slated at the time to set new records in participation and attendance, featuring more than 7,500 athletes and more than 150,000 spectators from all over the globe.[15]

1964, NOT 1945

For Japan, the Games marked a turning point in the country's twentieth-century identity and, in particular, offered an opportunity to provide the people with some separation between Japan's prewar and postwar identities. This was not the first time Japan attempted to attain this separation. In 1955, Japan had bid to host the 1960 Olympic Games. Memories of the war were still too fresh in the minds of many, though, and the bid was unsuccessful. Thus, to have the opportunity to host in 1964 offered a high-profile and symbolic way to close the door on a dark period in Japanese history. If the narrative of the first half of the twentieth century featured Japan as a revisionist, ultra-nationalist power that tried to change the international system only to suffer defeat and foreign military occupation, then the 1964 Games offered a way to write a new postwar narrative for Japan: Japan was no longer an aberrant actor in the international system but a peace-loving, affluent, and supportive member of that system. The Olympics celebrated this transition. As Ian Buruma aptly observed, on October 10, 1964 (the opening of the Tokyo games), Japan's decades of shame were over and the nation and its people rejoined the international community.[16]

This notion of closing the door on the past was evident in the news coverage of the Games. The *New York Times* in the run-up to the event wrote about how Japan, once an insular nation, went to the freakish extreme of instigating war throughout the Pacific in hopes of domination, only to suffer defeat. They describe the defeat in 1945 as not only military but a "crushing" psychological blow from which it took the nation two decades to recover. In this regard, "the Olympics . . . staged in Tokyo, symbolize for the Japanese the final absolution, the total welcome back into the family of nations."[17]

Japan performed well at the Olympics, winning sixteen gold medals (third behind the United States and the Soviet Union) and taking fourth in the overall medal tally. While there were many wonderful performances, the Japanese women's volleyball team stole the show. The team members were mostly local talent from Osaka who were extremely hard working and well coached. They had toured Europe before the Games and defeated every opponent, who had afflicted them with the derogatory nickname the "witches of the East." The team's performance generated a great deal of excitement in Japan as school children pasted posters of their favorite players on their bedroom walls. The country exhibited a sense of national pride that had been largely discouraged during the occupation period and in the early postwar years.[18] When the volleyball team defeated the Soviet Union for the gold medal, "The whole nation was glued to the TV screen and together shed tears of joy at the end of the game."[19] The performance of the women's team and Japanese athletes overall in the games took on much greater significance than merely playing well and winning gold, silver, or bronze medals before the home crowd. Each medal won was another nail in the coffin of 1945, sealing forever Japan's dark past and showing that the new Japan was excelling in its return to the community of nations. The idea, therefore, was that 1964 was not 1945—the Olympics were in effect a temporal wall between the two eras (analogous to what the 1972 Munich Games would mean for Germany and its past). Nowhere was this symbolism more apparent than in the opening ceremony, where crowds watched with glee the entrance of the Olympic torch to the stadium as it was passed ceremoniously from one distinguished athlete to the next. Yoshinori Sakai was given the honor of carrying the torch to light the stadium's Olympic flame, marking the start of the Games. Sakai, a young Japanese runner, was born only a few minutes after the atomic bomb was dropped on Hiroshima. There could not have been a more powerful way to make the point that the start of the Games symbolized the end of prewar and wartime Japan.

1936 AND 1964

At the same time that the 1964 Games meant the closure of one period in Japanese history, they also signified the continuation of another—the story of Japan as a great power returning to its rightful place in the world. In this regard, the common description of the 1964 Olympics as marking Japan's "coming-out" party on the world scene as a major power is not accurate. As discussed later, this may be an apt description of South Korea's and China's hosting of the Olympics, but the differences with Japan are subtle and important.

Japan was always a major power, even in defeat after 1945. Going back to the late nineteenth century, Japan was the only country in Asia to meet the modernization trends from the West. It defeated the two major powers in Asia, China and Russia, within the span of a decade. After World War I,

Japan's status as a great power was validated in its participation in the Washington and London naval conferences. Tokyo was originally selected in 1936 to host the 1940 games. At the time, the IOC viewed this as an entirely appropriate choice, commensurate with Japan's position as a world power. But the decision came under greater and greater scrutiny as imperial Japan's hegemonic ambitions led to the invasion of Manchuria and the outbreak of war with China. In 1938 imperial Japan in a dramatic move pulled out from hosting the event and was not invited by the IOC to participate in subsequent Olympics because of its wartime actions (the 1940 Games were relocated to Helsinki, Finland, and then cancelled outright with the outbreak of World War II). The question at the end of World War II, therefore, was not if Japan would reemerge as a great power, but when and in what form this inevitably would occur.

Japan's postwar economic recovery and return to the status of a major power coincided with the hosting of the Olympics. By 1964 Japan was the fifth largest industrial nation, having enjoyed a decade of unparalleled prosperity of 10 percent annual average growth. This period of "high growth," as it was known in Japan, was also marked by full employment. Soaring personal income levels were manifest in the 1960s phenomenon of the ubiquitous Japanese tourist groups. Japan became a GATT Article 9 country, which was symbolic of its ascension as an advanced industrialized nation and open economy. It became an International Monetary Fund Article 8 country in 1964, another sign of its advanced status.[20] It received full membership in the exclusive OECD club of nations in the same year and hosted the International Monetary Fund–World Bank conference.

For the Japanese, therefore, a connection was evident between 1964 and 1936—not in the sense of a return to ultranationalism and imperialism but in the world's acknowledgment of Japan as a great power. After 1936, the question was not if, but when would Japan be allowed again to host the Games commensurate with its major power status in the world. The answer was that the country would have to wait nearly two decades. In this sense, the 1964 games evoked the feeling of a long wait having finally come to an end. A *New York Times* curtain-raiser the week before the Games captured the atmosphere of the moment:

> It was as if Tokyo's 10 1/2 million people couldn't wait for the official beginning of an event to which they have looked forward for almost a quarter of a century. Tokyo was to have had the Games in 1940, but World War II intervened. The atmosphere in the city today was buoyant, as if in a culmination of 24 years of tense waiting.[21]

The Games were terribly important to Japan, and the long sense of waiting and self-absorption was evident in the lack of concern for almost anything else that was happening in the country or around the world at the time. Japan was in the midst of a political crisis, its prime minister beleaguered, but all was put on hold until after the Games. China exploded its first nuclear weapon during the Games (on October 16, 1964), but that did not even matter: "Who was faster, stronger or cleverer in 20 Olympic events seemed far more important for the moment to the crowds at the stadiums and other locations of the Games than who was prime minister somewhere or who was playing with explosives."[22]

The 1964 Olympics were also crucial for Japan's conception of its identity and the image it sought to present to the world. As much as the Games offered a willing Japanese population the opportunity to show the world that their nation's identity as a fascist and ultranationalist regime was no more, the Games also represented the culmination of the country's long awaited chance to return to the center stage. The 1964 Games did not herald Japan's coming out as newly developing country but its reintegration in the twentieth-century international system as a reformed global power. The proper comparison therefore is to Rome (1960) and Munich (1972) rather than to Seoul (1988) and Beijing (2008).[23]

THE SEOUL OLYMPICS OF 1988

Once known as the "hermit kingdom" Korea's games represent a kind of coming out party, for which Seoul's final countdown is already in progress today, Monday, September the twelfth, nineteen-eighty-eight.

–BRYANT GUMBEL, *THE TODAY SHOW*, SEPTEMBER 12, 1988

Unlike Japan, the ROK did not have a history as a major power when it was given the opportunity to host the Games in 1988. The Olympics became the primary vehicle through which the ROK propelled itself onto the world stage as a major power. This coming-out party, however, was not the only role that the Games played in constructing Korea's identity. An unpopular military regime in Seoul also sought to use the Games to validate its own legitimacy. Finally, Seoul's hosting of the Games marked a watershed in the Cold War competition between the two Koreas. This competition would lead tragically to bloodshed and terrorism.

From the division of the country in 1945 by the United States and Soviet Union to the end of the Korean war in 1953, Korea's story was of a small, postcolonial, half-country without a particularly bright future. After the establishment of two separate states in 1948, USAID officials predicted through the 1950s and early 1960s that South Korea would not advance beyond an agriculture-based economy that in the best of scenarios might eventually export light manufactured goods. These "expert" predictions proved wrong as the world witnessed three decades of unparalleled growth and the rise of the ROK to become the world's twelfth largest economy. The 1988 Seoul Olympics therefore represented a "coming-out" party of the grandest caliber to celebrate the country's arrival and to show off its accomplishments after three decades of hard work.

The idea for bidding to host the Olympics originated during the Park Chung Hee regime (1961–1979). Park was a general turned politician who took power in a military coup in 1961 and ruled the country with an iron fist for nearly two decades. In order to build an economic bulwark against the communists in the North, Park promoted export-led growth of the economy and focused on development of South Korea's steel and other heavy industries, largely with capital and technology borrowed from Japan. His strategy succeeded in turning South Korea virtually overnight into one of the world's biggest steel producers. This growth came at the expense of political liberties as the country, run under the "Yushin system," lacked all semblance of the democracy that Korea would later become. Park himself was a Japanophile, having been trained in a Japanese military academy when Korea was a colony of the Japanese. Park's contemplation of an Olympic bid was motivated by his desire to emulate the 1964 Tokyo Games but also by the need to legitimate a flawed authoritarian regime. The general-turned-civilian autocrat was assassinated by his own bodyguard in 1979 before he could act on his desires.

The idea of bidding for the Olympics was reintroduced under a subsequent military regime a couple of years later. Chun Doo Hwan was a middling general who took over the country in a military coup in December 1979, only two months after Park's assassination. He viewed the Olympics as an opportunity to demonstrate to the world the ROK "success story." Planners hoped for a carefully crafted production that carried several messages about Korean identity. First, hosting the Olympics would allow the world to see that South Korea was no longer a poverty-stricken, war-torn country. Second, through the Games, the world could witness the culmination of

Korea's transition from a nineteenth-century "hermit kingdom"—an intro-verted country unable to meet Western standards of modernization—to a strong, modern, prosperous, and cosmopolitan nation. Third, the Olympics would provide a stage upon which to show Korea's wealth and stability as a "success story" for which the Cold War was fought. Finally, the staging of the Games in Seoul would mark the final victory of the South over the North in economic terms—a competition that began in 1948 with the more endowed and developed North (as a result of the Japanese occupation) falling irrecov-erably behind the South by the 1980s. The Olympics validated the nation's view that it had earned standing among developed nations, surmounting untold obstacles after much hard work.[24]

The Koreans believed the stage upon which their "coming-out" story would be told was especially momentous because it was to be only the sec-ond Olympics held in Asia and the first in twelve years to have full par-ticipation because of the boycotts by the United States and Soviet Union of the 1980 Moscow and 1984 Los Angeles Games, respectively. Roughly 14,000 athletes and officials from 160 countries would descend upon Seoul, guar-anteeing that these would be the biggest Games ever. The fact that Seoul had unexpectedly beat out its former colonizer, Japan (and the city of Nagoya), to win the bid made the event even more significant a symbol of Korea's rise to greatness despite overwhelming historical odds. According to Don Ober-dorfer, Seoul won the bid over Japan simply because they "worked harder" at it. They appointed the Hyundai magnate Chung Ju-Young as the Seoul Olympic Committee chairman, and he and other ROK *chaebol* industrial-ists traveled around the world winning the votes of IOC delegates. Prime Minister Lho Shin-yong of South Korea led an intense lobbying campaign at the United Nations General Assembly in New York City. Seoul prepared detailed technical presentations, including an incredible scale model of the future Olympic Village. In case the IOC delegates were not interested in that, Seoul also brought a stable of fashion models to Baden-Baden, Germany, in September 1981 to gain favor with the mostly male IOC delegates.[25] In the end, Seoul won the bid over Nagoya by a two-to-one margin.

In staging the Olympics as a showcase of ROK development, the Koreans even had a dress rehearsal in the form of the 1986 Asian Games. After win-ning the bid in 1981, Korea rushed to renovate Seoul (which I discuss in a later chapter) in time. The Asian Games were the ROK's first opportunity to host an international sporting event, and they provided an early chance to show off new facilities, as well as a time to work out all the kinks for the real show two years later. Korea's athletes performed well in the Asian Games, amassing a total medal count higher than that of China (224 to 222).

There is no denying that Seoul had accomplishments to show off at its Olympic coming-out party. The country had experienced an astounding 12 percent annual growth rate. The year of the Games, the ROK broke $100 billion in total trade, buoyed by the phenomenal growth of exports at 27 percent per annum. Like Japan in 1964, the ROK also shifted IMF status to conform with Article 9. Having undergone political liberalization reforms just fourteen months before the games (see chapter 6), Korea could also showcase itself as one of the most successful cases of peaceful democratic transition in the world. The fact that the ROK athletes did well in the Summer Games, tallying more gold than any countries except the Soviet Union, East Germany, and the United States, only reinforced the image of a Korea rising from the ashes.

Korea's desire to display its confidence as an advanced, developed nation through the Summer Games, however, masked a national insecurity that occasionally seeped through. The Korean government and people both grew angry when NBC's coverage of the Games included segments on the history of military dictatorships, gender inequality, and the fact that Korean culinary habits included eating dog (spokespeople for the Koreans immediately sought air time to explain that this did not mean Koreans ate their own pets). The Seoul Olympic Organizing Committee filed complaints over the "casual and undisciplined" manner in which the American team entered the stadium during the opening ceremonies, waving "hi mom" at the television cameras and not marching in the orderly fashion in which the Seoul organizers had planned. More complaints were filed against NBC for giving inordinate television coverage to the roughing up of a New Zealand referee by Korean spectators after the decision in a close boxing bout went against Korea. The aggrieved Korean pugilist then staged a protest by sitting in the middle of the ring for hours after the bout. Ian Buruma wrote that the South Korean quest for portraying national power and identity in the games was so intense that it recalled for him the 1936 Berlin Games. The opening ceremonies, he notes, combined images of economic power with military patriotism and folk culture in a manner reminiscent of communist or fascist systems.

It was perhaps unfair to watch the opening ceremony in Seoul with Leni Riefenstahl's films and books by prewar chauvinists fresh in my mind. Yet, with all the banners bearing Coubertin's slogans, the uniformed athletes marching behind their national flags, the parades of folk dancers, the sacred flame, the thousands of children drilled to form gigantic flags and Olympic symbols, the chatter about Peace and Progress, one realized how profoundly old-fashioned South Korea . . . still is.[26]

The 1988 games were about much more than sports; they became an assertion of Korea's new national identity. But Korean insecurity stemmed from a national desire to portray a developing product as a finished one. The story of the Korean political and economic miracle was true, but it was still unfinished. Democracy had triumphed over dictatorship, but this democracy was still a fledgling. Economic growth was indisputable, but the Koreans still feared being viewed as a less-developed country.

> Power, miracle, power, power! One cannot escape it: these are the expressions of a country that is either superbly confident or racked by anxiety. Whenever one assumes it to be the former, evidence of the latter tends to break through.[27]

REGIME LEGITIMATION

Seoul sought the Games not only to show off its wares to the world but also to gain some political legitimacy. It is often forgotten that when the ROK won the bid in September 1981, it was a far cry from the democracy that it would become by the opening ceremony in September 1988. The IOC decision to award the Games to South Korea, in this regard, was very controversial. It came at a time when the military dictatorship in the ROK was widely seen as illegitimate. Having come to power in a coup, the Chun regime sentenced to death the opposition politician and democracy activist Kim Dae-jung. In the spring of 1980, Chun also turned the South Korean military against its own people to brutally suppress demonstrations in the southwestern city of Kwangju in Cholla province, killing hundreds if not thousands of citizens. Human rights groups strongly condemned the IOC's decision as irresponsibly sanctioning a human rights violator and pressed other countries not to recognize the decision.[28]

Unsurprisingly, the Chun regime saw hosting the Games as concerning much more than sport. Chun was a middling general who had violently taken power with a small coterie of peers. His rule was far from stable, which led him to crack down viciously against any perceived challenges. If one general could wrest power so quickly, so could others. The Olympics constituted a valuable and unique opportunity to gain some political legitimacy and consolidate his hold on power. As one study noted, for "many other nations of the world for whom South Korea was virtually an unknown entity, the decision to award the games automatically and almost immediately conferred the sort of legitimacy that could hardly have been gained in any other way."[29] Chun also sought to improve his position by negotiating a visit to the White House in February 1981 as the first major head of a foreign state to be the guest of President Ronald Reagan. President Reagan wanted to demonstrate America's strong support of South Korea as a frontline Cold War ally after the difficult years of the Carter administration, when the United States proposed the withdrawal of all its troops from the Korean peninsula. Reagan's invitation was harshly criticized by liberals at the time, who viewed it as bestowing legitimacy on a horrible regime. Few knew, however, that the quid pro quo for the visit was Chun's promise to commute the death sentence of Kim Dae-jung, who would later be the democratically elected president of Korea.

GAME OVER

The 1988 Seoul Olympics marked a turning point in the diplomatic and economic competition between the two Koreas. By hosting the world's biggest sporting event, the ROK was demonstrating an affluence and level of development that the DPRK had no chance of matching. The start of the Seoul Games, in this regard, truly marked the end of the inter-Korean competition for legitimacy.

At the time, inter-Korean relations were not nearly as amiable as they are today under South Korea's "sunshine" policy of engagement. Seoul and Pyongyang were locked in a zero-sum game of competitive delegitimation, in which each sought diplomatic victories at the other's expense. This animosity was driven by Cold War dynamics but also by genuine rivalry and competition from the 1950s through the 1970s. The DPRK was better endowed in terms of mineral resources and retained most of the heavy- and chemical-industrial development left by the Japanese colonists in the first half of the twentieth century. According to CIA figures, per capita GNP in the North rivaled that of the South at least until the 1970s. Moreover, while the DPRK dictatorship enjoyed the steadfast support of big-power communist patrons in China and the Soviet Union, the ROK was the model of political instability, suffering one coup after another and facing the prospect of the U.S. withdrawal of its 40,000 ground troops from the country during the Carter administration. The ROK's economy expanded rapidly, however, while the North reached the limits of its aged and unimproved industrial capacity. From the late 1970s the ROK started to irreversibly pull away economically from its northern rival. By the 1980s it was openly acknowledged by the world that the competition was over. In this context, when the ROK was given the Olympics it essentially meant "game over" in the inter-Korean competition for legitimacy and status in the world.

The DPRK did not initially respond for two months to news in September 1981 of the IOC's decision. The DPRK leader, Kim Il-sung, then proposed that the North cohost the Olympics and call them the "Chosun Games" after the ancient Korean dynasty. The proposal lacked credibility as the DPRK had never put in a bid with the IOC to host the Games, but in the spirit of sportsmanship, Seoul replied by offering the North a few events that it might host. Pyongyang was greatly offended by the ROK offer and threatened that it would lead the entire Eastern bloc of countries to boycott the Games. The threat was not only empty but also embarrassing for the DPRK as the Soviet foreign minister, Eduard Shevardnadze, stated publicly that his country had no plans to boycott the Seoul Olympiad on behalf of Pyongyang.

North Korea agreed to enter into negotiations with the ROK under IOC stewardship for a formula for cohosting. The ROK initially offered four events that could be held in the North. DPRK officials responded with the unrealistic proposal to host half of all Olympic events and then held out for at least a third. Seoul countered with a proposal to give the table tennis and fencing events (two DPRK favorites), but the talks ended in August 1987 without resolution.[30]

North Korea then chose to deal with the problem in its own way. Two spies were sent on a terrorist mission to blow up an ROK civilian airliner for the purpose of dissuading other countries from participating in Seoul's games. Three months after the failure of the inter-Korean Olympics talks, Korean Air flight 858 was blown to pieces while flying from Abu Dhabi to Seoul, killing all one hundred and fifteen passengers aboard. Kim Seung-il (seventy) and Kim Hyon-hui (twenty-five), posing as father and daughter, boarded the plan in Baghdad and disembarked at Abu Dhabi after setting their explosives. The two terrorists planned to escape from Abu Dhabi to Rome, where they would meet up with a support team, but because of flight complications, the two were stuck in Abu Dhabi for two days as they awaited a connection through Bahrain. Authorities caught up with them in Bahrain, where both tried to commit suicide by ingesting poison, but the younger Kim survived and later confessed to the entire plan.[31] The 1987 Korean Air bombing was a tragic example of how sport quickly can become political in a way that threatens lives. In the end, the DPRK's attempts to foil the ROK's coming-out party failed miserably, and Seoul successfully hosted the most well attended Olympic Games in three decades. (Before the start of the 1986 Asian Games in Seoul, a bomb went off an the main international airport in Seoul, and many believe this was associated with North Korea as well.) The

DPRK had to live with the stigma of its horrendous acts as the 1987 bombing became one of the stated rationales for keeping the North on the U.S. list of state sponsors of terrorism. To this day, when DPRK officials are asked about the event there is no sense of pride, only shame and discomfort at such a self-destructive act. In sum, the significance of the 1988 Seoul Olympics went far beyond the final score. The Games validated South Korea's view that it had arrived on the global stage after much hardship. This coming-out party, while celebrating the South Korean economic miracle, was also crucial to an unpopular regime's search for political legitimacy. The North's attempt to sabotage the Games through terrorism only reinforced the world's will to make the Games a success. This success was a stark reminder of how far behind the DPRK really was.

THE 2008 BEIJING GAMES

Sport and identity have been deeply intertwined for China. The 2008 Beijing Games represented a hybrid of the Korea and Japan cases. As the 1988 games had for Seoul, the Beijing Olympiad constituted a "coming-out" party that announced China's arrival on the world stage. Like Tokyo, however, China also sought to use the Games as a way to close the door on a difficult period in its national history and to start anew. By hosting a well-managed Olympics and by the strong performance of its athletes, the Chinese also used the Games to demonstrate the strength and legitimacy of their own system to the Chinese people and to the world. Finally, while the government tried to show the uniqueness of Chinese civilization and culture through the Olympics, China also sought to demonstrate that it was and ultramodern nation and that the city of Beijing was no different from Paris or Berlin. In spite of its accomplishments, however, insecurities and anxieties similar to the Korean case were evident.

COMING OUT CHINESE STYLE

The 2008 Olympics represented the crowning achievement of China's long effort after the Cultural Revolution to modernize and develop the country. Deng Xiaoping's 1978 modernization reforms emancipated the country ideologically from communism and marked its first cautious steps toward a socialist market economy. China then worked hard at modernization for three decades and on the thirtieth anniversary of Deng's campaign finally achieved its goal and marked its arrival on the world stage with the Olympics. As one commentary in a government-backed Chinese newspaper elaborated, "If the ideological emancipation in 1978 marked the starting point of China's journey toward a 'well-off society', Beijing's hosting of the 2008 Games signals that the country is taking off."[32] The physical "trophies" of this success included gleaming skyscrapers and state-of-the-art facilities built for the games, including the world's largest airport terminal and the most technologically advanced Olympic facilities ever constructed (see chapter 5). These structures were monuments to the country's economic growth rates, which were greater than 10 percent. Nowhere was the symbolism of China's rise and the Olympics more apparent than in its first manned spaceflight, a 2003 payload launch. The astronaut wrapped himself in the banner of the Beijing Olympics as China crossed the threshold of this new frontier. This was not, of course, the first time that China had used sport to mark transitional moments in its history. In 1955, the first National Worker's Games marked the establishment of the PRC and the CCP. In 1959, the First Chinese National games marked the tenth anniversary of the PRC. And the 1990 Asian games held in Beijing marked China's arrival as an Asian power.

China sought to create its own version of "shock and awe" in August 2008. The Chinese sought to use the Games to show off to the world China's advancements but at the same time create a sense of awe at China's culture and civilization. This "shock and awe" strategy was apparent in the celebrations on August 8, 2007, which marked the beginning of the one-year countdown to the games. The Chinese threw a party for one million guests (literally), inviting the IOC president, Jacques Rogge, and also such world-renowned Chinese personalities as the NBA star Yao Ming. The ceremonies culminated with fireworks and everyone singing "We Are Ready!" a song ostensibly meant to assure the world of Chinese preparations for the games but symbolically indicating China's readiness to ascend the stage as a global power.

While the parties, skyscrapers, and stadiums exuded the confidence of a new China, strong and ready, one could not help but feel that the hard-working Chinese were trying too hard. They wanted so badly for the Games to be remembered as the greatest Olympics ever, where Chinese athletes won gold medals and everyone marveled at China's modernity and were humbled by its vast civilization. The slogan "One World, One Dream" for the Beijing Games meant for Chinese that, finally, Beijing was truly at the center of the universe. Not unlike the Korean case, however, this intensity reflected insecurity as much as it did self-assurance. The supreme overconfidence, even arrogance and haughtiness, covered up a deeper anxiety that China would not meet the standard and that any failure in the execution of, or performance in, the Games would reveal to the world the real China. China exhibited the hypersensitivity seen in Korea when their tactics to frame the event did not go exactly as planned, whether this came in the form of complaints about international press coverage or protests over NGO attempts to embarrass the Chinese during the Olympic torch relay. In the run-up to the Games, for example, almost every Chinese official I met at the White House and in Beijing touted China's greatness in hosting the Games. NGOs, media stars, and activists then started to call on Beijing to improve its human rights record, its environmental measures, and its foreign policy (see chapter 6) and advocated boycotts of the Games without such changes. With their plans to focus the Games only on sports and China's greatness gone awry, Chinese foreign ministry and Olympic Organizing Committee spokespeople became visibly upset in press conferences, accusing the world of a conspiracy to sabotage the Beijing Games and to rob China of its moment in the sun. They railed against attempts to play "Cold War politics" with the Olympics, referencing the politically motivated boycotts of 1980 and 1984. All Chinese officials not directly involved in the Games subsequently refrained from any public discussion out of anxiety that the mere mention of the Games would be an opportunity for political linkage. I once sat through a sixty-minute PowerPoint presentation by a high-level Chinese official in charge of technology and environment where the word "Olympics" was not mentioned once as he explained all the efforts by China to improve its air and water quality. When I asked about how much the preparation for the Olympics has spurred this activity (answer: a lot), he responded by rote that the Olympics are about sports and nothing else.

I will discuss how the Olympics affected Chinese nationalism later, but here I would first draw attention to China's hypersensitive response to any negative events before and during the Games. The anger of the Chinese reactions was intense, greater than what any previous Olympic host had displayed. The Chinese were clearly angry over the attempts by NGO groups, for example, to disrupt the Olympic torch processions in March and April 2008 in San Francisco, London, and Paris, among other cities. As the South Koreans had done in 1988, the Chinese complained publicly about attempts to ruin their cherished moment in the sun. Sympathizers organized counterprotests calling for "sport purism" and allowing the Games to progress without politics. But Beijing's hypersensitivity sometimes spilled over and became its own foreign policy issue. When the torch procession went through Seoul in April 2008 for instance, thousands of Chinese students studying in Korea were encouraged by the Chinese embassy to come out for the event. As many as 6,000 students, armed with PRC flags and t-shirts (there are about 37,000 Chinese students studying in the ROK, more than in any other foreign country), gathered at the start of the torch procession at the Seoul Olympic Stadium (site of the 1988 Games) and in the city center. But as citizens of a democracy with a vibrant civil society, South Koreans also came out in droves to express their views about the Beijing Olympics. Some were pro-Tibet, and others protested China's labor abuses and refoulement of North Korean defectors. An ugly dynamic ensued in which the Chinese students started to surround protesting South Koreans as they felt compelled to "defend China's honor" against attempts to spoil the ceremony by demonstrators. Clashes between the two groups occurred, and Chinese students threw bottles, rocks, and metal pipes at the South Korean demonstrators. The fighting in some places spilled into major South Korean hotels as foreigners and others looked on in horror. Video of the attacks spread like wildfire across South Korean media, and it soon became a major diplomatic incident. Prime Minister Han Seung-soo said that the ROK would take diplomatic and legal action to restore the "pride and dignity" of Koreans. The PRC ambassador was summoned into the ROK foreign ministry for a formal protest. Seoul promised to deport the instigating Chinese students and to restrict visa entries for future students. A prominent South Korean legislator visiting Washington at the time of the incident trembled with anger as he promised that Koreans would never forget and expressed outrage at the audacity of the Chinese students to attack their Korean hosts in their own country. The interrelatedness of insecurity and identity was evident in Korea during the 1988 Seoul Games, but for the Chinese this sensitivity took on a new intensity. The fact that this violence erupted in South Korea is ironic but, in retrospect, not entirely unpredictable given the two countries' similar feelings of Olympic insecurity.

GHOSTS OF TIANANMEN

This anxiety and insecurity stems from China's desire to use the Games not only to tell a story about a new, modern China but also to close the door on two dark chapters in China's history. China defines its own identity and prestige in relation to the West and to Japan. In a deeper historical sense, the Olympics were to mark the end of China's story as the "sick man" of Asia. In Chinese eyes, their country was victimized in Asia as the object of Western and Japanese imperialism for centuries, its territory carved up and its sovereignty violated. For three hundred years, China was ruled by the foreign Manchu dynasty. The country then lost territories like Nepal, Burma,

Indochina, Korea, and Taiwan to stronger powers. Its ports of Hong Kong and Macao and its mineral resources were also taken on a long-term basis by Western countries. In this sense, the Chinese see centuries of disgrace and dishonor in their relations with the West, Russia, and Japan. Even the physical image of sick Chinese old men was popular in the West as representative of the country. The 1893 World's Fair in Chicago actually had an "opium den" exhibit featuring real Chinese opium addicts.[33]

The Olympics represented the closing of this dark chapter in Chinese history. Just as the 1964 Games laid to rest Japan's ultranationalist past, the 2008 Games symbolized the end of centuries of humiliation, victimization, and shame. Hosting the world in grand Chinese fashion and ceremony meant that China would finally draw respect, recognition, and equality from the world. As a woman who attended the August 2007 countdown party explained, the Olympics "is a dream that has lasted for a century. . . . We want foreigners to discover Chinese culture and to know that China is a strong country now."[34] The intensity of the Olympic spirit therefore stemmed from much more than a love of sport; it was an assertion of a new Chinese identity. With this intensity, however, came a nagging anxiety that even the smallest foul-up in the performance or execution of the Games could ruin Beijing's best-laid plans.

The Olympics were equally important to the ruling Chinese elite as an instrument to eradicate the ghosts of the Tiananmen Square massacre of 1989. For the world, this event remained deeply embedded in their views of China, and the Chinese felt they had to live with the stigma of Tiananmen for over a decade. The Games gave the world images of a new China—peaceful, prosperous, and stable—rather than tanks plowing down unarmed students. The Chinese first attempted to do this with their bid for the 2000 Olympics. The bid was made in 1993, and China was one of the two finalists for selection, but it lost out to Sydney, Australia, by two votes. For the Chinese, this was an extremely humiliating experience. After all, China was a great country compared to the smaller and remote Australia. The Australians had already hosted the Games (1956 Melbourne), which favored Beijing. Moreover, the IOC president, Juan Antonio Samaranch, was openly in favor of awarding the Games to China. China's failed bid, however, showed that the blood of Tiananmen was still very much on the world's minds.

It is, therefore, no small coincidence that China utilized the physical space of Tiananmen to host several huge celebrations related to the Olympics. The July 2001 celebrations in the square (when Beijing won the bid) certainly offered the world a very different image from 1989: "Instantly the sky was ablaze with the colours of an exuberant fireworks display and, soon after, top leaders headed by President Jiang Zemin and Premier Zhu Rongji, acknowledged the enthusiastic acclamation of an ecstatically joyful crowd gathered in front of the Millennium Monument. Soon Tiananmen Square was alive with a heaving, flag-waving throng, embracing each other, unfurling streamers, singing patriotic songs, and dancing in delight."[35] The August 2007 countdown party for a million people was also held in Tiananmen Square, as was the ceremony marking the arrival of the Olympic torch to China. While there were other symbolic as well as logistic reasons for using this locale, the world's coming to associate Tiananmen Square with the Olympics rather than the lone student standing in front of a parade of tanks constituted part of a larger plan, as noted by the *Economist*: "Hosting the Olympics would wipe out the humiliations of the four years since the quashing of the Tiananmen Square protests and put their country back among the world elite."[36]

Performance, not just symbolism, was very important to the identity China sought to portray at the Games. This was because the whole story of a new China that was strong and prosperous, that closed the door on its sick man image, and that erased the memories of Tiananmen also required robust and athletic play. China could not merely host the Games; they needed to rack up a lot of gold as a substantive validation of China's rising status and place in the world. While China was first represented in the Games in 1928 in Amsterdam, their first athletes did not compete until 1932, and they did not win gold until 1984, when Xu Haifeng won the pistol shooting competition. Chinese athletes subsequently took fifteen gold medals at the Los Angeles Games, and sixteen gold medals at both Barcelona in 1992 and Atlanta in 1996. It was not until Sydney in 2000 that China took twenty-eight golds and placed fourth overall in total points, and at Athens in 2004, China accumulated thirty-two gold medals, second only to the United States (see table 4). The story of China's rise would not have been complete without their athletes bettering the record at Athens. Anything short of first place, given the identity-stakes behind the Games, would have been a failure.

Given all that was at stake, it is not surprising that China was so hypersensitive to Western media coverage of the Games. Anything less than positive reports, absent any political (i.e., negative) commentary, was deemed by some Chinese as hurtful, and by others as confirming an ages-old Western conspiracy to deny China its rightful place in the world. As I discuss later, this led to a reactive and negative nationalism rather than dissent within the Chinese system. The history of this issue goes back to the 1992 Barcelona Games and 1996 Atlanta Games, when some Chinese viewed the coverage

TABLE 4 SUMMER OLYMPICS MEDAL TALLY FOR AUSTRALIA, CHINA, JAPAN, THE KOREAS, 1896–2004

YEAR	AUSTRALIA: (TOTAL) GOLD/SILVER/BRONZE	CHINA: (TOTAL) G/S/B	JAPAN: (TOTAL) G/S/B	SOUTH KOREA: (TOTAL) G/S/B	NORTH KOREA: (TOTAL) G/S/B
1896	(2) 2/0/0—10th place	–	–	–	–
1900	(5) 2/0/3	–	–	–	–
1904	–	–	–	–	–
1906	(3) 0/0/3	–	–	–	–
1908	(4) 1/2/1	–	–	–	–
1912	(6) 2/2/2	–	–	–	–
1920	(3) 0/2/1	–	(2) 0/2/0	–	–
1924	(6) 3/1/2	–	(1) 0/0/1	–	–
1928	(4) 1/2/1	–	(5) 2/2/1	–	–
1932	(5) 3/1/1	–	(19) 7/7/4—7th place	–	–
1936	(1) 0/0/1		(20) 6/4/10—6th place	–	–
1948	(13) 2/6/5	–	–	(2) 0/0/2	–
1952	(12) 6/2/3	–	(8) 1/6/1	(2) 0/1/1	–
1956	(35) 13/8/14—3rd place	–	(16) 4/9/3—9th place	(2) 0/1/1	–
1960	(22) 8/8/6—5th place	–	(19) 4/7/7—9th place	–	–
1964	(18) 6/2/10—8th place	–	(29) 16/5/8—4th place	(3) 0/2/1	–
1968	(17) 5/7/5—	–	(25) 11/7/7—6th place	(2) 0/1/1	–
1972	(17) 8/7/2	–	(29) 13/8/8—6th place	(1) 0/1/0	(5) 1/1/3
1976	(5) 0/1/4	–	(25) 9/6/10—7th place	(6) 1/1/4	(2) 1/1/0
1980	(9) 2/2/5	–	–	–	(5) 0/3/2
1984	(23) 3/8/12—10th place	(31) 15/7/9—7th place	(30) 10/6/14—8th place	(19) 6/6/7	–

YEAR	AUSTRALIA: (TOTAL) GOLD/SILVER/BRONZE	CHINA: (TOTAL) G/S/B	JAPAN: (TOTAL) G/S/B	SOUTH KOREA: (TOTAL) G/S/B	NORTH KOREA: (TOTAL) G/S/B
1988	(14) 3/6/5	(28) 5/11/12— 7th place	(14) 4/3/7	(33) 12/10/11— 5th place	–
1992	(26) 7/9/10— 9th place	(52) 16/21/15— 4th place	(21) 3/8/10	(27) 11/5/11— 8th place	(10) 5/0/5
1996	(41) 9/9/23— 5th place	(49) 16/22/11— 4th place	(14) 3/6/5	(27) 7/15/5— 8th place	(5) 2/1/2
2000	(58) 16/25/17— 3rd place	(58) 28/16/14— 3rd place	(18) 6/7/5	(28) 8/10/10— 10th place	(4) 0/1/3
2004	(49) 17/16/16— 4th place	(63) 32/17/14— 3rd place	(37) 16/9/12— 6th place	(30) 9/12/9— 10th place	(5) 0/4/1

SOURCE: COMPILED FROM HTTP://WWW.DATABASEOLYMPICS.COM.

of their national team's performance as overly critical. For example, when the Chinese team entered the Olympic stadium at the opening ceremonies in 1992, NBC coverage referred to the Chinese athletes as products of an old-style East German sports machine, "using who knows what methods" to win Olympic gold.[37] At the 1996 Atlanta Games, television commentary on the Chinese team's entry included the fact that China represents one-fifth of the world's population, enjoys 10 percent economic growth, and offers a huge consumer market, but it also included reference to human rights abuses, intellectual property rights violations, threats to Taiwan, and rumors of performance-enhancing-drug use by its athletes (although none had been caught at the Barcelona Games). This led to complaints against NBC. Westerners sympathetic to China, such as Susan Brownell, saw this as unnecessary China bashing by the American media, which are still tainted by memories of the Cold War in their coverage of China. Others viewed it as typically critical reporting that aimed to give a full picture of the subject to the world audience.[38] These same debates were resuscitated on a grander scale during the 2008 Games. While there were indeed both positive and negative things that occurred that were clearly newsworthy, the intense debate and recriminations over the relative balance between these two types of

YEAR	CHINA (TOTAL) GOLD/SILVER/BRONZE	JAPAN (TOTAL) G/S/B	SOUTH KOREA (TOTAL) G/S/B	NORTH KOREA (TOTAL) G/S/B
1924–1952	–	–	–	–
1956	–	(1) 0/1/0	–	–
1960	–	–	–	–
1964	–	–	–	(1) 0/1/0
1968	–	–	–	–
1972	–	(3) 1/1/1	–	–
1976	–	–	–	–
1980	–	(1) 0/1/0	–	–
1984	–	(1) 0/1/0	–	–
1988	–	(1) 0/0/1	–	–
1992	(3) 0/3/0	(7) 1/2/4—10th place	(4) 2/1/1	(1) 0/0/1
1994	(3) 0/1/2	(5) 1/2/2	(6) 4/1/1—10th place	–
1998	(8) 0/6/2	(10) 5/1/4—10th place	(6) 3/1/2	–
2002	(8) 2/2/4—10th place	(2) 0/1/1	(4) 2/2/0	–
2006	(11) 2/4/5—10th place	(1) 1/0/0	(11) 6/3/2—10th place	–

SOURCE: COMPILED FROM HTTP://WWW.DATABASEOLYMPICS.COM.

news underlined how much value the Chinese placed on using the Olympics as an ideational space in which to present a new, modern, and positive identity to its people and to the world.

NO SPITTING!

Events like the Olympics create pressures on any society to conform to a global standard. I will deal with the effects of these socialization pressures on politics and foreign policy in a later chapter. Here, my focus is on China's perceived need to advance through the Games the image of China as a civilized, advanced, and modern society. The physical facelift undertaken by Beijing, razing traditional *hutong* neighborhoods and constructing parks, five-star hotels, and other buildings, has been part of this effort. Conforming with the idea of a "high-tech" Olympics, the Chinese invested hugely in information technology side by supporting the 300-plus events at 70 venues with over 10,000 computers, 1,000 servers, 5,000 results-systems terminals, and 4,000 printers, all staffed by over 4,000 techies.[39] But the Olympic organizers understood that the longest-lasting impressions of a modern China were to be had through people-to-people interaction as tens of thousands of foreigners descended on the country in the summer of 2008. For this reason, organizers went to inordinate lengths to "prepare" the people of China for the Games. The Beijing Tourism Bureau undertook massive "Wen Ming" (civilizing) campaigns, distributing more than 2.8 million pamphlets teaching Chinese Western public courtesies and proper etiquette, particularly in the presence of foreigners. One campaign stated that "No Smoking" really means no smoking. In keeping with a tradition that began at the 1992 Barcelona Olympics, Beijing Olympic organizers, beginning in January 2008, strove to make the Games tobacco-free by instituting a smoking ban in public places, including sport venues, hospitals, and schools. The Beijing Health Bureau trained more than 100,000 people to act as inspectors. The problem was that some 350 million Chinese population men smoke. The Beijing health and transportation bureaus instituted in October 2007 a "Green Taxi, Smokeless Cab, Health for All" campaign for Beijing's 66,000 cabs and a ban on smoking in other forms of public transportation.[40] Chinese nicotine fiends, who could be fined up to twenty-eight dollars, could barely abide by these rules, and the police (who also smoke) could hardly enforce them. Restauranteurs and bar owners strongly resisted the new law and succeeded in getting their establishments excluded. The ban raised such an uproar that the government relaxed the restrictions almost immediately for fear of popular unrest. Another campaign focused on advocating patience and politeness when waiting on line rather than the notorious Chinese habit of cutting. Hospital administrators and city officials, for example, conducted a campaign where they handed out long-stem roses to those waiting for pharmaceuticals or to pay bills. The Beijing Capital Ethics Development office, the official watchdog of etiquette improvement, started to enforce a 50 yuan (US$6.50) fine for spitting in public. The Xicheng District Health Bureau set up a group of volunteers who operated a "shame" movement, distributing tissues to spitters and asking them to wipe their expunged matter off the street and place it in paper bags. To reduce litter, trash cans were placed every 300 feet on main thoroughfares in Beijing. CNN reported that Beijing cabbies—a much-used form of transportation by foreigners—were pulled over by the etiquette police for spot inspections to make sure that they were brushing their teeth, showering, and maintaining basic hygiene so as not to be off-putting to Olympic spectators. In the run-up to the Games there were reports of a "social cleansing" operation by the police to clear the streets of Beijing of homeless, street vendors, and prostitutes before August 2008. But the police would do this with smiles on their faces. Known for their rudeness and indifference, Beijing's finest were asked to turn over a new leaf and underwent foreign-language training and "smile lessons" in preparation for the Games.[41] There were even regulations on *how* to smile—for hostesses of the Games, the smile must expose at least six teeth.[42]

Correct English translations have always been a major challenge for Chinese businesses and facilities. As I noted earlier, restaurant goers were treated to more systematic translations of menu items thanks to an effort by the Beijing Tourism Bureau to issue standardized English terms to replace such strange "Chinglish" as "steamed crap" or "chicken without sexual life." The effort extended to correcting more than 6,500 traffic and public signs. So a public park in Beijing dedicated to ethnic minorities with the sign "Racist Park" and a proctology hospital with a huge flashing neon sign, "Hospital for Anus," were among those given more accurate terms. As was done in Korea, hotline services were created so foreigners could pick up a phone to get just-in-time translations into English, Spanish, French, and other languages. The king of Spain himself, Juan Carlos I, came to China in June 2007 to inaugurate the Spanish-language call center. As Yu Debin, deputy head of the Beijing Travel Administration Bureau, noted, "It is a huge effort that costs a lot of money, but we must correct the mistakes to make the city ready for the world." All of these efforts represent a part of China's coming of age, and the Chinese view that the Olympics constituted the validation of decades of hard work and the creation of a strong (albeit insecure) new country that is no longer seen as the sick man of Asia.

4

GREASING THE WHEELS OF DIPLOMACY

You have opened a new chapter in the relations of the American and Chinese people. I am confident that this beginning again of our friendship will certainly meet with majority support of our two peoples.

—ZHOU EN-LAI TO U.S. NATIONAL TABLE TENNIS TEAM MEMBERS,
APRIL 14, 1971, GREAT HALL OF THE PEOPLE

With these historic words to a visiting delegation of American ping-pong players by the Chinese premier, a new era opened in Sino-American relations. This rapprochement would have effects far beyond Asia as the world welcomed the wealth of economic and geostrategic benefits created by the meeting of East and West. Who would have thought that a ping-pong ball could help facilitate this sea change in world politics? Sport is more than sport. It is a tool of diplomacy. Sporting events can carry a political significance that goes far beyond the final score. This significance is measured not only in terms of status and reputation, as I described in the previous chapter, but also by how countries and governments can be spurred to overcome diplomatic obstacles. Sport offers a symbolic, high-profile, and yet tactful tool for diplomatic statecraft that can accomplish what a standard embassy demarche could not dream of. In Asia, where tactfulness, symbolism, and subtlety are highly valued, sport has been unusually central to policy, arguably more so than elsewhere in the world.

Sport matters for diplomacy in two basic ways. First, sport offers an "out-of-the-box" tool for creating openings and progress between estranged countries that ordinary foreign-ministry negotiations cannot use. Second, politicians have not been averse to using sport as a tool of coercive diplomacy by boycotting certain sporting events or banning offending countries from participation. In this sense, sport has been used as a form of sanction that sends high-profile and symbolic political messages of disapproval.

GREASING THE WHEELS

Sport is a diplomatic lubricant. It can create the goodwill that might be needed to enhance a negotiation process. Or it might be the icebreaker—the event that gets a process rolling by creating some unexpected diplomatic traction. We need to be clear about the limitations of this argument, however. Sport is rarely itself the sufficient condition for diplomacy. If it were, we might be able to solve many problems with Iran, North Korea, or Burma merely by organizing a sporting event! Sport is most effective as a facilitating condition rather than as a specific cause of diplomatic breakthroughs (or breakdowns). Sport can be the symbolic step that comes at a moment when diplomatic currents are primed to move in a positive direction. It can create momentum or accelerate a process once the underlying conditions are right. In this regard, timing is everything. Should the sporting event come before any groundwork has been laid, then it won't be nearly as effective. On the other hand, if the diplomatic grounding is fertile enough, then sport can be tremendously helpful—not only by creating political goodwill but also by appealing directly to the general public in ways that can help political leaders press forward over the objections of entrenched interests. It provides leaders with a good barometer of public opinion and can catalyze grassroots support. For any secretary of state or foreign minister, it is easier to build a new initiative when you know the policy is supported by the public. Sport in this sense gives leaders the opportunity to tap grassroots support and build momentum for change over reluctant bureaucracies or opposition political parties.

In the late 1990s, for example, the onset of the Khatami regime offered a possible opportunity for thawing relations between the United States and Iran. In 1998 a small delegation of American wrestlers went to Iran to compete in the Takhiti Cup. The five wrestlers and five officials, constituting the first U.S. sport delegation to go to Iran since the revolution, met with a warm reception and standing ovations when they entered the arena. But this moment of goodwill did not lead to a broader improvement of relations. In 1999 Major League Baseball's Baltimore Orioles and the Cuban national baseball team played exhibition games in the United States and in Havana. The Orioles won the game played in Cuba (3 to 2), and the Cuban team won the game in the United States (12 to 6). These exhibition games undeniably created goodwill on both sides. Baseball is the national pastime in both countries and is strongly linked to American and Cuban national identity; in Cuba it had been played as a sign of resistance against colonial Spain's law banning the game in 1868 as a vehicle of Cuban insurrection.

The games allowed for a new narrative to U.S.-Cuban relations other than the Bay of Pigs invasion and the October missile crisis. Yet the timing of these baseball games did not comport with the state of diplomacy between the two nations; hence, the games were fun, but led to nothing substantive in terms of improved relations. By contrast, 2008 arguably offered an opportunity for baseball diplomacy as conditions in the difficult bilateral stasis entered a state of flux. Fidel Castro, Cuba's longtime leader, handed over power to his brother as his health deteriorated, bringing the country its first leadership transition in over forty years. On October 24, 2007, President Bush announced a new initiative to establish a multi-billion-dollar freedom fund for Cuba to help encourage a democratic transition in the country. When the ground shifts in this manner, the opportunity for sport—baseball in this case—to help shape positive movement should not be underestimated.

I encountered similar experiences with sport diplomacy during the Six Party Talks (involving the United States, Japan, China, Russia, and the two Koreas) from 2004 through 2007. As we worked at the beginning of the second Bush administration to restart the multilateral denuclearization talks after a year-long boycott by the DPRK, we received inquiries from the office of Congressman Jim Leach (R-Iowa) about inviting the DPRK wrestling team to the United States. Leach, a former Princeton wrestler, saw an opportunity in his capacity as chairman of the House Subcommittee on East Asian and Pacific Affairs to try to jumpstart the talks by creating some political goodwill through having the DPRK participate in the annual Dan Gable Iowa Wrestling Classic. Although Leach's intentions were honorable and meant in the best spirit for moving forward the diplomacy, there was absolutely no diplomatic momentum at the time that a sporting event of this nature could catalyze.

From late 2005, however, the pace of negotiations picked up considerably. In September 2005 we achieved the Six Party Joint Statement, comprising a set of principles and quid pro quos of economic and energy assistance for the North's denuclearization; in February 2007 we negotiated the first implementation of the Joint Statement, which led to a shutdown of the North Korean Yongbyon nuclear reactor facility and the reintroduction of IAEA inspectors to the country after their expulsion five years earlier; and in October 2007, the Six Party Talks produced the second implementation agreement, which promised a permanent disablement of Yongbyon and a complete declaration of all nuclear activities by the DPRK. In the midst of these negotiations, I took a trip to Pyongyang with Governor Bill Richardson of New Mexico and the former secretary of veteran affairs Anthony Principi to retrieve the remains of six American servicemen killed in action during the Korean war. The issue of sports diplomacy again came up. Staying at the guest house in Pyongyang, I turned on the television in my room late one night to one of the two channels, both state-run, permitted in the country (all other channels such as CNN and BBC showed blank screens reading "Connection Unavailable"). The North Korean women's soccer team was in the process of trouncing their opponents from Taiwan 8 to 0. The next morning as we drove from Pyongyang to the DMZ with the soldiers' remains in tow, my DPRK counterpart and I discussed the quality of the DPRK women's soccer team and the possibility of exhibition matches in the United States against NCAA collegiate women's teams. With some diplomatic momentum already established with the February 2007 agreement and the establishment of a "working group" on U.S.-DPRK political normalization, the idea of a sporting event that might create public interest and some goodwill had a much better chance of succeeding. My North Korean counterpart was enthusiastic and discussed the possibility of other cultural exchanges that would bring Americans to the North. Though not related to sport, the North eventually relayed an invitation for the New York Philharmonic Orchestra to come to North Korea in February 2008. Their trip was carefully prepared with the help of the State Department, and though some members of the orchestra had personal difficulties with performing in a country so replete with human rights abuses, the event came off well, creating some public interest in both countries. Events of this nature can help to begin a process of normalizing relations between two longtime adversaries.

Sport is most effective as a diplomatic tool when there is already some momentum on the ground generated by any number of variables, including changes in domestic politics or a leadership transition. Then sport can create new channels of communication, provide a vehicle for displaying goodwill, and tap the public's support for a change in policy that might otherwise be opposed by entrenched bureaucratic interests.

PING-PONG DIPLOMACY

In Asia, sport diplomacy has been unusually effective. The seminal case of sport diplomacy in Asia, if not the world, is ping-pong diplomacy and the opening of U.S.-China relations in the 1970s. The rapprochement after three decades had ramifications for international politics far beyond the bilateral relationship. Much of this was difficult to fathom, at least for the general public, before a ragtag collection of American ping-pong players found themselves suddenly thrust into the world spotlight and crossing new diplomatic frontiers.

The United States and Chinese national teams participated in the thirty-first World Table Tennis Championships in Nagoya, Japan, from March 28 to April 7, 1971. Table tennis hardly ranked among the top sports in the United States then as it did in Asia, but the Americans fielded a team of enthusiastic players from all different walks of life. This collection of unassuming soon-to-be diplomats included a DuPont chemist, a Long Island University professor, an IBM programmer, a psychology major from the University of Cincinnati, a banker, a U.N. employee, and a housewife from Grand Rapids, Michigan. The American team was outplayed by the superior Asian teams, though, finishing at the bottom of the rankings in both men's and women's play. But the historic unfolding of events took place on the sidelines of the tournament. According to the captain of the Chinese national team, Zhuang Zedong, he attempted to reach out to the Americans when a fortuitous set of events put members of the two teams in direct contact. Glenn Cowan, a boyish-looking hippie member of the U.S. team from Santa Monica, California, was looking for someone to practice with before his match. He asked a Chinese player to hit with him and the two started to practice. When Japanese tournament officials saw this, they knew the political implications and tried to shutter off that part of the hall so that nosy reporters would not see. The two players practiced for about fifteen minutes, but then the American inadvertently missed the bus to the match facility. Not wanting to be late, Cowan jumped on another team bus headed to the arena; it happened to be the bus of the Chinese national team. Cowan walked down the aisle of somber-faced athletes who made no eye contact or attempt at communication with him. At the time, there were no diplomatic relations between the United States and China, and official interaction between the two was extremely circumscribed. Diplomats had specific instructions about the nature and extent of conversation they could have with their counterparts. While such instructions would have no relevance for American citizens, in particular a good-natured and free-wheeling ping-pong player from southern California, they presumably affected the behavior of the stone-faced Chinese players when they saw the long-haired American. But Zhuang, a three-time world champion, took the initiative to welcome Cowan and presented him with a silk portrait landscape that he inexplicably had on his person.[1] Cowan sought to return the gesture and rifled through his bag but found nothing but a comb. He later found Zhuang, however, and presented him with a red, white, and blue tie-dyed t-shirt emblazoned with a peace symbol and words from the Beatles song "Let it Be," which a bemused Zhuang accepted.[2]

FIGURE 8. "US PING PONG PLAYERS AT GREAT WALL," *TIME* COVER, APRIL 26, 1971

Folklore has it that Chairman Mao Tse-tung was initially skeptical about the idea of using the American ping-pong team's visit to Asia as an opportunity for diplomacy. Japan, which hosted the tournament and had been steadily improving unofficial trade ties with China, reportedly conveyed to the Chinese the American delegation's desire to receive an invitation to visit China after the tournament, but Mao expressed disinterest. However, he was apparently delighted to hear about Zhuang's chance encounter with Cowan and noted that the young Chinese athlete was a pathbreaking diplomat wise beyond his years. Mao apparently changed his mind thereafter, and on April 7 the PRC conveyed an invitation to the U.S. team's captain, Graham Steenhoven, to visit China for exhibition matches at the conclusion of the Nagoya championships. According to some reports, the U.S. captain sought instruction from the American embassy about how to proceed, and, as Kissinger recalls, the embassy recommended that they accept the invitation.

From April 11 through 17, 1971, the American ping-pong team made the historic trip to China. The event was widely covered in the American and world press and was heralded as a new opening to China. *Time* magazine's cover story on April 26, 1971, read, "The Ping Heard Round the World." Glenn Cowan and this unassuming group of ping-pong-paddle-toting pioneers were the first Americans to enter China since the revolution in 1949. Images of their trip to the Great Wall, the Chinese opera, and other sites were plastered on the front pages of *Life* and *Time* magazines, and every detail of their trip was recorded as representative of a new thaw in U.S.-China relations. ATT reported that China accepted its first long distance call from the United States in twenty-five years while the team was there.[3] Premier Zhou En-lai received them in the Great Hall of the People and proclaimed their arrival as a historic moment of reengagement between Americans and Chinese. Zhou said, "The Chinese and American people used to have frequent exchanges. Then came a long period of severance. Your visit has opened the door to friendship between the peoples of the two countries."[4] Cowan asked Zhou what he thought of the hippie movement in the United States, to which Zhou responded diplomatically that youth are often dissatisfied with the current situation and are always in search of a greater truth. Back in Washington, President Nixon applauded the team's historic visit, noting also that "I was quite a ping pong player in my days at law school . . . I might say I was fairly good at it."[5] The popularity of the team's visit to China, according to some reports, led Nixon to announce the relaxation of the U.S. embargo on China in the midst of their stay (April 15) and this eventually paved the way for Nixon's historic trip to China in February 1972. The resulting rapprochement in U.S.-China relations permanently changed the strategic environment in Asia—all because of ping-pong.[6]

Ping-pong diplomacy was undeniably important to the rapprochement in Sino-American relations in 1972. It offered an out-of-the-box channel for demonstrating good intentions that no other form of diplomacy could replicate. But it unintentionally contributed to an underlying strategic decision by the Nixon administration to engage China. Unknown to the public at the time were systematic and aggressive diplomatic efforts by Nixon and National Security Advisor Henry Kissinger to open ties with Beijing. The ping-pong tournament came at a critical point in these secret contacts and helped facilitate the diplomacy, but if the strategic decision had not already been made, ping-pong alone would not have led to Nixon's breakthrough visit to China in February 1972. Sport was a necessary but not sufficient condition for the breakthrough.

Nixon's personal beliefs about opening China antedated his run at the presidency. As a Wall Street lawyer in 1966, Nixon went to Asia for a client (Coca-Cola) and wrote what later became a famous *Foreign Affairs* article arguing for the importance of engaging with China. He saw no alternative: "Taking the long view, we simply cannot afford to leave China forever outside the family of nations, there to nurture its fantasies, cherish its hates, and threaten its neighbors. There is no place on this small planet for a billion of its potentially most able people to live in angry isolation."[7]

Nixon and Kissinger acted on these beliefs in short order. Fifteen days after he took office in 1969, the White House ordered a review of U.S. policy to China and approved the resumption of ambassador-level talks through Warsaw, Poland, which had been suspended since 1967 and constituted the primary channel of communication between the two estranged countries. During a trip to Romania late in the summer of 1969, Nixon declared that the United States would deal with communist countries on the basis of pragmatism and foreign policy not ideology and internal policies, and he conveyed messages through President Yahya Kahn of Pakistan and Romania's Nicolae Ceaușescu, expressing his desire to open a dialogue with Beijing. In November 1969, during a refueling stopover in Guam, Nixon announced a new doctrine for U.S. policy in Asia that called for the gradual disengagement of U.S. ground troops from the Vietnam War and for Asian nations to take more responsibility for their own defense (this became known as the "Nixon Doctrine"). As evidence of his intentions, the United States ended the Seventh Fleet's patrolling of the Taiwan Straits; lifted a travel ban on American visits to China; allowed tourists to bring back $100 worth of goods from the country; relaxed diplomatic rules of engagement;

and started to refer for the first time to "Red" China by its official name, the People's Republic of China.

Progress made in 1969, however, was impeded in May 1970 when the Chinese protested U.S.-backed incursions into Cambodia. Relations then worsened in July 1970 after an altercation between Chinese fighter planes and a U.S. intelligence plane off the Chinese coast. Kissinger nevertheless pressed forward with his secret diplomacy and in October and November 1970 engaged in a set of communications with Premier Zhou through Kahn in Pakistan on a possible high-level visit to China by a U.S. official. The discussion, though hampered by Beijing's precondition that the entire agenda of such a visit should focus only on Taiwan, continued to move forward, and by January 1971 the Chinese had put into play the idea of Nixon's visiting China. On April 1, 1971, Nixon made the decision to lift the trade embargo on China. This decision was made before the Chinese invitation to the ping-pong team (April 7), but the announcement was later timed to take place during the team's visit to China (April 15).[8] In May and June 1971 Kissinger engaged in a set of secret missives with Premier Zhou on a Nixon visit. In order to maintain secrecy, Kissinger recalled that he sent these on plain white paper

FIGURE 9. PRESIDENT NIXON AND MAO TSE-TUNG SHAKING HANDS

SOURCE: © BETTMANN/CORBIS..

without White House markings to maintain anonymity.[9] In July 1971, Kissinger traveled to the region ostensibly to hold meetings with Yahya Kahn in Pakistan. Using the pretext of sickness and bed rest, Kissinger gave the traveling press a free weekend in Pakistan while he made a secret trip to Beijing to iron out the details of the presidential visit. Upon Kissinger's return to Washington, the White House made a televised announcement on July 15 that shocked the world: President Nixon would go to China.

The point of this brief historical excursion is to highlight that while the ping-pong tournament was important in bringing about the change in U.S.-China relations, its effectiveness was magnified by two years of substantive diplomatic contacts. Kissinger pressed these contacts not just because of the president's personal beliefs but because he understood the wider geostrategic forces at work in the region and in political debates at home. First, the opening to China was dictated in part by proximate U.S. needs in Vietnam. The Nixon administration took office faced with a domestic political imperative to reduce American involvement in the unpopular Vietnam conflict. The Nixon Doctrine's call for Asians to bear the greater burden of their own ground defense (while the United States maintained air and naval support and the nuclear umbrella) established the policy pretext for a drawdown in Southeast Asia. However, to implement a drawdown without corresponding improvements in relations with China would, despite any policy justification, look like a unilateral admission of defeat. Conversely, if hostilities in Vietnam continued, then improved relations with China were necessary to ensure that the conflict would not escalate into a direct confrontation between the two countries. Hence, at either end of the escalation/de-escalation continuum an opening to Beijing was critical. Indeed the joint communiqué that emerged from Nixon's China visit (the February 1972 Shanghai Communique) helped to clarify intentions on both sides regarding Vietnam. The United States asserted that it would continue to support the South Vietnamese but that these actions posed no threat to China. China in turn reserved the right to support the North Vietnamese, but the purpose of such support was to check Soviet influence in Hanoi rather than to oust the United States and overthrow Saigon.

Kissinger and Nixon also understood that the Sino-Soviet split was a critical new development in the regional balance of power that redounded to U.S. interests. Brewing since the 1950s, disagreements over spheres of influence and ideology within the communist monolith became full blown with armed border clashes in 1969, causing Moscow and Beijing to view each other as the proximate threat. Kissinger understood the ramifications of this split for power dynamics in Asia. The United States could occupy a unique geostrategic pivot position between these two communist adversaries as each would seek improved relations with the United States in order to preempt any condominium arrangements sought by the other that might isolate either Beijing or Moscow in this new three-way power dynamic. For this reason, the conditions were ripe for the United States to achieve Sino-American rapprochement as well as U.S.-Soviet détente.

Third, U.S. domestic politics favored an opening to China. Prominent Democrats such as Senators Edward Kennedy and Mike Mansfield were pressing the new Republican administration for a change in U.S. policy toward China, calling for the recognition of China in the United Nations and the removal of U.S. troops from Taiwan. Mansfield, as Senate majority leader, pressed to visit Beijing as a way to help reduce tensions over Vietnam, which Democrats believed might escalate into a U.S.-China conflict.[10] Indeed, during Kissinger's secret visit in July 1971 to Beijing, he made clear that Nixon did not want the Chinese to receive any other American politicians, particularly Democrats, before his scheduled visit in February 1972. As James Mann observed, "The Nixon White House wanted an exclusive franchise on visits to China."[11]

A confluence of geostrategic forces therefore provided the conditions for an improvement in Sino-U.S. relations. The Sino-Soviet split, the imperatives for a drawdown in Vietnam, and a new president's personal interest in China prepared the diplomatic ground for an event like ping-pong diplomacy. If ping-pong did not create the breakthrough, then exactly how did it play a critical role in facilitating the events that followed? For one, the overture to the ping-pong team came at the right time. As noted earlier, Beijing's response to the secret overtures from the White House from 1969 blew hot and cold. By the beginning of 1971, however, momentum started to build when the Chinese raised the possibility of Nixon's visiting China, but the key sticking point was the Chinese insistence that the sole agenda item for the visit be about Taiwan. Nixon and Kissinger responded that this was not possible and they had not heard from Chou En Lai for quite some time. In this environment, the news of the ping-pong team's trip was fortuitous. Kissinger believed the Chinese outreach to the American team was a goodwill gesture designed to convey a positive signals regarding the coterminous secret communications taking place.[12] The overwhelmingly successful visit gave both sides the confidence to press forward with the secret discussions, which ultimately led to Kissinger's visit only three months later. After the ping-pong team's visit Chou later sent confirmation through the Pakistanis that Beijing dropped the condition that the talks be only about Taiwan.

The ping-pong team's visit also facilitated diplomacy through its effect on public opinion. Though difficult to imagine in today's world, where technology makes almost any society relatively transparent, China was a closed book, particularly after the Cultural Revolution. It was a mystery, closed to the rest of the world. Moreover, until the April 1971 visit there was little news about the emerging Sino-American rapprochement. The only hint available was Nixon's *Foreign Affairs* article from 1966. Much of the public news on China instead tended to be negative, focusing on defections by Chinese diplomats or altercations between U.S. and Chinese planes. Meanwhile, the entrenched bureaucratic interests of the "Taiwan lobby" kept close watch to prevent any changes in U.S. policy. Thus Nixon and Kissinger's quiet and intensive diplomatic efforts were taking place in a vacuum, without public exposure and therefore without any real sense of the level of public support. In this regard, the ping-pong team's visit made eminently clear what the world thought of a Sino-American thaw. The public's fascination with a potential new chapter in Sino-American relations could not have been more enthusiastic. It acted as a counterforce to the power of the entrenched interests of the Taiwan lobby. Ping-pong therefore provided a clear indication of popular support that made it easier for the United States and China to press forward with rapprochement in ways that might not otherwise have been possible. As the *Time* cover story of the trip stated so aptly:

> Probably never before in history has sport been used so effectively as a tool of international diplomacy. With its premium on delicate skill and its onomatopoeic name implying an interplay of initiative and response, Ping Pong was an apt metaphor for the relations between Washington and Peking.[13]

ASIAN SPORT DIPLOMACY

Two of the least known but most successful cases of sport diplomacy in Asia took place on the Korean peninsula around the 1988 Seoul Olympics and the Asian Games. In each case, the government of the Republic of Korea used the sporting event as an effective tool to overcome Cold War barriers with its two major communist neighbors, the Soviet Union and China. Though these cases are not as well known as ping-pong diplomacy, they represent an effective use of sport to engineer diplomatic breakthroughs that fundamentally changed the geostrategic environment around the peninsula. The ROK used the 1988 Seoul Olympics to engage successfully with Moscow, eventually leading to the establishment of diplomatic relations in 1990. And the 1986 and 1990 Asian Games (hosted by Seoul and Beijing, respectively) gave the

ROK and China a pretext for crossing the Cold War divide despite China's alliance with its communist North Korean neighbor.

KOREAN NORDPOLITIK

The establishment of diplomatic relations between the ROK and the Soviet Union in 1990 was widely seen as a breakthrough in ending the Cold War in Asia. The Soviet Union became the first major power in Asia to have diplomatic relations with both Koreas (China and Japan did not, nor did the United States). The ROK used sport as a diplomatic tool in their larger strategy of "nordpolitik," or "northern policy." Modeled on West Germany's "ostpolitik," the Korean version, formed under the Roh Tae Woo government in 1988, stated that the ROK would seek normal relations with communist nations on the basis of pragmatism and economic benefits, rather than determining policy through ideology. Seoul would do this while maintaining three core policy principles. First, the new foreign policy outreach would be grounded in a stable domestic-political situation at home; second, the outreach would be grounded in strong relations with traditional allies (i.e., the United States); and third, it would be grounded in a strong economy.

Nordpolitik was a clear expression of South Korean confidence at the time.[14] Politically, the country had just gone through a peaceful transition to democracy in 1987 (which I discuss in the next chapter). The economy was running at an extraordinary 12 percent annual growth rate, creating an economic gap that the rival North Korean regime could not overcome. By any measure, the competition of social systems between the two that had raged during South Korea's days of postwar poverty, and as recently as the 1970s, was now over, with Seoul emerging the clear winner. In this sense, Roh's nordpolitik declaration of July 7, 1988, was not just about establishing diplomatic relations across the Cold War divide with Soviet bloc countries but, by doing so, also achieving the ultimate diplomatic victory of isolating the North from its communist patrons.

Nordpolitik's stated objective of normalizing relations with the Soviet Union was by no means an easy task. There was a history of mutual hostility and nondialogue between Moscow and Seoul. The Soviet–North Korea defense treaty, tens of millions of dollars in Soviet aid, and ideological support for Pyongyang made Moscow in South Korean eyes one of the primary patrons of the North Korean threat. Similarly, the Soviets saw South Korea as a forward base for U.S. ground, air, and naval assets in the region, as well as the third leg in the "iron triangle" (the United States–South Korea–Japan) designed to encircle and contain them. During the détente years in the early 1970s, as part of the efforts by President Park Chung-hee of the ROK to improve relations with communist countries, the Seoul participated in some private, academic exchanges, but, on the whole, nondialogue and mutual recrimination formed the dominant narrative for the relationship. Tensions reached their height in 1983 when a South Korean civilian airline (KAL 007) was shot down by a Soviet fighter plane, killing more than 200 passengers. This tragic incident resulted in the suspension of all bilateral dialogue, including nonofficial, private exchanges.

By the late 1980s, however, a series of developments pointed to a potential thaw in relations. In July 1986 Soviet leader Mikhail Gorbachev made a speech in Vladivostok calling for a new, more active and engaging role for the Soviet Union in Asia. In an effort to reduce tensions with China, Gorbachev also announced his intention to unilaterally draw down forces on the Sino-Soviet border. In July 1988, Roh announced the inauguration of the new nordpolitik policy, responding to Gorbachev's speech by calling for improved relations with communist countries based on pragmatism and economic gain. Gorbachev responded in September 1988 with a declaration at Krasnoyarsk, in which he explicitly stated his intentions to improve relations with the ROK. These declarations were followed by a series of economic contacts and semiofficial political meetings between the two sides from 1988 through 1990. These contacts led to the establishment of trade offices by KOTRA (Korea Trade Promotion Association), backed by the South Korean government, and the Soviet chamber of commerce in the summer of 1989. Consular functions were added to these trade offices in February 1990. These burgeoning contacts were finally consummated at the highest political level in June 1990 in San Francisco. Presidents Roh and Gorbachev held the first ROK-USSR summit in postwar history in a hotel room and agreed in principle to establish formal diplomatic relations. Relations were established in September 1990, followed by two additional summits in Moscow (December 1990) and on Jeju Island (April 1991) in which the two leaders reaffirmed their new relationship. The Soviets provided a formal apology for the first time for shooting down KAL 007 in 1983, and the two countries inked a major economic agreement, including a $3 billion ROK loan to the Soviet Union.

SPORT AND NONSPORT FACTORS

How does one explain the shift from decades of nondialogue to full diplomatic reconciliation in a period of five years (i.e., 1986 through 1990)? And what role did sport play? The prevailing explanation, of course, is the end of the Cold War. The end of the bipolar conflict in Europe had the effect of liquidating security and ideological barriers that impeded any sort of inter-action throughout the postwar period. Just as the ROK established trade and consular relations with Eastern European countries and the Soviet Union in 1989 and 1990, democratic elections and the demise of communist rule were taking place in Poland, Czechoslovakia, and Hungary. East Germany lost a massive outflow of people to the newly democratic states as they sought a way to get into West Germany. The Berlin wall fell in November 1989, and German unification occurred in October 1990. On the South Korean side, the end of the Cold War enabled Seoul to improve relations with Moscow without opposition from traditional partners, particularly the United States. Indeed, what facilitated the Roh-Gorbachev meeting in San Francisco in June 1990 was Gorbachev's earlier meeting with President George H. W. Bush in Washington, which effectively marked the end of the ideological hostility between the two superpowers.

An equally important factor leading to ROK-Soviet normalization was Gorbachev's new political thinking and program of domestic reform. Aimed at weakening the communist party's grip on domestic and foreign policy, perestroika represented a more pragmatic view that made a priority of re-invigorating the faltering Soviet economy. Soviet policy initiatives in Asia flowed directly from this. From Moscow's viewpoint, the Soviet Union was physically a part of Northeast Asia but had not yet enjoyed the benefits of the region's phenomenal economic growth. Gorbachev sought to tap into these benefits through a combination of diplomatic initiatives and tension-reduction measures. This was the purpose of Gorbachev's 1986 Vladivo-stok speech. It called for a unilateral withdrawal of Soviet troops from the Sino-Soviet border, reducing tensions with China and enabling Gorbachev to meet with Deng Xiaoping in May 1989 (a historic visit obscured by the demonstrations in Tiananmen Square). Gorbachev also proposed a forum for regional security cooperation in the speech and laid out plans for the development of Siberia to solicit Asian investment. Of the Asian countries, South Korea was seen as a particularly good fit for Soviet needs. It was a source of consumer goods and could provide foreign capital and technol-ogy for development of Siberia. In return, the ROK would gain access to a new export market and potential returns in terms of the development of natural gas, oil, and coal reserves. Moreover, the Soviet hope was that the ROK could play the role that Japan had not. Soviet attempts at eliciting Japa-nese economic cooperation on Siberia in the 1970s fell flat as a result of un-certainties in Japanese assessments of the economic viability of the projects and the absence of a resolution of the longstanding issue of the northern territories. Seoul was a particularly good target, therefore, for Gorbachev's initiatives: There was economic complementarity; there was hope that ROK interest in Siberia might spur Japanese interest again; and, finally, there was the view that outreach to a frontline Cold War state like Korea might help to remove Moscow's stigma as the region's threatening power. As a result, Moscow undertook a policy of creeping engagement to show good faith in improving relations with Seoul. In addition to the Vladivostok and Krasnoyarsk speeches, this included such practices as a more lenient handling of South Korean fishing boats caught violating Soviet territorial waters. Moscow also liberalized visa policies, allowing ethnic Korean populations living in different parts of the Soviet Union (e.g., Sakhalin) to visit Korea, and the Soviet government allowed for more cultural and academic exchanges with South Korea.

South Korean incentives for normalizing relations derived from the nordpolitik policy of the Roh government and the economic rationales I have already described. But an equally important motive for Seoul was winning the diplomatic competition with North Korea. At the time, relations among the two Koreas and the major powers in the region were seen in entirely zero-sum terms—that is, no one side could improve its situation without the other side being made worse off. In this light, having one of the North's primary Cold War patrons officially extend diplomatic recognition to its archrival in the South was considered the ultimate diplomatic victory in further isolating the North.

From the ROK perspective, other benefits could come from normalizing relations with the Soviet Union. Seoul calculated that a newly cooperative relationship with Moscow would affect the nature of the Soviet–North Korea defense treaty. The Kremlin indeed watered down its "automatic intervention" commitment to the DPRK after normalization with the ROK. Finally, normalization with the Soviets could pave the way for an ROK seat in the United Nations. It is often underestimated how important an objective this was for Korean foreign policy. Because of Cold War politics and the veto held by the two communist powers on the U.N. Security Council, the ROK was unable to become a member of the international organization as a divided country. Communist thinking at the time, supported by the DPRK, was that a two-Korea formula for the U.N. would cement the division of the peninsula as permanent. This constituted a source of great indignation for the crafters of South Korean foreign policy over the years as it reinforced the notion that South Korea was a "pariah state" and not truly a member of the international community without U.N. membership. Soviet recognition of the ROK would remove a major political obstacle to the goal of a U.N. seat, which the ROK finally achieved in 1991.[15]

WOOING THE SOVIETS WITH SPORT: THE 1988 OLYMPICS

Sport played a critical role in facilitating the breakthrough in Soviet-ROK relations. Sport provided a proximate event, the activities around which each side could send clear signals of its interest in improving relations. While the strategic and domestic forces were conducive to an improvement in relations, an event like the 1988 Olympics was in many ways the trigger that enabled an accelerated diplomatic reconciliation to progress.

When Seoul won the bid in 1981 to host the Games, many thought its lack of diplomatic relations with Eastern European countries and the Soviet Union would be an inhibiting factor in the success of the event. The United States had just led a boycott of the 1980 Moscow Games, and the Soviets were expected to boycott the 1984 Los Angeles Games. Since the ROK was a frontline Cold War ally of the United States, there were real concerns that Moscow would again choose not to attend the Seoul Games. The ROK government adopted a two-pronged strategy: First, the Seoul Olympic organizing committee undertook a full-court press early to win Soviet agreement to participate in the 1988 Games. Second, the government sought to use the Games as an opportunity to build goodwill and facilitate high-level meetings to achieve the expressed goals of nordpolitik.

Seoul's courting of the Russians began at the 1984 Los Angeles Games. Representatives of the Soviet sports ministry were in attendance despite the official boycott in their capacity as officers of the international cycling federation. South Korean officials sought out these and any other Russian officials present to convey their enthusiasm for Soviet participation in the 1988 Games. The ROK explained how the Olympics could be the beginning of great economic opportunities for Korean business conglomerates in the Soviet Union. They pointed to the opening of trade-promotion offices between the ROK and Hungary (all facilitated by the Daewoo chairman Kim Woo Chung) as an example of the opportunities available to Moscow. While Seoul's improving relations with other Eastern European countries was presented to Moscow as evidence of Seoul's nordpolitik intentions, it also put subtle pressure on the Soviets to follow suit. As the ROK moved forward with countries like Hungary in trade relations, they also gained public commitments from such governments that they would attend the Seoul Olympics. This made it even more difficult for the Soviet Union to consider a boycott that would not be honored by its satellite countries. Thus Seoul's fast-paced attempts to improve relations with Hungary, Poland, Czechoslovakia, Bulgaria, and others and gain commitments to attend the Games also served to preempt any Soviet consideration of a boycott. Though this was never stated explicitly as a strategy, it was a subtext of Seoul's smile diplomacy toward the Soviets.

As a political gesture intended to thaw relations and display the often overemphasized Asian diplomatic sense of "trust," Seoul offered to allow a Soviet ship to call at Incheon port for the duration of the Games if Moscow preferred its delegation not to stay in Seoul proper. The offer of Incheon was significant not just because it was unprecedented but also because it was where MacArthur had landed during the Korean War. As a further gesture of "trust," Seoul also asked if the Soviet Union could make available certain portions of its airspace in conjunction with the Games. This, too, was significant in the aftermath of the 1983 shooting down of KAL 007 and was meant as a sign of the ROK's willingness to move on. The first indicator of the success of the ROK's engagement strategy came in April 1986. Seoul hosted a meeting of the National Olympic Associations and pressed hard for Soviet attendance. Roh Tae Woo, who would become South Korea's president in 1987, spearheaded the effort, which succeeded in bringing thirty Eastern European countries and the Soviets to the meeting. In many ways, this was the icebreaker that ensured Soviet attendance at the Olympics two years later.

The ROK government used the Soviets' agreement to participate in the Games as an opportunity to build as much goodwill as possible to promote nordpolitik objectives. The government followed through on its promise to allow a 12,800-ton ship, the *Mikhail Sholokov*, to dock at Incheon harbor for over a month as it housed Soviet athletes and officials. In August 1988, before the start of the Games, Roh sent the special envoy Park Chul-un to Moscow to convey a private letter to Gorbachev supporting his reforms and conveying Seoul's desire to seek normalized diplomatic relations.[16] President Roh agreed to receive a Soviet consular delegation during the Games as a demonstration of mutual interest in expanded diplomatic contacts. He used the Olympics as the pretext for inviting various trade and cultural delegations from the Soviet Union to meet with South Korean corporate executives. Both the Moscow Philharmonic and the Bolshoi Ballet were invited to perform at the national theater. These performances received rave reviews and were hugely popular among the South Korean public. The state-run Korean Broadcasting System invited Nelli Kim, a half-Korean Soviet gymnast who participated in the 1976 and 1980 Olympics, to give interviews and gymnastic performances. All of these events created excitement at the prospect of a new relationship with a longtime adversary. The public's enthusiasm and appreciation were on full display at the opening ceremonies of the Games, when the Soviet delegation entered the stadium to a standing ovation and the second loudest cheers, after only the Korean delegation.

Soviet government officials came to Seoul as spectators, but this provided the opportunity for official contacts that paved the way for improvements in relations. As a result of these contacts, new shipping and air routes were opened with Moscow. Gorbachev's Krasnoyarsk speech, in which he explicitly proclaimed his intention to improve relations with Seoul, came on September 16, 1988, the day before the opening ceremonies in Seoul. The Soviet Union eventually sent more than 6,000 athletes and tourists in what became the most well attended Games in recent Olympic history. Seoul's success in using sport to facilitate nordpolitik diplomacy was manifest in the flurry of diplomatic activity taking place after the Games' conclusion. In February 1989, the ROK established diplomatic relations with Hungary. Two months later, trade offices were established with the Soviet Union. In November and December 1989, diplomatic relations were established with Poland and Yugoslavia. Czechoslovakia, Bulgaria, and Romania followed in March 1990. And in September 1990, the ROK established full diplomatic relations with the Soviet Union.

Given all that was riding on the 1988 Seoul Olympics for the ROK government, it was determined not to allow a no-show by the Soviets to spoil their coming-out party. The efforts to woo the Russians to the Games were a clear success, not only for the Olympic movement but also for nordpolitik. Sport did not cause the September 1990 normalization between these two longtime adversaries, but it was instrumental in the pace of the diplomacy and as a vehicle for displaying good intentions. Without the Seoul Olympics, normalization might not have come for quite some time.

ENGAGING CHINA

South Korea's normalization of relations with China in 1992 is perhaps one of the most understudied but successful cases of engagement.[17] The reestablishment of political ties between these estranged countries constituted the second major step in ending the Cold War in Asia. And as in the case of the Soviet Union, sport was used as an effective tool of diplomacy. In particular, the two countries' interactions over the preparations for the 1986 Asian Games in Seoul and the 1990 Asian Games in Beijing helped pave the way for the breakthrough in diplomatic relations.

The barriers to improved relations between the ROK and China were hardly insubstantial. Between 1945 and 1980, the relationship was entirely adversarial. The two were combatants in the Korean War when the Chinese intervened in September 1950 preventing a U.S.-led unification of the peninsula. From that point onward, Sino-ROK relations were characterized by nondialogue and hostility that were arguably even more intense than what existed between the ROK and Soviet Union. China proclaimed a relationship as close as "lips and teeth" with the communist North Korea, and provided a security commitment to the North "sealed in blood" from the Korean War. The fact that ROK combat forces constituted the second largest ground contingent in the Vietnam War after the U.S. forces only worsened Sino-ROK relations. Despite any historical and cultural affinity between the two societies, this was a quintessentially Cold War relationship.

Ties between China and South Korea started to change in the 1980s. Economics was the primary engine as indirect trade through third countries (e.g., Hong Kong, Japan) steadily increased. In 1979, for example, trade stood at $40 million and increased to $222 million in 1984 and to $518 million in 1985. An important and unexpected event contributed to the emerging thaw in relations in May 1983 when a hijacked Chinese civilian airliner was forced to land in Korea. Seoul and Beijing were put in the position of having to engage in direct negotiations on the return of the crew and aircraft to China, which went smoothly for both sides. Resolving this incident produced goodwill that led to an increase in cultural and academic exchanges. Trade continued to increase, and a big jump in 1986 ($1.5 billion) pushed China's share to 80 percent of South Korea's total trade with socialist countries. By 1989, the trends were clear; total bilateral trade between the ROK and China exceeded by ten times total trade volume between China and the DPRK. In addition, by the late 1980s China was the second largest investment target for South Korea (measured in terms of the number of projects). The period culminated with the establishment of trade offices in October 1990.

After the opening of trade offices, the relations accelerated toward normalization, a process punctuated by a number of cooperative acts. In November 1991, the ROK played an important facilitating role, as host of that year's Asia-Pacific Economic Cooperation meetings, in bringing China to the summit despite attendance by Taiwan and Hong Kong. This event enabled meetings between Foreign Minister Qian Qichen and Trade Minister Li Lanqing of China with President Roh of the ROK. At the same time, China acquiesced to South Korea's bid for U.N. membership despite DPRK objections. The two concluded a series of bilateral trade agreements, which granted most-favored-nation status to each other, and various other investment agreements. Finally, in August 1992, the two formally established diplomatic relations.

What were the determinants of this diplomatic outcome? Clearly the permissive condition, as was the case with the Soviet Union and the ROK, was the end of the Cold War in Europe. A more specific cause, however, was the desire of both China and South Korea to alienate rival regimes through normalization. For Seoul, China was the ultimate prize in the zero-sum diplomatic competition with the DPRK. Having already made substantial inroads with Eastern European countries and the Soviet Union, the ROK saw China as effectively completing the circle of new relations that would isolate the North. Similar incentives existed on the Chinese side. Like Seoul, Beijing saw relations with Taipei in zero-sum terms, and normalization with Seoul would have the effect of further isolating Taiwan. Beijing's requirement for normalization was that Seoul must adopt a one-China policy, which naturally meant the end of diplomatic relations with Taiwan. Taiwan-ROK relations had a rich history as Cold War allies going back to the days of Syngman Rhee and Chiang Kai-shek in the 1950s and 1960s. The two viewed each other as the first line of defense against the communists in Asia. Chiang offered to send troops to Korea during the 1950 war. Taiwan was also the first government to recognize the ROK when it was established in 1948. Despite this history, Seoul abruptly and unceremoniously ended relations with Taipei in 1992.

There were also economic incentives for improving relations. China badly needed South Korean capital and technology and was intrigued by the ROK's model of economic development, which focused on capitalist export-oriented growth without giving up political control. This "strong state" model of development practiced by Korea in the 1970s and 1980s offered much to Deng's modernization program. Conversely, the ROK saw in China cheap labor and a large export market, particularly as it faced growing protectionist sentiment in traditional markets like the United States. Improved economic relations would benefit both countries in terms of trade—the ROK from the import of Chinese mineral resources (coal, petroleum) and agricultural and fishery products, and China South Korean electronics, consumer goods, and textiles.

In contemplating normalization with the ROK, Beijing had to consider the impact this would have on relations with its traditional communist ally in the North. The Chinese were comparatively more sensitized to being perceived as abandoning North Korea than the Soviets, who made the decision abruptly in 1990 with little advance consultation with Pyongyang. Throughout the growing economic engagement with the ROK during the 1980s, China would tell the DPRK that they pursued a dual-track approach of maintaining old ties with traditional allies but not restricting the potential for new partners in the region. In typical fashion, foreign ministry diplomats would refer to their position with North Korea as a "door that is always open," and their position with South Korea as a "door that is closed . . . but not locked." An important structural factor that prompted Beijing to go ahead with normalizing ties with the ROK despite DPRK protests was the end of the Sino-Soviet split. This reduced the strategic value of the DPRK to both communist powers. The position Pyongyang had previously enjoyed as a country courted by both the Soviets and the Chinese was lost with Sino-Soviet reconciliation; Pyongyang had gone from a valuable ally to a political and economic liability for both Beijing and Moscow. China took the step across the Cold War divide with South Korea two years after the Soviets, but with equally devastating impact for the DPRK's bilateral relations as it suspended trade credits and moderated the nature of its defense commitment.

DIPLOMACY AND THE ASIAN GAMES

What role did sport play in facilitating the improved Sino-ROK relations? A confluence of structural factors (e.g., the end of the Cold War, the end of the Sino-Soviet split) and domestic factors (e.g., zero-sum diplomacy with DPRK and Taiwan; economic complementarities) inclined Seoul and Beijing to improve relations. A fortuitous set of events surrounding the tenth and eleventh Asian Games in 1986 and 1990, however, helped to facilitate the transition from largely economic cooperation in the 1980s to political cooperation and eventual normalization.

The two summer Asiads—a slimmed-down regional version of the Olympics—were scheduled to be held in 1986 in Seoul and in 1990 in Beijing. For Seoul, the Games were effectively a dress rehearsal for the 1988 Olympics, and planners worked feverishly to complete most of the construction for the Olympic venues in time for the 1986 event (which I discuss in more detail in next chapter). As I noted, Seoul wanted to ensure maximum participation for the Olympics after the boycotts in 1980 and 1984, so the effort started with ensuring maximum participation at the 1986 Asiad from countries across the Cold War divide. The organizing committee lobbied China to send a large delegation. The plan was for the Chinese officials and athletes to come to Seoul, perform well in the competitions, and generally have a good time. Through this experience, broadcast throughout Asia, the Asiad could build goodwill and change Chinese and South Korean popular perceptions, which were largely antagonistic.

The plan worked. China ended up having the largest delegation at the Games. The Chinese team performed well, tallying the most gold medals (ninety-four) and coming in second in the total medal count (to the ROK hosts). Visiting athletes and officials praised the Koreans' hospitality and friendliness. Visiting dignitaries, moreover, returned to China with a newfound respect and interest in Korea's modernization. Chinese government-run media outlets gave glowing commentary on the way Korea had combined Western modernity with Confucian traditions. The Communist Party journal *Hongqi* (Red Flag) and the prestigious literary journal *Renmin Wenxue* (People's Literature) were awash with lengthy observations of the Seoul Asiad. As Chae-jin Lee noted, these reports,

> praised the neatness and modernity of Seoul, the bustling South Gate market, the majesty of the Kyungbok Palace, the modern facility of *Chungang Ilbo* (a major South Korean newspaper), and the beautiful students at Ewha Women's University. [One article] observed that Korean girls always smiled and wore modern dress but observed traditional customs. . . . [The Chinese author] was impressed that many South Koreans volunteered to work for the Asian Games. He vividly described the opening and closing ceremonies that emphasized Korean traditions.[18]

Because of the superior performance of their athletes, the Chinese had every incentive to broadcast the Seoul games widely at home. This had the effect of conveying to a wider Chinese audience images of a cosmopolitan Seoul, which starkly contrasted with the destitute and poverty-stricken picture of the DPRK. The DPRK's state-run newspaper, *Nodong Sinmun*, blasted Seoul's successful games as a plot to perpetuate the peninsula's division.[19] The overall experience was an important step in building political goodwill to complement the burgeoning economic interactions taking place at the time.

Fours years later, China found itself in frantic preparations for the Asian Games. This was the first major international sporting event the country had hosted, and there was a great deal at stake in terms of international reputation. After all, in 1978 Deng Xiaoping stated that China's modernization would lead to hosting the Olympics one day, and Chinese officials believed that the time had come. They calculated that a strong showing as the hosts of the 1990 Asiad would be the prelude to an Olympics bid. The problem they faced, however, was minimal support from other countries in the region and from the world more generally because of international outrage over the Tiananmen Square massacre in June 1989.

The ROK went out of its way, against the climate of international opinion, to help support Beijing's preparations for the Games. While the United States, Japan, and the European Union imposed sanctions, the Roh government displayed a pronounced ambivalence to the international campaign against China and tried to use the opportunity to expand political and economic cooperation. In a memorable statement, then-foreign minister Choi Ho-joong announced: "Out of political consideration for social stability, China will leave open the possibility for improvement of relations with us. We will also continue to exert efforts to improve relations with China both on governmental and private levels."[20] Having just hosted the 1986 Asiad and the 1988 Olympic Games, Seoul was in a good position to make these efforts, and they lavished every manner of assistance on Beijing. This included political support, technical support, logistics, and financial assistance. President Roh personally lobbied Asian leaders, many of whom he had just hosted for the Seoul Olympics, to avoid any consideration of a boycott of Beijing's Asian Games because of Tiananmen. More than 22,000 South Korean tourists came to Beijing for the games. The Korean conglomerate Hyundai and other carmakers donated more than 400 vehicles to China for the transport of athletes and officials at the Games. The ROK provided assistance to Chinese tourist industries that had been adversely affected by Tiananmen, and Korean companies provided over $15 million in advertising revenues.[21] Three major *chaebol* conglomerates in Korea, Samsung, Lucky-Goldstar, and Daewoo each spent between three million to five million U.S. dollars on advertising in China, and one estimate put total ROK government and private sector support of the Chinese Asian Games at about US$100 million.[22] A newspaper report captured the phenomenon: "A flood of South Korean advertising and contributions for the Asian Games is intended to promote Beijing-Seoul ties that could benefit the economies of both nations and contribute to peace on the Korean Peninsula."[23] President Roh dispatched a relative to lead the presidential delegation to the games in Beijing, a move intended to convey a personal commitment at the highest levels to improved political relations. Key government officials were added to the delegation so that low-profile, high-level talks could be had on the establishment of trade offices and normalized relations. The North protested to China about South Korea's assistance, but Beijing gladly accepted it. General Secretary Jiang Zemin of the CCP also reportedly rejected DPRK leader Kim Il-sung's requests to limit the size of the South Korean delegation, not to fly the ROK flag at the Games, and to reduce the prominence of advertising billboards for ROK companies at the Games.[24]

In the end, China hosted a successful Asiad. Their athletes excelled in competition, winning the gold, silver, and overall medal counts. Now, because of

Seoul's help, the Chinese could move to the next stage—during the closing ceremonies of the Asian Games, a large banner was unfurled stating that since China had hosted a successful Asian Games, ought it not seek the Olympics? President Yang Shangkun of China met with the attending IOC chairman, Juan Antonio Samaranch, and told him formally for the first time that China intended to bid for the 2000 Olympics. Four months after the conclusion of the Asian Games, in October 1990, the Chinese formed a Beijing Olympic organizing committee to follow through on Yang's promise to Samaranch. While South Korea's help was not solely responsible for these developments, it was extremely successful in conveying political intentions in a way that normal diplomacy could not. The ROK and China established trade offices shortly after the conclusion of the 1990 games, which then made normalization a foregone conclusion less than two years later.

SPORT AND DIPLOMATIC CONFLICT

Just as sport can contribute to diplomacy, it can also be a tool of diplomatic conflict. This can occur in one of two ways. Sport can be used as a punitive instrument of statecraft either as a sanction or ban against a target state, or nations can protest against or boycott sporting events.

As I noted in chapter 2, boycotts or bans provide governments with a low-cost, high-profile way of conveying disapproval over a particular policy. They register protest with minimal risk of escalation into war or other forms of conflict. Much to the consternation of athletes, bans and boycotts have often been used by governments precisely because they are symbolically powerful but less costly than an economic embargo and, relatively speaking, fairly easy to enforce. They also give politicians the ability to claim that they are "doing something" about the problem. By the same token, lifting a ban on participation in a sport event can have huge implications for a country's identity and international recognition. Invitation to an international sporting event carries all the connotations of statehood and therefore, as I discuss below, has been a huge issue in cross-straits relations between Taiwan and China.

The most well known sport boycott by a government is, of course, the American boycott of the 1980 Moscow Olympics. President Jimmy Carter's decision came in early 1980 and was intended as a protest of the Soviet invasion of Afghanistan in 1979. The United States undertook a period of intense diplomacy to rally supporters of the boycott. It was not easy. Countries such as France, Ireland, Finland, and Greece opposed the boycott. Such stalwart allies as West Germany, Japan, and Canada honored it, but the British did not, succumbing to strong protests from their athletes. The South American states, wanting to demonstrate independence from the U.S. position, all opposed the boycott (except Chile). In the end, thirty-three nations honored the boycott, and thirty more (including China) did not formally respond to the Soviet invitation to the Games, which constituted the lowest participation rate since the 1956 Melbourne Games. The Soviets reciprocated in 1984, leading a boycott of the 1984 Olympics in Los Angeles that was less widely honored (140 countries participated in the Games).

While the practice of Olympic boycotts and bans garnered world attention in 1980 and 1984, these were not the first instances by any means. The history of the Games is littered with such occurrences. In 1956, Spain and Switzerland did not participate in the Melbourne Games to protest Soviet actions in Hungary (it was also at these Games that fifty Hungarians defected). Egypt, Iraq, and Lebanon also boycotted the Melbourne Olympics in protest of the Suez Crisis. Earlier, the 1920 "Games of Renewal"—the first Olympics after World War I, held in Antwerp to memorialize Belgium's suffering during the war—were originally slated to be held in Hungary; however, as Hungary had been a German ally in the war, it was banned from hosting the Games. Similarly, Germany, Austria, Bulgaria, and Turkey were all banned from the Games of Renewal.

The use of boycotts also extended to regional games. Israel had been a regular participant in the Asian Games until 1962, when Indonesian leader Sukarno, as host that year, banned Israel from participating as an act of solidarity with other Muslim states and in protest of U.S. Middle East policy. Indonesia's ban quickly became an international political incident. The IOC intervened and called upon Jakarta to abide by the Olympic ideal of forbidding any form of political or racial discrimination in sport. Sukarno did not acquiesce, and the IOC banned Indonesia from participating in the 1964 Tokyo Games.[25] Sukarno responded by hosting "Games of the New Emerging Force," dubbed the new "anti-Imperialist" Olympics. Israel participated in the next two Asiads, but in 1974 the games were hosted by Iran, which reinstituted a ban against Israel.[26]

The interest in boycotts has waned in the aftermath of the 1980 and 1984 Games. When the idea of boycotts arose in the run-up to the Beijing Olympics (discussed in next chapters), the IOC was strongly opposed, maintaining that these were anachronistic tools of a bygone era. President Bush resisted all pressures from activists and the Congress for boycotting the Games, insisting that he would go only for the sports. A March 2008 survey found almost 80 percent of the British population not in favor of a boycott of the Games.

The chair of the IOC, Jacques Rogge, claimed that boycotts never achieved their purposes. The 1980 and 1984 boycott-plagued Summer Games were still considered successes. Former Olympians also rightly expressed their strong opposition to the use of athletes' dreams for political bludgeoning. As 1992 100-meter gold medalist Linford Christie of Great Britain stated, "Athletes have one chance every four years to compete at the Olympics and they should be allowed to do that. People are very hypocritical on this issue; we condemn China but then we all use Chinese electrical goods."[27]

CHINA AND TAIWAN

The question that naturally arose with the 2008 Games in Beijing was whether the sport could help create reconciliation between Beijing and Taipei. The lack of any progress was not a surprise, however, given the tortured history between the two parties. Participation in the Olympics, because of its strong connotations of statehood, was an issue of intense diplomatic conflict between the two governments. From 1924, the Republic of China was recognized by the IOC as the sole representative of China through its administrative body, the China National Amateur Athletic Federation. The ROC participated in the 1932 Los Angeles Games, 1936 Berlin Games, and 1948 London Games. After the CCP revolution in 1949 and the move of the ROC government to Taiwan, the ROC maintained its ties with the IOC and continued to claim representation in international sport for all of China. It did not take long for the PRC to challenge this claim. In October 1949 it formed the All-China Athletic Federation, which claimed jurisdiction over all Chinese Olympic activities.[28] Thus began decades of acrimony and mutual recrimination during which the sport world had to decide effectively whether it would follow a one- or two-China policy.

The first battle took place at the 1952 Helsinki Olympics. Beijing sought to represent China, sending its first delegation with strong encouragement from the Soviet Union, which had just joined the IOC in 1951. The IOC would only allow one national committee to represent China, yet neither Taiwan nor China was willing to negotiate a combined committee (and team). The IOC authorities faced a dilemma where its decision would be interpreted as sanctioning either a one- or two-China policy. They tried to skirt the issue temporarily with a makeshift formula whereby each national committee was permitted to send athletes to Helsinki only in those sports for which the country's national sport federation was recognized by the international sporting federation. While this would have enabled both governments to send athletes, Taiwan protested vigorously on the grounds that it had been the representative of China at the Olympics since 1932. When the IOC did not respond to its appeal, the ROC boycotted the Helsinki Games. Meanwhile the PRC delegation had difficulties with visas for the Games (since many countries did not yet recognize the PRC), and only arrived in time for the closing ceremonies, where the small group proudly watched the national flag of the PRC raised at the Olympics for the first time.

After the difficulties in Helsinki, the IOC chose to adopt a two-China policy for the 1956 Melbourne Games, recognizing and extending invitations to both Chinas. This drew the PRC's ire and led Beijing to announce a boycott, charging that the IOC was violating its own Olympic Charter, which stated that only one team could represent a country in the Games. A heated exchange of letters followed between the IOC chair, Avery Brundage, an American, and the Chinese Olympic Committee, in which the politics of the Sino-American Cold War was readily evident despite protestations to the contrary. The Chinese Olympic Committee excoriated Brundage:

> As for your remark "There is a seperate [sic] Government in Taiwan," Mr. President, you must not forget how this situation is brought about. . . . That these traitors are able to survive in Taiwan until today is due to the political, economic, and military aid openly given by the U.S. Government and open interference in the internal affairs of our country by the U.S. Government. . . ."

China Olympic Committee representative Dong Shouyi personally attacked Brundage as "a faithful menial of the US imperialists bent on serving their plot of creating "Two Chinas."[29] China withdrew from the IOC and nine other international sporting organizations, demanding a rescission of the two-China policy. Beijing's boycott of the Olympic Games continued for three decades through the cultural revolution years while Taiwan participated in all international sport events.

China participated in the Asian Games and games sponsored by non-aligned states after its withdrawal from the IOC, but it would not do so without assurances that Taiwan would not participate. The Indonesians hosted the 1962 Asian Games, and Sukarno quietly promised Beijing that Taiwan would not be there even though, officially, no host of the Asian Games could make such a commitment. In the end, the Taiwanese team never received their credentials for the Games through some delivery "mishap." The IOC banned Indonesia for this and for its exclusion of Israel. But Sukarno established the Games of the New Emerging Force in

1963, and these constituted China's first full-scale participation in an international sport event.

Nixon's opening to China in 1971, followed by the admittance of the PRC to the United Nations and the expulsion of Taiwan, were watershed political events that became the springboard for China's reentry to international sport. In 1972 Willi Daume of the IOC invited the PRC to send an observer delegation to the 1972 Munich Games. But because German authorities would not ban Taiwan from participating, China declined the invitation. The American opening to China, however, triggered a movement among several nations to get China back into the IOC. At the same time, Lord Michael Morris Killanin replaced Avery Brundage as IOC president in 1972, and in contrast to Brundage was seen as sympathetic to China and antagonistic toward Taiwan. Japan, in particular, having been the first of the East Asian countries to normalize relations with China in September 1972, played a leading role in pleading China's case. In 1973 Japan's national Olympic committee petitioned the IOC and the national Olympic committees to reinstate China and to expel Taiwan. This petition comported with Beijing's own strategy, which was not simply to try to rejoin the IOC with Taiwan as a standing member, which would only reinforce a two-China policy. Yet Beijing knew it was unfeasible for them to continue a self-defeating boycott of international sport. Hence, Beijing sought to rejoin the IOC by seeking membership in only those international sport federations in which Taiwan was not a member (a minimum of five memberships was necessary to qualify for IOC membership).[30] As China reentered the sport world, it was only a matter of time before hosts would want Chinese participation even at the expense of Taiwan's. At the October 1974 Asian Games in Iran, the organizing committee voted in favor of inviting the PRC and not Taiwan. Because of China's refusal to join any sport federation in which Taiwan participated, more and more sport federations began to solicit Chinese membership and expel Taiwan. In 1974 the international sport federation for weightlifting made the switch, as did the international sport federation for fencing. By 1975, China has succeeded in getting Taiwan expelled from nine sport federations.

Beijing sought an invitation for the 1976 Montreal Olympics but only on the condition that Taiwan was banned. Chinese authorities argued this on the grounds that China was the only recognized representative of China in the United Nations after Taiwan's expulsion. The appeal fell on sympathetic ears in Canada since Ottawa had already given diplomatic recognition to the PRC and followed a one-China policy, severing diplomatic ties with Taiwan. At the same time, Canadian authorities still did not want to ban Taiwan since they had competed in every Olympics since Melbourne in 1956. The

IOC proposed an interim solution where Taiwan would participate under the name "Taiwan–Republic of China," but the delegation would not be able to fly the national flag at the Games; they would have to participate under the Olympic flag. Though well-intentioned, the proposal was strongly opposed by both Beijing and Taipei. China's protest was over the fact that this solution would effectively constitute a two-China policy. And Taiwan disliked the proposal because it found disgraceful the notion that the delegation would not be able to fly their national flag at the Olympics. Taipei rallied supporters to its side, and a mini diplomatic crisis ensued in which Montreal faced the prospect of boycotts by either China or Taiwan (and the United States) based on the outcome of the Olympic dispute. The crisis continued up until a couple of days before the opening ceremony, when the Taiwanese, sensing that their demands would not be met, packed their bags and left Montreal under protest.[31]

After the Montreal fiasco, the IOC in 1977 and 1978 sought trilateral negotiations with China and Taiwan to find a workable solution. Taiwan declared that it would only meet with the IOC and would not participate in a three-way meeting with China. From the perspective of Taipei's delegates, the standing precedent was that they were still the representative of China, with many more years experience and membership in the IOC than Beijing. If they were to meet with the PRC for the purpose of revising Taiwan's participation status, this would essentially be admitting acceptance of a change in the historical precedent. The IOC continued with its plan and held bilateral discussions with the PRC in 1979, three sessions in Uruguay, Puerto Rico, and Japan. The IOC proposed a two-China solution again that the PRC predictably rejected, demanding that the IOC expel Taiwan. Beijing took this hard-line position as it sought to leverage what at the time was a wave of international opinion in favor of recognizing the PRC as China.

The IOC then proposed a formula in which the PRC and the ROC would both participate, but the ROC would use the name "Chinese Taipei." Beijing jumped at this offer because it was tantamount to IOC acceptance of a one-China policy with the PRC as the true representative of China in the IOC. They would participate under their name and national flag; Taiwan, on the other hand, could not. Finally, the name "Chinese Taipei," made it sound as though Taiwan was a province of China. The new IOC chairman Juan Antonio Samaranch presented the formula to Taiwan and pleaded with them to accept it, promising that the Olympics would always treat Taiwan as an equal and with respect. In the end, Taipei agreed only because it would otherwise lose out completely, but it adopted a strategy of trying to protest the right to fly the national flag through the courts of the host country.

The thirteenth Winter Olympic Games in Lake Placid, New York, in 1980 was the first opportunity to try out the new IOC formula as China returned to the Games after being absent since 1958. Beijing pressed the point that they would only welcome Taiwan's participation under the name "Chinese Taipei" as per the IOC resolution in Nagoya, Japan. Taiwan proceeded to file a court case with the New York district court demanding the right to participate under the ROC name. On February 11, two days before the start of the Games, the Justice Department and State Department filed statements with the New York State Supreme Court upholding the IOC stance. Taiwan boycotted the Lake Placid Olympics. While Taipei disliked the IOC's "Chinese Taipei" formula, it soon became the only way they could participate in international sport. Various sport federations followed the IOC model. Taiwan eventually acceded to the model and later appealed to reenter various sporting federations, including the Federation for International Basketball, the Federation for International Gymnastics, and the fencing and rowing federations based on this IOC formula.[32] Since 1984, both the PRC and ROC have participated in every Olympics in accordance with the 1979 agreement.

THE 2008 TORCH CONTROVERSY

Although a workable formula for PRC and ROC participation in international sport has prevailed, the protracted dispute over the 2008 Beijing Olympic torch relay made clear to all that sport would continue to be an outlet for cross-strait diplomatic conflict. The 2008 torch relay, took place between March 25 and August 8, 2008, before the start of the twenty-ninth Games in Beijing. The torch traveled from the Pananthinaiko Stadium in Athens to Beijing, following a route through six continents, and was the object of numerous protests (as I discuss later). The planned route originally included a stop in Taipei between Ho Chi Minh city in Vietnam and Hong Kong. Taiwan authorities, however, rejected the plan because it would imply that Taiwan was part of China since it was adjacent in the relay to Hong Kong. In response, Taiwan demanded that a new route be planned and that Taiwan be allowed to fly the national flag and play the national anthem during its twenty-four-kilometer portion of the torch relay. Ten months of useless negotiations ensued, and in the end the IOC declared in September 2007 that the Taipei leg of the torch relay would have to be dropped since no agreement could be reached. President Chen Shui-bian of Taiwan declared that the PRC was not acting in good faith in trying to use the torch relay to blur Taiwan's status as an independent state. The head of Beijing's Olympic

Organizing committee criticized the "vile precedent" set by Taipei in trying to change the terms set by the IOC in 1979 on Taiwan's participation.[33]

As much as sport can help to create diplomatic breakthroughs, it has also been a tool of diplomatic conflict. As the examples in this section show, it is the athletes in the end who are most victimized by the use of bans and boycotts. Despite all the dashed dreams and expectations of the victim-athletes, these actions did not achieve their ultimate policy objective, yet sport's appeal as a tool of diplomacy for politicians is unassailable. The U.S. boycott of the Moscow Games did not affect subsequent Soviet actions in Afghanistan. In the seven-year run-up to the 2008 Beijing Olympics, the calls by different groups for a boycott of the Beijing Olympics were loud and constant. Human rights groups, nongovernmental organizations, media personalities, and politicians at one time or another all called for a boycott of the Beijing Games to protest China's human rights record, its trade imbalance with the United States, Chinese product safety, and Beijing's policies toward Darfur, Burma, Tibet, and Xinjiang, among other issues. The actor Mia Farrow, also goodwill ambassador for UNICEF, dubbed the 2008 Games as the "Genocide Olympics" and called on corporate sponsors to boycott the Games in protest over Beijing's lack of efforts to prevent the killings and pillage in Darfur.[34] Fred Hiatt, the editorial page editor of the *Washington Post*, derided the Games as the "Saffron Olympics" and called for the United States to boycott the Games if China did not change its hands-off policy while the military regime in Burma brutally put down democracy demonstrations.[35] Indeed, the question of how much sport can create change is still an open one. It is this question to which I now turn.

5

THE OLYMPIC FACELIFT

Officially, everyone professes confidence that [the country] will be ready when the ceremonial torch is finally lit in the great National Stadium. Still, the race between construction workers and the Olympic flame bearer is likely to be uncomfortably close. . . . The futuristic looking National Gymnasium, where swimming and basketball games are to be held, is swathed in scaffolding. . . . Construction here is admittedly so far behind that Olympic judoists may have to duck wet paint signs.

–NORMAN SKLAREWITZ, "TOKYO RACES TO FINISH OLYMPIC PREPARATIONS BEFORE OCTOBER 10 OPENING," *WALL STREET JOURNAL*, 23 JULY 1964

With just six months to go before the Games, the capital is pockmarked by 10,000 or so construction sites. The wrecking ball has laid waste whole neighbourhoods and displaced thousands of residents. . . . Even without the Olympics, [the city] would have developed. But the Olympics accelerated the whole process.

–"OLYMPICS SPEEDS UP BEIJING TRANSFORMATION, "AGENCE FRANCE PRESS, 5 FEBRUARY 2008

To what extent and in what manner is sport an agent of change in world politics? The preceding chapters have reviewed ways in which sport has been inextricably intertwined with national identity. Sport can also be a tool of diplomacy, facilitating breakthroughs or operating as a manner of diplomatic conflict. But sport can register as more than a symbol or a tool—it can be an agent of change. This change is both physical (this chapter's discussion) and political (chapter 6). When nations bid for a world sporting event, this creates tremendous impetus for physical change and development of the host city that would not otherwise be possible.

This chapter's epigraphs offer descriptions of the frantic preparations that a city undergoes as it prepares to host the Olympics. The fact that the two descriptions are hardly distinguishable, despite having been written more than forty years apart, highlights not only the just-in-time nature of the preparations but also the vast scale and size of the project. Cities that host a sporting mega-event like the Olympics undergo massive and rapid physical transformation. This is more than just a couple of stadiums; it is a general package of infrastructure, environmental, transportation, airport, tourism, and athletic-facility construction and upgrades on a scale unprecedented in the country's history. This change, moreover, is usually compacted into a short time frame. Once a country wins the bid to host the event, a race begins to complete in five to seven years what might otherwise take well over a decade. Many of the physical features of cities like Seoul, Tokyo, and now Beijing—everything from their skylines to their parks—are the result of the physical "facelift" the metropolises underwent as they put their best face forward to the world for the Olympic Games.[1]

In some cases, the race to be ready for the Games takes place from a standing start, with very little infrastructure already in place. Sochi's successful bid to host the 2014 winter Olympics, in this regard, required a massive $12 billion dollar capital commitment by President Vladimir Putin of Russia in order to be credible. One of the stories to be written in the run-up to these Games will surely be the massive transformation of this sleepy Black Sea resort into a world-class winter sports mecca by Russia's newfound oil and gas wealth.

Much of the facelift we see in these Olympic cities, however, consists of an acceleration of upgrades or construction projects that might already have been underway. Some national Olympic committees and cities, in this regard, adopt a conscious strategy of bringing the Games home in order to jump-start upgrades or win federal funding for projects they had already planned. In preparation for the 1996 Summer Games, Atlanta received $609 million in federal funds to speed up transportation, public-housing, and inner-city-gentrification projects that included the construction of apartments, hotels, and a new stadium that would become the home for the Atlanta Braves baseball team.[2] Salt Lake City received more than $1.3 billion in federal assistance on an accelerated basis in order to meet the Olympic timeline to build a new light-rail line and finish reconstruction of an interstate highway.[3] Barcelona used the hosting of the Games in 1992 to gain the funding for turning an abandoned port area into a new marina and beach. Sydney used the Games in 2000 to prioritize the cleaning up of Bush Bay and the building of a new railway system. As I discuss later, China had made the decision to uproot the heavy industry complexes in the Beijing metropolitan area because of their pollution as early as the 1980s, but entrenched financial interests made it difficult to implement the decision. It was only with the Olympics and the premium placed on making the city look modern and reducing pollution that the move took place. In short, as one group of experts observed, "the Olympic Games have emerged as an important tool of urban and regional renewal through their ability to justify redevelopment and enhancement."[4]

The cost of the transformation is huge and sometimes crippling. The Rome Games of 1960 cost more than $50 million in public-works projects. Munich in 1972 spent over $850 million in their preparations; Moscow, as much as $8 billion; and Beijing, over $40 billion. These kinds of numbers present hosts with a huge financial gamble. On the one hand, there are clear incentives to seeking a bid in terms of promoting city redevelopment and modernization, gaining world media attention, and reaping increased tourist and business revenues.[5] Cities also experience an economic and employment upturn in the run-up to the Games because of the increased public spending and construction projects. The PRC National Bureau for Statistics, for example, predicted that Beijing city productivity would increase by 2 percent annually and that over 2 million new jobs would be created in the run-up to the 2008 Olympics.[6]

While there is a boom associated with pre-event development, there is a bust associated with postevent costs. Most public-investment studies show that investment in sport facilities offers little net economic gain.[7] The huge facilities have little sustained use after the games. And while the national government may help with public borrowing in order to finance the construction projects before the games, the burden often falls to the city's taxpayers to pay off the loans after. For example, in the run-up to the 2002 World Cup, Japanese city and prefectural governments floated bonds to cover 70 percent of the new stadium construction costs, but soon after the event, the cities were stuck with huge bills.[8] The stadiums were not a good source of revenue after the World Cup, in spite of the city planners' search for corporate sponsors for the facilities in order to maintain financial viability. Prefectural governments such as Niigata were saddled with over 80 percent of the scheduled repayment of loans and interest in their budgets, while the cities were stuck with the maintenance costs of the stadiums.[9] The most disastrous case of financing was the Montreal Olympic Games in 1976, which suffered a net loss of some $1.2 billion. Montreal taxpayers ended up footing the cost of the Games for years through a seventeen-cent tax on cigarettes.[10]

Montreal's financial difficulties were so prominent a deterrent to hosting that Los Angeles was the only candidate city with a serious bid for the 1984 Olympics. The U.S. Olympic Organizing Committee developed a business plan, however, that turned the Games into an economic success. Under the leadership of Peter Ueberroth, the planners developed a private nonprofit cooperation, the L.A. Olympic Organizing Committee, which aimed to finance the Games through the sale of television rights and corporate sponsorships. Obtaining over $300 million in broadcasting rights and between $5 million and $15 million each from some thirty-four corporate sponsors ensured that as little financing as possible would be required from the city. The city imposed a tax on Olympic tickets and a hotel-occupancy tax to cover its costs. Deals with corporate sponsors were also made to refurbish existing athletic facilities rather than building new ones at prohibitive cost. Atlantic Richfield refurbished the facilities while AT&T provided the telecommunications. GM provided the official cars, and Coca-Cola provided Coke. Total revenue for the L.A. Games ended up being over $1 billion while costs were $467 million.[11] The success of the L.A. Games would become the business model for all future Olympics.

The shiny new structures that serve as evidence of sport's role as an agent of physical change sometimes end up as monuments of financial failure, and the promises of an economic boom after a mega-event often go unfulfilled. Yet the allure of hosting a sporting mega-event is still strong. As one study noted, "Despite the almost unanimous conclusion of numerous studies that public investment in sports facilities yields only minimal economic benefits, officials continue to push for new facilities and public money continues to be spent on them."[12] The cachet of being an Olympic city or World Cup host is irresistible.

TOKYO'S OLYMPIC TRANSFORMATION

In the cases of Tokyo and Seoul, the physical change wrought by the Olympics transformed the cities into the ultramodern metropolises that we now know today. The opening ceremonies of the Tokyo Games in October 1964 represented Japan's rejoining the international community after the Second World War. The Japanese displayed a newly rebuilt city of Tokyo and sought to impress the world with their hospitality, organization, and technology.

In preparation for this day, as much as $3 billion was spent in overhauling the city.[13] Much of today's Tokyo is a direct result of these preparations for the 1964 Games. The elevated expressways that lead picturesquely into the city from the airport and run above Tokyo's canal and waterway system were constructed for the Games at a cost of $469 million. City officials did away with the ordinance prohibiting construction of buildings taller than ten stories, which allowed for the huge skyscrapers that now adorn the Tokyo skyline. The subway system was expanded and a new monorail linked Haneda airport with city center. Japan's signature Shinkansen "bullet train," a $1 billion state-of-the-art project boasting the fastest trains in the world, was constructed in time to open for the Olympic Games and connected Tokyo and Osaka travelers in only four hours (at eighty mph).[14]

The preparations went beyond infrastructure and transportation, however. Tokyo's public sanitation system at the time had one of the worst reputations among developed countries. Though hard to imagine today, in 1964 it was common to see open-air refuse trucks and an above-ground sewage system in the streets of Japan's capital city. This was considered unacceptable by Western standards, so the government spent some $38 million on new underground sewers, $15 million on a new public incinerator plant, and another $3 million for river cleanup.[15]

Hotels were another priority. Tokyo was still a small town in the 1960s by international standards. Yet planners estimated some 11,000 athletes and over 150,000 tourists would flood the city, so the government provided $60 million in subsidies to develop the hotel and tourism infrastructure, including the flagship 1,100-room New Otani Hotel (the attendance numbers ended up being smaller than predicted, leaving some disappointed innkeepers with surplus rooms). In order to prevent culture shock, hotel bathrooms were all refitted with Western-style toilets rather than Asian squat toilets. Hoteliers also faced a "bed dilemma." The majority of the beds in Japanese hotel rooms were considered too small for Westerners' frames. The vision of Olympic tourists sleeping uncomfortably, their ankles hanging off their beds, would not have comported with Japanese hospitality. So a decision was made to install new beds in the hotels. The problem was that no domestic manufacturer had designs for the larger Western bed, hence manufacturers were requested to make a specially designed bed for the games.

Part and parcel of the Olympic facelift in Tokyo was city beautification. Thousands of trees were planted, and new parks were added to give the city a greener look. Olympic facilities were state-of-the-art not only in technology but also in design. The new Yoyogi National Gymnasium, designed by the Japanese architect Tange Kenzo, won worldwide acclaim and the Pritziker Award as one of the most beautiful new structures of the twentieth century.[16] Tokyo became a new city in the few years before the Olympic games. The New York Times summed up the city's transformation: "The new trees, the flower gardens planted along miles of parking strips and the soaring tracery of overhead highways rushed to completion in time to handle Olympic traffic are among the improvements that have given Tokyo a wholly new aspect. It is unlikely that visitors to the Olympics will go away

FIGURE 10. YOYOGI NATIONAL STADIUM

SOURCE: © ANGELO HOMAK/CORBIS

repeating an old criticism that Japan's capital, for all its charm and vibrance, is an ugly city."[17]

SEOUL'S FACELIFT

The scale, scope, and pace of Tokyo's pre-Olympic transformation was matched only when the Olympics next came to Asia, in 1988. For Seoul, the Games represented the opportunity to make a statement about South Korea's emergence from the ashes of the Korean War and arrival on the global stage as a prosperous and developed nation. For the political regime, as well, hosting a picture-perfect Olympics was critical for domestic legitimacy. The city of Seoul underwent a similar pattern of upgraded infrastructure, environmental cleanup, enhanced tourist and hotel services, and city beautification. And like Tokyo, the Seoul we know today is largely a product of the preparations for the Olympic games.

While the ROK government had already planned for some infrastructural upgrades as part of its five-year development, the preparation for the Games enabled a rapid acceleration and prioritization of these projects. The first step was Kimpo airport, where a new international terminal and runways were constructed.[18] In a massive multiyear project, city planners built a new thirty-seven-kilometer multilane expressway on the southern side of the Han river bisecting the city of Seoul, that came to be known as the "88 Olympics Expressway." Large parts of downtown Seoul were dug up for most of the first half of the 1980s as a new state-of-the-art subway system was constructed in time for the 1986 Asian Games.

The Chun regime undertook a massive cleanup of the Han River at a cost well over $300 million. The river was the main waterway through the city and was terribly polluted, an externality of the ROK's booming but environmentally unfriendly economic growth rates. The Han River redevelopment project included massive dredging and drainage work, the construction of raised embankments along the river, and the addition of parks, bicycle paths, and other public leisure spaces, all of which served to make the river a site for watersports, fishing, play, and city cruises. As some authors describe it, this project was arguably the most aesthetically important physical mark left by the Chun regime on Korea, all in preparation for the Olympic games.

Until the early 1980s, most of the electrical wiring in Seoul was above ground. In preparation for the Games, the government undertook a project to move all power and telephone lines underground. Also inspired by the desire to make the metropolis look new and modern to the world, neon lighting emerged in Korea with the Olympic Games, and Seoul today, down to the crosses on its Christian churches, is awash in gaudy and multicolored neon every evening.

While the Chun regime was no longer around to host the Games because of the democratic transition in 1987 (which I discuss in the next chapter), in the five-year run-up it did tie its international and domestic legitimacy to the Olympics; hence, there was no detail too small in terms of putting the best face forward. New international broadcasting facilities and a new foreign press center were built. The planners knew that the first image of Seoul that would be broadcast around the world would be from the Olympic torch relay, so the government undertook a massive campaign to beautify everything along the planned route. Homeowners found their roofs painted, roads repaired, doors replaced, streets and alleyways cleaned, and sidewalks awash with new flowers. As was the case in Tokyo, thousands of trees were planted, and parks were built to give the city more green spaces. In addition, local governments and municipal authorities financed public-education campaigns aimed at reducing noise pollution, teaching over seven million merchants how to cater to Westerners, and improving public etiquette (e.g., standing on line, preventing spitting). For many Koreans, the changes being wrought by sport were not only visible but also an intrusion on their daily lives. In the end, however, the national project of hosting the Olympics could not have come to Seoul without such a physical transformation, one that touched the life of every city dweller.

PHYSICAL CHANGE AND BEIJING 2008

From my time as a White House official at the Six Party talks in 2006 and 2007, I recall the daily commute from the U.S. embassy in Beijing to the Daoyutai complex where the talks were held. I would look right and left along the main thoroughfare and lose count of the number of cranes and construction projects underway in the run-up to the 2008 Olympic Games. Where construction was not readily visible, huge billboards announcing the Chinese theme "We Are Ready!" obscured the demolition and rebuilding of entire city blocks. The energy and pace of the preparations were palpable.

The 2008 Beijing Games showed like no other event how sport transforms a city's physical appearance. Beijing certainly underwent the same sort of physical transformation that had occurred in the Tokyo and Seoul Olympics, but on an unprecedented scale. The Olympics Games not only represented China's "coming-out" party but were also meant to mark the crowning achievement of Deng Xiaoping's era of modernization reforms, and the end to the centuries-old view of China as the sick man of Asia. For this reason, Beijing spared no expense in preparation for the Games, spending over $40 billion, which was the largest amount ever laid out for a set of Olympic Games. More than 400 miles of new expressways, 4 new subway lines, a new airport terminal, and 37 new stadiums in 6 cities were built at an estimated cost of *another* $6/ billion to ensure China's pre-Olympic facelift.

Terminal 3 at Beijing International airport, constructed as one of the "showpieces" for the Games, constituted the biggest part of a $4.6 billion expansion of the airport. Shaped to look like a cross between a dragon and an imperial palace, the state-of-the-art terminal, priced at $2.8 billion, is the largest air-terminal building in the world, with a footprint of one million square meters, making it larger than the Pentagon. With 8 levels and 120 departure gates, the facility is designed to handle 43 million passengers per year. China also opened a newly built third runway at Beijing airport, increased from seven to thirteen the levels of Chinese airspace to allow for more flights, and built a new airport at Guangzhou and a second passenger terminal at Shanghai International Airport. Chinese authorities made it clear that since the airport is the first window into China for the 500,000

tourists from around the world expected to arrive for the Games, it would represent Chinese modernity on the grandest scale.[19]

Chinese hospitality was not restricted to air transportation. In October 2007, Beijing opened the first of four new subway lines in preparation for the Games. The power of sport to promote physical change in a host city gave Beijing its first new line in over forty years; the last time China built subways they were part of a civil defense plan to defend against Soviet attack! Each of the new state-of-the-art lines cost well over $1 billion. Even the two older lines were substantially refurbished with the addition of over 260 new air-conditioned and handicapped-accessible cars. To deal with the expected influx of tourists, a light railway connecting the city system to the airport opened in June 2008; more than 2,500 new buses were added to the streets of Beijing and well as China's first magnetic levitation train.

Historically, stadiums in communist China were always considered a reflection of the party-state's power and prestige. In 1959, for example, China built the 80,000-seat Workers' Stadium to celebrate the tenth anniversary of the CCP, complete with a special "Chairman's Platform" in the best part of the stadium.[20] The modern Olympic era has seen its share of iconic sport venues, and Beijing sought to break new frontiers in technology and aesthetics with its own pair, the Bird's Nest and the Water Cube. The former is a $400 million, 91,000-seat stadium that housed the opening and closing ceremonies of the Games. Assessed to be one of the most expensive Olympic structures ever built, the stadium, with its intersecting ribbons of steel woven in patterns resembling a bird's nest, is already revered as an architectural wonder. This is a far cry from the first modern stadium built in Beijing at the Xian Nong Temple in 1937—a 10,000-seat dirt soccer field.

FIGURE 12. "THE WATER CUBE": BEIJING OLYMPIC NATIONAL AQUATICS CENTER

SOURCE: © CSPA/NEWSPORT/CORBIS

Completed in January 2008, the $200 million Olympic aquatic center—the Water Cube—won *Popular Science*'s 2006 award for "What's New in Engineering." A steel structure covered with specially designed translucent lightweight Teflon pillows that resemble a space-age bubble wrap, the aquatic center uses a technology developed by two physicists in Ireland to replicate the structural properties of soap bubbles. The energy-efficient structure, housing 17,000 spectators for the Games, can inflate and deflate according to temperature changes as it holds in light and heat. It uses solar energy to heat the pool and features double-filtered recycled water. The Olympic Village and some other stadiums also boasted such facilities, with heat, lighting, and water systems entirely powered by hybrid photovoltaic and thermal power.[21] Why did the Chinese invest in such over-the-top facilities? These buildings became the iconic symbols of the Olympic Games, and, for the Chinese, served more than a utilitarian purpose. The billions of dollars put into these facilities conveyed to the world that the Great Wall would no longer be the only image of China. The Bird's Nest and the Water Cube are the face of a new China, strong, cutting-edge, chic, and prosperous.

SMOGLYMPICS?

The most publicly scrutinized aspect of Chinese pre-Olympic preparations was the environmental cleanup. Desperate to prove the critics wrong that the Beijing Olympics would be played in a haze of Chinese smog and dust, the Chinese went on a crash course. From the start it looked to be a losing battle. By the 1990s, eight of the ten most polluted cities in the world were located in China, and almost all major Chinese cities, including Beijing, exceeded the WHO guidelines for safe levels of sulfur dioxide concentrations and showed three times the recommended level of particulate matter in the air. Ninety percent of China's sulfur dioxide emissions and fifty percent of particulate emissions are from coal. Seventy-five percent of river water in urban areas was unfit for fishing or drinking. Media attention focused in particular on Beijing's air quality and how it might hamper the conduct of the Games. Jacques Rogge, head of the IOC, forewarned on the occasion of the August 2007 Olympic countdown celebrations in Beijing (when the air was like pea soup) that some endurance events like the marathon might have to be postponed if air quality was poor. Tennis star and 2004 gold medalist Justine Henin announced that she might not defend her medal because of her concerns about the air given her asthma (she dropped out of an earlier tournament in China for similar reasons). Marathon world record holder Haile Gebrselassie considered not competing given Beijing's air quality. Some national teams, including the United States and Australia took well-publicized precautionary measures to guard against the ill effects of competing in China's foul air. Randy Wilber, a consultant to the United States Olympic Committee, called for U.S. athletes to arrive at the last possible moment before competition, remain indoors, and wear masks to protect their respiratory systems to the best extent possible.[22] The British Olympic Association were also considering masks for their athletes. The teams of several countries, including Germany, Britain, Sweden, and the Netherlands, rented out practice facilities in nearby Korea and Japan, flying into Beijing only for the competitions.[23]

This was not the first time that air quality was an issue for the Summer Games. Smog was a major issue for the 1968 Mexico City Games and the 1984 Los Angeles Games. Indeed, in the latter case, radical measures not unlike those employed by the Chinese were used to clear the skies of the Los Angeles basin and provide city dwellers with a view of the San Gabriel Mountains, which they had never enjoyed before.[24] There were similar concerns in advance of the 1988 Seoul Games, where there were more cars and less public transport than in Beijing. But for Beijing, the scrutiny was particularly intense. The Olympics became the generator of a long-needed environmental overhaul of the city. The government devoted some $16 billion to this effort, and, according to Sun Weide, spokesperson for the Beijing Organizing Committee for the Games of the Twenty-ninth Olympiad, undertook 200 measures to clean the air. The "blue-sky program" started in 1998 with the overall goal of improving Beijing's air quality from level 3 to level 2 on the international scale by closing many polluting smokestack factories. Once prestigious signs of Mao-era industrialization, heavily polluting plants like the Beijing Shougang Group Steel plant and Beijing Number 2 Chemical Factory were finally either shut down or moved out of Beijing despite deeply entrenched bureaucratic interests.[25] Hundreds of polluting factories were reportedly retrofitted with scrubbers and other pollutant-reducing innovations, shut down, or moved outside city limits. Five regions surrounding Beijing were enlisted in the effort: Tianjin, Heibei, Shanxi, inner Mongolia, and Shandong.

The government developed programs to increase by four times the use of clean energy sources such as natural gas, solar power, and geo-thermal power by the start of the Games. In order to promote clean public transportation, 70 percent of the taxis and 90 percent of the buses in Beijing were replaced with clean-energy vehicles.[26] Authorities also undertook a massive forestation of Beijing as part of a city-beautification campaign that also aided the environmental cleanup effort. Over 28 million trees were planted, creating greenbelts along the second, fourth, and fifth ring roads to help absorb carbon dioxide.

Two of the more novel attempts were cloud-seeding and car bans. In order to help wash away pollution in advance of key outdoor events, Beijing authorities prepared silver iodide, salt, and dry ice to induce rain for the purpose of clearing the air days before an event. They also experimented with methods to delay rainfall in order to reduce the likelihood of a downpour on the roofless Bird's Nest (the original design called for a roof, which was eventually scrapped because of cost overruns). The Chinese government has practiced weather-modification techniques since the 1950s and employs 37,000 people in a weather bureau that has 30 aircraft, 4,000 rocket launchers, and 7,000 anti-aircraft guns (the program is second only to the Soviet Union's, which used cloud seeding to prevent radioactive rain in the aftermath of the Chernobyl disaster).[27]

On any given day, there are three million cars on Beijing's streets and 1,200 new car registrations. So the authorities decided to ban one million cars from the city in order to reduce air pollution. This "temporary traffic management program" as it was termed by Beijing city officials was first experimented with in November 2006 for three days during the China-Africa summit, which NASA satellites reported to coincide with a 40 percent decrease in nitrous oxide levels in Beijing. (I was in Beijing at that time for a round of the Six Party Talks and did notice that the air was clearer.) A more publicized ban was again attempted in August 2007 for four days, when 6,500 police officers were mobilized to monitor the ban and fines of thirteen dollars were meted out for violators.[28] Beijing city officials planned to ban more than 1.65 million cars from the city for the duration of the Games.

The results of the cleanup effort have been mixed. Spokespeople for the Beijing Organizing Committee claimed that the number of blue-sky days steadily increased from 100 in 1998 to 165 in 2000, 224 in 2003, and 241 in 2006.[29] While there was no denying progress in the cleanup efforts, the Chinese continually faced setbacks and sometimes embarrassingly so. During the 2007 car ban, for example, air pollution levels actually rose, much to the dismay of the Beijing Olympic organizing committee.[30] On the very day that Beijing held a special environmental forum designed to showcase their blue-sky program, the air visibility was less than fifty meters. Particle dust from construction was so bad that the elderly and children were advised to stay home. Similarly, haze on the day of the August 2007 celebrations of the one-year Olympic countdown reduced visibility to a few hundred meters in Beijing, prompting the IOC head's remark about the possibility of postponing some of the endurance events at the Games if the air quality did not improve. Athletes expressed concern that China's metrics for clean air do not account for ozone levels, which have the worst effect on respiratory systems.

As one reporter noted, "In a half-hour of walking Monday, my throat was raw, and my breath was shorter. Run? Only with a portable oxygen tank."[31] Or as another reporter put it, China's fast-track environmental cleanup effort is like an athlete trying to get in shape by walking on a treadmill and eating double cheeseburgers at the same time.[32] When Beijing unveiled the new Water Cube aquatics facility in January 2008, black grime and soot were noticeably visible on the structure's white bubble-like membrane.[33] Despite these and other incidents during the Games, the Beijing Organizing Committee and the IOC continued to preach the virtues of Beijing's environmental cleanup efforts before and during the Games.

MEANINGFUL CHANGE?

Is the physical change seen in Beijing, particularly regarding the environment, meaningful? While the iconic stadiums will endure, will the environmental practices set a new standard for Chinese behavior? In the aftermath of the Olympics, some will maintain that the blue-sky program and other related efforts amounted to no more than a very expensive ($16 billion) makeshift effort to avoid the public embarrassment of a smoglympics. But it is difficult to deny that the Games awakened many Chinese to environmental issues that they might not have otherwise confronted. When a government budgets that much money and goes to the lengths that Beijing did, it is bound to have an effect on wider practices and ways of thinking. What results is a sense that growth in China is no longer acceptably achieved at any price but must take into consideration the effects on the environment.

Signs of meaningful change are governmental plans that have timelines extending beyond the end of the Games. In September 2007, for example, the China State Council approved an environment plant cleanup aimed at reducing the discharge of major pollutants by 10 percent by 2010, long after the Olympic Games. Environmental conservation is gradually being built into the process of doing business in China. Subsidies are provided for companies that use clean fuels. Parking fees have increased in order to make public transportation more appealing. One of the most important ways to monitor longer-term change will be in terms of enforcement. Some of the most effective aspects of China's pre-Olympics environmental cleanup had less to do with new rules than with the effective enforcement at the local level of rules already on the books. In 2007, for example, environmental protection agencies gave local governments the tools to enforce punishment against polluters. These included allowing local banks to deny loans to violators, the levying of energy consumption surcharges on companies that use energy inefficiently, the ability of local governments to compel polluters to issue public apologies for their bad practices. The fact that these enforcement practices extended outside of Beijing constituted another sign that the environment was being taken more seriously. Provincial officials in Heilongjiang closed one hundred polluting businesses that were sending industrial runoff into Russia. Provincial government officials in Shanxi closed an entire county of coal mining plants that were found to be polluting waterways, and dairy plants in inner Mongolia were shut down for polluting the Yellow River. Emblematic of China's new thinking on the environment was Tai Lake in Wuxi. A totally polluted and unusable body of water was gradually cleaned up and salvaged through the closing of more than 1,340 factories that sent their waste into the lake.[34]

Finally, the world will encourage China to maintain its commitment to the environment. Many groups have sought to use Beijing's pre-Olympic emphasis on new cleaner technologies as a way to press longer-term changes in Chinese energy practices. The World Wildlife Fund, for example, sponsored a conference in October 2007 aimed at promoting best practices on the environment more widely in China. China used only certified timber for construction of the Olympic Village; one project at the WWF conference was to get China to use only certified timber for all construction projects. Another was to promote wider use of solar panels after their introduction in the stadiums built for the Olympics.[35]

Skeptics will still argue that the fact that Beijing's showing during the 2008 Games was not a complete environmental disaster offers no window on the longer-term prospects for change. Pollution is just being transplanted from one part of the country to another—in this case, from Beijing to cities like Tianjin and Hebei province, which remain terribly polluted. Plants closed for the Olympics will eventually be reopened after the Games, and cars will eventually be allowed back into the city, raising pollution levels. At least in the immediate aftermath of the Games, however, the Olympics appears to have precipitated a shift in thinking in China. Growth is still king, but not without adequate consideration of the environment: "[C]ities are taking measures that show that their officials are beginning to make the environment a higher priority than raising the gross domestic product, a fundamental shift in thinking for a country that can attribute much of its early development to being the place to which others outsourced their pollution."[36] As one expert concluded, "The commitment, the profile, the energy behind the state's environmental protection efforts far exceed anything we've seen in China's history."[37]

6

CATCH-22

China's economic, military and diplomatic ties to the government of Sudan continue to provide you with the influence and the obligation to press for change. . . . the decisive hour for Darfur is now. There must be meaningful and measurable progress on the ground for Darfuris within the next few weeks. The world needs China to lead here. So many lives are at stake.

–STEVEN SPIELBERG, AMERICAN FILM DIRECTOR AND AN ARTISTIC DIRECTOR FOR THE BEIJING OLYMPICS, TO PRESIDENT HU JINTAO OF CHINA, 15 NOVEMBER 2007

It's up to [Steven Spielberg]. I am going to the Olympics, I view the Olympics as a sporting event. . . . I am not going to go and use the Olympics as an opportunity to express my opinions to the Chinese people in a public way because I do it all the time with the President.

–PRESIDENT GEORGE W. BUSH, 14 FEBRUARY 2008, *BBC* INTERVIEW

People in China enjoy extensive freedom of speech. . . . No one will get arrested because he said that human rights are more important than the Olympics. This is impossible.

–FOREIGN MINISTER YANG JIECHI OF CHINA, 28 FEBRUARY 2008

In the preceding chapters, I have shown how sport precipitates tremendous physical change, turning cities into six-year construction sites before the Olympics and totally remaking everything from airports to highways to beds and lavatories. But how deep does this change go? Does physical change lead to deeper political change. If so, how might this happen?

The history of sport in Asia shows that sporting events creates certain pressures for change upon the host government in domestic and international policies. What may have once been a standard way of doing business changes as new audience costs become associated with a government's behavior under the international spotlight. This prompts short-term changes in policy in order to avoid embarrassment and undue scrutiny, but these short-term changes can lead to more permanent change as states become socialized to the new behavior. Taking the case of the Beijing Games, China clearly wanted to use the Olympics to enhance internal credibility and control, showcase its economic growth, delegitimize Taiwan, improve its international stature, extinguish memories of the Tiananmen Square massacre of 1989, and establish the PRC as a global player. However, illiberal regimes that host an event like the Olympics face a catch-22—they seek to use the Games to improve their international stature, but the absence of any change while under the microscope of international media scrutiny only serves to undercut their reputation and stature. In the run-up to the Games, the Chinese sought to deal with this dilemma by making tactical changes in certain aspects of human rights and foreign policies, particularly in Africa and in Burma.

Sport creates two types of pressure for political change: tactical and ideational pressure. The former refers to the dynamic in which hosting a global sporting event like the Olympics puts the country in question and its practices under the international spotlight for the six years before the Games and for years thereafter. The spectacle of the event attracts tens of thousands of people who are interested in examining every aspect of the host nation's society and politics. The same magnet attracts every nongovernmental organization that seeks to change aspects of politics and society by essentially shaming the host country into succumbing. The continual drumbeat of NGO pressure and media scrutiny begins six years before the Games and grows particularly loud about twelve to fourteen months in advance of the event. As more people pay attention, advocates mobilize to channel that attention away from sport and toward the country's aberrant behavior. The result is that the government and its Olympic planners have more to think about than merely building stadiums and infrastructure. As one observer noted, "the seven-year run-up to the 2008 games is more likely to unnerve the authoritarians themselves, as tremendous pressure is brought to bear on the regime to open more political space and to maintain its current moderate foreign policy."[1]

The other type of pressure that prompts political change is less tactical and more ideational. In addition to the media microscope, sport creates socialization pressures on a regime, particularly an illiberal one, because of the gap between the regime's aberrant practices and the values that sport privileges. Based on fair competition, rules, best efforts, and rewarding merit and performance, sport and sporting competition inherently privilege values that are classically liberal in nature. The Olympics and the concept of Olympism is not merely a sport; it is a collection of values and prescribed practices about humanity and its treatment.[2] Avery Brundage believed Olympism should surmount all racial, religious, and political barriers and prejudices and should engender fair competition, cohesion, and integration.[3] It is worth noting that elements of the Olympic spirit were hardly liberal. The Games were largely attended in the beginning only by white males. At the 1904 Games in St. Louis there were "anthropological days" in which natives of African, North American, and South American tribes poorly showed their skills, thereby confirming the myth of white racial superiority. Coubertin, the founder of the modern Olympic movement, was not in favor of women's participation in the Games. With decolonization in Africa, Avery Brundage, the IOC chair at the time, did not allow African countries to have equal representation in the IOC.[4] This early history notwithstanding, the IOC Charter's similarity with the universal declaration of human rights is hardly coincidental:

> The goal of Olympism is to place sport at the service of the harmonious development of man, with a view to promoting peaceful society concerned with the preservation of human dignity. . . . the practice of sport is a human right. Every individual must have the possibility of practicing sport, without discrimination of any kind and in the Olympic spirit, which requires mutual understanding with a spirit of friendship, solidarity, and fair play. . . . Any form of discrimination with regard to a country or a person on grounds of race, religion, politics, gender, or otherwise is incompatible with belonging to the Olympic Movement.[5]

The link between Olympism and liberalism is therefore inescapable. This ideational aspect of sport is more powerful than people realize. A government that hosts the Olympics is expected to embrace the ideals and values consistent with the Olympic social movement, explicitly in the competitions themselves and implicitly in their overall role as hosts. This naturally puts pressure on a host government to address practices that are inconsistent with the ideals.

The ideational pressure for political change is particularly acute for illiberal regimes that host the Games. They feel compelled to find some way, however gerrymandered, to close the gap between ideals and practices. One might expect that authoritarian regimes should merely act like sports purists, hosting the event flawlessly and ensuring that their teams perform well. That's what Hitler tried to do in 1936, after all. In the twenty-first century, with twenty-four-hour cable news and tens of thousands of tourists armed with camera cell phones, however, illiberal regimes cannot ignore the ideational pressures to conform because the costs of not doing so impinge directly and immediately on their reputations. And sport events have tremendous reputational value for regimes seeking to enhance their legitimacy and stature. Illiberal regimes face another catch-22: They host the Olympics to improve their prestige, but hosting the Games forces them to adjust illiberal practices to liberal Olympic ideals. Not doing so has potentially damaging implications for the prestige so desperately sought through the Games.

China sought to circumvent this problem by supplanting Olympic ideals with its own. It introduced several concepts for the 2008 Games. The first was a "clean and green," environment-friendly Olympics, and the second was "high-tech" Games demonstrating China's cutting-edge prowess. Both of these were chosen in no small part because they are value-neutral concepts focused largely on modernity while eschewing any of the liberal values associated with Olympism. The third theme of "Chinese-style" Olympics focused on Chinese culture and history and also safely circumvented any notion of universal values inherent in Olympism. The fourth theme of "harmonious Olympics and society" talked amorphously about how the Games were for the people, which meant essentially that the Games would help propel the Chinese people across the $1,000 per capita GDP threshold—a worthy economic aspiration, but hardly an Olympic value. These gerrymandered ideals highlight the specific problem for Beijing's illiberal regime as it tried to devise a rationale for the Olympics that allowed it to gain the benefits of prestige without sacrificing any real political change or liberalization.

Political change engendered by sport, then, is a function of the media microscope and the deceptively powerful ideals of Olympism. These create tactical and ideational pressures on the regime for change. Groups inside and outside use the Olympic microscope to organize and demand change. This in turn creates new audience costs and calculations for the leadership about its own practices. What was once a standard way of doing business now has new costs associated with it, including the fear of being boycotted, labeled a pariah, and embarrassed before the world. These forces compel political change.

THE OLYMPICS AND KOREAN DEMOCRATIZATION

A large digital clock sat atop City Hall in the center of Seoul. The clock counted down the days, hours, minutes, and seconds before the opening day ceremonies of the September 1988 Seoul Olympics. In many ways the clock acted as a running scoreboard of the race against time as Seoul worked feverishly to complete the roads, hotels, stadiums, and subways in time for the Games. In this regard, the clock was a vivid and daily reminder of what was at stake for Koreans in 1988. But no one knew that the clock would also time the countdown of the ROK's move to democracy.

The most historic case of sport leading to political change is the impact of the Seoul Olympics on Korea's democratic transition in 1987. In retrospect, ideational pressures were strong. When the Games were awarded to Seoul by the IOC, the ROK government was a military dictatorship with practices anathema to the Olympic ideal. The yawning gap between practices and ideals was something the Chun regime had to contend with. Tactical pressures were also strong. Political dissidents, democracy activists, and international human rights groups leveraged the international attention heaped on Seoul to corner the Chun junta into choosing between democracy or martial law, all under the glaring spotlight of the Olympics. Chun and his cronies, a group of middling generals who had taken power in a coup, desperately sought to gain domestic and international legitimacy through the Games. Their stakes in avoiding an Olympic failure were real and critical. This confluence of forces made the Seoul Olympiad a very important agent of political change.

The ROK decision to bid for the Summer Games was made during the last months of dictator Park Chung-hee's government in 1979. Park Jong-kyu, then head of the Korea National Olympic Committee, discussed the idea with President Park. The rationale was typical of a developing Asian country under authoritarian leadership; Park wanted to host the Games to show off the ROK's economic prowess and gain international stature and legitimacy. Park was assassinated in October 1979 by his own bodyguard, ending nearly two decades of dictatorial and brutal rule. Hopes surfaced after Park's death for political liberalization in the ROK, but after only a couple of months of ineffective transitional rule, the country suffered a military coup by a group of generals led by the relatively obscure Chun Doo-hwan. Chun cracked down on all dissent within the country and in May 1980 ordered a brutal suppression of demonstrating South Korean citizens in the southern city of Kwangju. He subsequently sentenced to death Kim Dae Jung, the democracy activist and future winner of the Nobel Peace Prize.

Chun was not popular. He faced international criticism and demands that he allow for political liberalization. The general desperately sought to gain legitimacy and solidify his hold on the country through two actions. In December 1980, he decided to follow through on the late president Park's idea to bid for the summer Olympics. Though a long shot, Seoul's winning the Games would provide the country with a national project to focus its attention. Meanwhile, Ronald Reagan came into office in Washington desirous of reaffirming the U.S. commitment to staunchly anticommunist Cold War allies like the ROK and distancing himself from the Carter administration's policy of disdain for allies with poor human rights records. In February 1981, Chun engineered an invitation from the White House to be Reagan's first major head of state visitor (in tacit quid pro quo, Chun commuted the death sentence against Kim Dae Jung). Despite boisterous political opposition and radical student demonstrations, the Chun regime steadily consolidated power, and in September 1981, the IOC at Baden-Baden, Germany, awarded the 1988 Games to Seoul.

The IOC decision, a surprise that undercut the favorite candidate, Nagoya, Japan, was roundly criticized by human rights groups. In their view, the Games were being handed to Chun, a military dictator, only fifteen months after the Kwangju massacre. Commentators drew comparisons between this decision and a similarly ill advised one in 1968, when the Mexican military gunned down unarmed students in the run-up to the Mexico City Games. Others went so far as to compare the decision to the 1936 Berlin Olympics.

The Chun regime, therefore, faced immediate pressure before the Games, which would come to a head in the summer of 1987. With Chun's single seven-year term as president coming to an end, there were growing calls among the South Korean body politic for political liberalization, including revision of the constitution and the institution of a direct presidential-election system. By the spring, the traditional demonstration season in Korea, a combination of students, laborers, and radicals were out in full force demanding that the unpopular Chun regime relent to the peoples' will. In April 1987, Chun, rather than relenting, chose to suspend all debate on constitutional revision. His stated rationale was that the ROK could not suffer such political disarray while hosting the Olympics, and he offered to revisit the issue after the successful Games. Meanwhile, Chun appointed his friend and military coup compatriot Roh Tae-woo as the government party's candidate, essentially anointing him into the position as Chun's successor. These actions met with widespread disapproval, and mass demonstrations raged in the streets of Seoul amid tear gas and Molotov cocktails.

By June 1987, the constitutional crisis in Seoul had captured international attention. Unarmed students were lionized in the world media as democracy fighters against riot police, the latter dressed in sinister-looking Darth Vader–like urban combat gear and armed with rubber bullets, tear gas, and water cannons. The demonstrations spread among the Korean population, for the first time encompassing the burgeoning middle class, who, with their newfound affluence, also demanded political freedoms. White-collar workers, nurses, and office workers started to join the street protests alongside radical students. Major newspapers were all stationing their Asia-based reporters in Seoul to document the unfolding of an incredible grassroots democratization story. NGOs and international human rights groups mobilized to ensure that the world would scrutinize every move made by the Chun regime in response to the demonstrations.

The city of Seoul was a mess. Streets were strewn with garbage, burning vehicles, and tear gas canisters, all the remains of clashes between demonstrators and riot police. Parts of the city were entirely shut down. Amid the chaos, there was speculation that Chun might respond by declaring martial law, and even send in combat troops as he had done in bloody crackdown in Kwangju in 1980. The United States monitored the situation in Seoul and sent both public and private messages to the Chun regime emphasizing the need for a peaceful resolution to the strife and tacitly advising against any military action. A stressed and chain-smoking Chun considered imposing martial law, but then in a bombshell announcement on June 29, Chun's handpicked successor Roh Tae-woo announced landmark concessions. Roh's "June Declaration" accepted all of the political opposition demands for constitutional revision, provided political amnesty to Kim Dae Jung, and committed to hold direct presidential elections in December 1987. Because the political opposition remained divided and fielded two candidates for the presidential election, Roh eventually won with only 34 percent of the vote. But the events of 1987 were seen as a watershed in South Korea's transition to democratic rule. Today, it is still seen as one of the most successful and peaceful cases of democratic transition in world history.

Sport played a quiet but critical role in the political transformation of the Republic of Korea. There is no denying that other socioeconomic and political factors mattered. The June 1987 transition could not have happened without a vibrant and organized South Korean democratization movement. The country's economic growth, affluence, and levels of high education also gave rise to a middle class that would not live under the yoke of military dictatorships any longer. Restraint by a close ally, the United States, through quiet diplomacy also played a role. But hosting the Olympics was crucial to the democratic outcome in 1987 in several ways.

First, the Olympics had the effect of illuminating the domestic political crisis to the world and constraining the government's behavior. The stark reality faced by the Chun government was that all of the political events in Korea of the 1980s took place against the backdrop of the upcoming Olympic Games. This made domestic developments in Korea an international story. At the height of the crisis, all three major U.S. networks were broadcasting from Seoul, reporting on a daily basis about the situation. The reporting was critical of the Chun government and conveyed legitimacy on the democracy activists supported by churches and the middle class.[6] Every move that Chun contemplated against the demonstrators would be examined under the microscope of world opinion. This spotlight forced Chun to be on his best behavior. As Han Sung-joo observed, "Internally, the [Seoul] Games played a pivotal role in bringing democracy to South Korea, if only because intensifying world scrutiny made it difficult for the government to deal harshly with those demanding expanded freedoms."[7]

Second, the journalism about the crisis was not only antigovernment and prodemonstrators; it also drew clear links between resolution of the democratic crisis in Korea and a successful staging of the Seoul Olympics. The moniker, "barbed wire Olympics?" became affixed to the ROK government's handling of the domestic political revolution taking place under their noses. NBC, *Newsweek*, and other media outlets ran cover stories expressing concern that the military dictatorship in Seoul faced a stark choice between its continued repression and hosting a successful Games. NBC, the official broadcaster of the Olympics, held off on opening its office in Seoul to televise the Games as it waited out the crisis.[8]

Third, the Chun regime became very concerned that an unresolved political crisis so close to the staging of the Games might cause the risk-averse IOC to pull the Games from Seoul. There was already mounting pressure on the IOC from human rights groups to undertake such a measure. The IOC chair, Juan Antonio Samaranch, faced the question in almost every press conference he gave. Some athletes also made public the possibility that they might not attend the Games. In a major step that underlined the seriousness of the situation, the cities of Berlin, Los Angeles, and New York all expressed their willingness to act as last-minute alternate sites if the political turmoil in Seoul imperiled the staging of the Olympic Games. For the Koreans, the talk of losing the Games brought back sickening memories of the last ill-fated attempt by Korea to host an event of this scale. In 1971, Park Chung-hee sought to host the 1976 Asian Olympics and won the bid but later had to forfeit it because the country could not afford the $34 million necessary to build the facilities, a terribly humiliating experience for the country. The prospect of losing an even bigger event so critical to enhancing the ROK's global prestige—this time, not for reasons of money, but because of visions of the Games being played under barbed wire and clouds of tear gas—was unfathomable. The IOC's concerns became readily apparent in June 1987 (only two days before the June declaration) when IOC member Alexandru Sipercu went to Seoul carrying a letter from the IOC expressing concern about the civil unrest's effects on Seoul's ability to host the games.[9]

Finally, the pressure and stakes of the Olympics were felt personally by Chun's anointed successor, Roh Tae-woo. Roh understood that a refusal to allow some political change would result in worldwide criticism and would destroy the prospect of a successful Olympics. As sports minister and then later as president of the Seoul Olympic Organizing Committee, Roh was an instrumental figure in Seoul's bid in 1981 and the subsequent preparations for the Games. He played a key role in hosting the 1986 convention of national Olympic associations, which sought to ensure there would be no Soviet or Eastern bloc boycott.[10] Roh therefore internalized the importance of the Olympics to ROK prestige and understood the link between the democratic crisis and a successful staging of the Games more than any other Korean politician. Indeed, when he made the June 29 declaration, he mentioned the Olympics several times. He pleaded for an end to the civil unrest with his concessions: "At a time when the Olympics are around the corner, all of us should be responsible for preventing the national disgrace of being mocked and derided by the international community because of a division in the national consensus."[11]

The catch-22 that the Olympics presented to Roh and the ROK leadership could not easily be ignored. The Games brought the desired prestige to the country but also brought world attention to the internal forces of democratization. Roh and his regime were forced to succumb to these pressures or risk national humiliation by losing the Games or permitting them to operate under martial law in clear defiance of the Olympic spirit. There is no denying that other forces pushed the country toward democratization, but as a *Los Angeles Times* story observed, none of these was nearly as important as the Olympics. September 1988 (the opening of the games) was supposed to be Korea's shining moment—the potential that this could turn to disaster was a key reason for Roh's political concessions.[12] In his first press briefing after taking office, in April 1988, President Roh mentioned the Olympics at least six times, and in his first speech to the National Assembly, he shared his personal anxieties of Olympic political change: "All nations of the world, which a year ago watched with concern and anxiety the chaotic situation in the country due to host the Olympics, are now amazed at our dramatic democratic development. The world perception of Korea has thus completely changed. There is an almost universal appreciation that having achieved an economic miracle, Korea is now working a political miracle also."[13] The result is that the Seoul Games have become the most important case of progressive political change related to sport in the modern Olympic era.

POLITICAL CHANGE AND BEIJING 2008

How much political change have the Olympics effected in China? The physical change wrought by the preparations for the Games on the city of Beijing was undeniable. To what extent did the change go deeper in politics and society? Beijing contended with the same catch-22 as its Korean counterparts two decades earlier. Indeed, the level of tactical and ideational pressure on the regime for change, the call for boycotts, and the demands for political change were deafening when compared with Seoul. In the run-up to the Games and in its immediate aftermath, Beijing sought to contend with these pressures with calibrated changes in policy designed to release some of the pressure and allow for a successful staging of the Olympics. Though many changes were transparently tactical, they constituted change nonetheless.

"GENOCIDE OLYMPICS" AND "TEAM DARFUR"

Like the ROK, China followed a path of rapid urbanization and the growth of a middle class that enjoyed unprecedented prosperity. It pursued this economic growth and liberalization under an authoritarian political system. Like Seoul, Beijing adopted sport and the Olympics as an important marker of its external success and as a means of asserting domestic legitimacy, which is why it faced the same catch-22. As I noted earlier, China sought to deal with the obvious gap between its illiberal political system and the liberal values embodied in the Olympics by coming up with value-neutral themes of a "high-tech," environment-friendly Olympics that, while hardly offensive, were chosen precisely because they skirt the core values of freedom, fair competition, and dignity of the individual inherent in the modern Olympic social movement.

"Face" is important to the Chinese, and a lot of it was on the line in the Olympics. The Chinese contended with tremendous internal and external pressure as many groups tried to leverage the Olympic spotlight to embarrass Beijing into altering its policies. I focus in particular on three policy areas—human rights, Africa, and Burma—largely because it is in these three issues where the gap between the liberal ideals of Olympism and Chinese practices were most apparent. China's domestic human rights abuses are well known, and Beijing externalizes these policies in its foreign relations with such places as Sudan and Burma. China accounts for 80 percent of Sudan's oil exports and provides arms and other forms of economic assistance to the Khartoum regime irrespective of the genocide taking place in Darfur, which has left 250,000 people dead and millions homeless. In Burma, China conducts over $2 billion worth of business and weapons sales with the regime on an annual basis, again without any condition or concern for the internal political and social situation. Cooperative actions by Beijing in other areas of behavior, such as combating nuclear proliferation in North Korea or Iran, joining a climate-change regime, rectifying the trade imbalance with the United States, appreciating the value of the reminbi, or addressing product-safety concerns could be explained by basic national interest rather than by any pre-Games pressures by advocacy groups.

FIGURE 13. BEIJING 2008 OLYMPIC TORCH RELAY

SOURCE: © VASSILIS PSOMAS/EPA/CORBIS.

FIGURE 14. BEIJING 2008 OLYMPIC TORCH RELAY

SOURCE: © VASSILIS PSOMAS/EPA/CORBIS

The media spotlight on Beijing led to scrutiny more intense than that faced by the host city of any previous Games. This was the first time in nearly three decades that the Summer Games were hosted by an authoritarian regime (Moscow in 1980 was the last). More than 21,600 press passes were authorized for the games, and estimates are that an additional 10,000 freelance journalists showed up without credentials to get a piece of the Olympic action. NBC planned to present more than 3,600 hours of television coverage, which is more than the combined total broadcast hours of all previous Summer Olympics in the United States. On NBCOlympics.com, the network also planned to provide live streaming broadband video coverage for the first time ever. Countless blog sites were set up to cover all aspects of Beijing's behavior, which China sought to control through the issuing guidelines on blogging during the Games. With 500,000 tourists expected to descend on Beijing, all armed with cell-phone cameras, the Chinese Communist Party faced the most comprehensive and intense media scrutiny and penetration in its history.

This spotlight was used by various groups to put intense pressure on the regime to change certain illiberal policies. The actress and UNICEF goodwill ambassador Mia Farrow authored an important *Wall Street Journal* op-ed article on March 28, 2007, calling the 2008 Games the "Genocide Olympics" because of Beijing's hands-off policies in Sudan. She called for an Olympic boycott by corporate sponsors unless Beijing used its substantial economic and military influence to force the Khartoum regime to stop the genocide in Darfur. Farrow also attacked film mogul Steven Spielberg for agreeing to act as a consultant to the Games, denigrating him as the Leni Riefenstahl of the Beijing Olympics, a reference to the German filmmaker who documented the 1936 Nazi Olympics. Farrow's campaign then led Spielberg to write an open letter to President Hu Jintao of the PRC in April 2007, in which he stated that if China did not change its policies in Darfur, he would withdraw from his work on the opening ceremonies of the Games.

> There is no question in my mind that the government of Sudan is engaged in a policy which is best described as genocide.
>
> I have only recently come to understand fully the extent of China's involvement in the region and its strategic and supportive relationship with the Sudanese government. I share the concern of many around the world who believe that China should be a clear advocate for United Nations action to bring the genocide in Darfur to an end.
>
> Accordingly, I add my voice to those who ask that China change its policy toward Sudan and pressure the Sudanese government to accept the entrance of United Nations peacekeepers to protect the victims of genocide in Darfur. China is uniquely positioned to do this and has considerable influence in the region that could lead efforts by the international community to bring an end to the human suffering there.[14]

In February 2008, Spielberg announced his resignation as artistic advisor for the Olympic opening and closing ceremonies. Other entertainers, including George Clooney, Richard Gere, Angelina Jolie, Brad Pitt, and Matt Damon used their star power to draw attention to Chinese government malpractice and called on Beijing to take responsible action or face boycotts.[15] Uma Thurman applauded Spielberg's action and called for other media personalities associated with the Beijing Games to take similar action given Beijing's "appalling" human rights record.[16] Quincy Jones, who was composing theme music for the Games, also considered withdrawing support. Eight Nobel Peace Prize laureates wrote an open letter in February 2008 to President Hu Jintao demanding an end to China's trade with and aid to the Khartoum regime to force an end to the atrocities in Sudan.[17] Charles, the Prince of Wales, declared he would not attend the opening ceremonies of the Beijing Games in opposition to China's handling of the Tibet issue. PRC officials complained that there was a global conspiracy aimed at ruining their Olympics. As another PRC official noted wryly, the level of public scrutiny and pressure would not be nearly as intense if not for the Olympics.[18]

In addition to movie stars, human rights groups mobilized to put maximum pressure on Beijing. Olympic Watch was established to monitor China's actions across a range of issues, including Tibet, Xinjiang, religious freedom, and media censorship.[19] Human Rights Watch drew attention to China's liberal use of capital punishment and demanded a moratorium before the Games.[20] Amnesty International launched a major campaign focused on China's crackdown on the Uighur population in Xinjiang, and another major campaign, "Gold for Human Rights," in spring 2008. The Free Tibet Campaign dubbed the Beijing Olympics the "Games of Shame." The World Association of Newspapers and the World Editors' Forum wrote letters to Premier Wen Jiabao of China calling for the release of thirty journalists and fifty "cyber-dissidents" held in Chinese prisons. Advocacy groups also organized around the Chinese government's labor and civil rights abuse of millions of migrant workers brought into Beijing to build the Olympic sites like the Bird's Nest who were forced to live in makeshift housing and work under terrible conditions. The Geneva-based Center on Housing Rights and Eviction publicized cases on behalf of individuals like Sun Ruoyu, one of thousands of Beijing residents forcibly evicted from their homes as the Chinese government razed entire neighborhoods for the Games.[21]

Much of the pre-Olympics pressure on China focused on a boycott of the Games. But a boycott became less likely after President Bush accepted President Hu Jintao's invitation during their bilateral meetings at the September 2007 APEC meetings in Sydney, Australia. The IOC also came out strongly against boycotts, calling them "a thing of the past, not of the present nor the future," and it maintained that even the 1980 and 1984 boycott-blighted Games were a success.[22] When the Beijing government's crackdown on the demonstrations in Lhasa, Tibet, in March 2008 drew more calls for boycotts, both the organizers for the 2010 Winter Olympics in Vancouver and the 2014 Games in Sochi, Russia publicly opposed in principle the concept of boycotts. Pro-Tibet NGOs then adjusted their strategy and focused instead on using the Games to maximize pressure on the regime and to embarrass the PRC leadership. (Chinese activists, by contrast, never wanted a boycott; they wanted to capture the attention of the world through the Olympics.) For example, Freedom House called on President Bush to meet with Chinese dissidents and human rights activists while attending the Beijing Games.[23] The *Washington Post* editorial page called on Bush to demand the release of a prominent Chinese AIDS activist and human rights blogger whom Chinese authorities sought to muffle until after the Olympics through a seven-month detainment.[24] Besides media personalities like Spielberg and Quincy Jones, other high-profile individuals, such as director Ang Lee and choreographer Ric Birch (who worked on the 2000 Sydney Games opening ceremony) were also asked to withdraw their cooperation on human rights grounds. NGOs also targeted corporate actors. The combination of corporate social responsibility and corporate sponsorship of the games offered an outlet of pressure for NGOs that was not as readily apparent in previous Olympics.[25]

Politicians got into the act as well. In August 2007 the U.S. Congress introduced three "sense of Congress" resolutions, one calling unconditionally for Bush to boycott the Games, and another calling for a boycott unless China "stops engaging in serious human rights abuses against it citizens and stops supporting serious human rights abuses by the governments of Sudan, Burma, and North Korea."[26] Following Mia Farrow's lead in labeling the Games the "Genocide Olympics," congressional leaders like Donald Payne and Maxine Waters introduced resolutions referring to the "blood Olympics" and calling for worldwide boycotts in protest over China's poli-

FIGURE 15. BEIJING 2008 OLYMPIC TORCH RELAY IN LONDON

SOURCE: © ANDY RAIN/EPA/CORBIS

FIGURE 16. BEIJING 2008 OLYMPIC TORCH RELAY IN PARIS

cies toward Sudan.[27] Senator Sam Brownback (R-Kansas) and Governor Bill Richardson of New Mexico, among other U.S. presidential candidates in 2007 and 2008, called for divestment from Chinese companies that do business with Sudan. Lord Mark Malloch Brown, Britain's minister for Africa, Asia, and the United Nations, broke from traditional British sport purist affinities and stated that he "very much raised [with China] the linkage to the Olympics and the public relations costs if the (human rights) issues were not handled correctly."[28] In February 2008 the Christian Union, a Dutch conservative Protestant party, began a transnational campaign to bring together conservative European political parties and American neoconservatives to press for national Olympic teams to boycott the opening ceremonies of the Beijing Games to protest policies in Darfur and China's horrid human rights record at home.[29]

Every time that Beijing organizers sought to showcase their Olympic preparations to the world, protest groups mobilized in an effort to embarrass the country for its human rights practices. At the March 2008 Olympic torch-lighting ceremony in Athens, Greece, in which the Olympic flame is lit by the rays of the sun in a simple but elegant start to its five-month journey, members of BOCOG (the Beijing Organizing Committee for the Olympic Games) proudly began their presentation to the audience and before international broadcasts. Suddenly, an anti-PRC government demonstrator who slipped through security cordons interrupted BOCOG president Liu Qi's remarks and unfurled at the podium a black banner showing five interlinked handcuffs instead of the five Olympic rings. Security guards quickly whisked the man away but not before the image was captured around the world. A Tibetan woman lay on the road to obstruct the beginnings of the torch relay but was removed by police. The Chinese response? Television and newspapers did not report the incident, the former operating on a delayed broadcast that enables censors to cut to pretaped scenes during any undesired obstruction. *China Daily*'s headline stated unapologetically, "A Perfect Start on the Road to Gold."[30]

The August 2007 one-year countdown celebrations in Tiananmen Square, in which the Chinese threw a party for a million people, featured fireworks, media stars like Jackie Chan and Yao Ming, and the theme song "We Are Ready!" But news stories focused on the call from Human Rights Watch for the IOC to join their demand for a ban on capital punishment in China. Reporters Without Borders held an unauthorized press conference to demand the release of one hundred dissidents, free speech activists, and journalists imprisoned in China.[31] Protesters climbed the Great Wall and unfurled a banner revising the Olympics theme of "One Dream, One World" to "One Dream, Free Tibet 2008." As the fireworks streamed over Tiananmen Square, critics on blogs around the world drew analogies between these celebrations on the square once stained by the blood of prodemocracy demonstrators and the Nazi regime's use of a site in Berlin for mass executions in 1935 and the Olympics in 1936. They asked if all future Olympic venues will be used by illiberal regimes in this way. [32] Activists used the international legs of the Olympic torch relay in London, Paris, and San Francisco, among other places, to protest Chinese human rights abuses and to embarrass China during its much-cherished time in the limelight. The torch was snuffed out by demonstrators, and some of the torch bearers were trampled in the process. In San Francisco, the crowds of demonstrators forced organizers to take detours and use decoy routes to finish a much-abbreviated course while transporting the torch on a bus. In Seoul, the torch runner's path was kept confidential in order to avoid the chaos of London and Paris, with only the start and end announced (there were still massive demonstrations at both spots). Jill Savitt, director of Olympic Dream for Darfur, an NGO created expressly for the purpose of leveraging the Games to pressure China, guaranteed that such protests would continue throughout the torch relay.[33] In a telling bit of irony, the only city in which the Olympic torch procession went as planned and in an orderly fashion, without demonstrators and "Free Tibet" signs, was in North Korea. The imagery being forced on the public was too much for Beijing to ignore: "Child labor. Forced abortions. Religious persecution. Jailed dissidents. Cultural clashes in Tibet and ethnic conflict in Africa. For China, the run-up to next summer's Olympics in Beijing is looking like a marathon through a human rights minefield."[34]

In perhaps the worst nightmare of Beijing organizers, athletes even became energized in expressing their outrage at Beijing's record. "Team Darfur," a group of some 250 athletes from 42 countries founded by a 2006 Turin gold medalist in speed skating, Joey Cheek (USA), organized for the purpose of using the Beijing Games to voice their concerns about China's policies in the western Sudan. These athletes included former Olympian gold medalists, and the group planned to wear red, green, and black sweatbands to show allegiance to the cause. Belgian steeplechaser Veerle Dejaeghere considered making political statements during the competition, such as wearing a "Free Tibet" t-shirt during the Games.[35] There were rumors that t-shirts imprinted with "Democracy Rocks" were being circulated among the Beijing athletes and that athletes were to shave their heads in silent but visible allegiance with the Tibetan and Buddhist monks in Lhasa and in Yangon. Concern over these and other athletes' disruptive behavior led some national Olympic committees to seek prior agreements from their athletes that they would not make political statements during the Games. When this met with public outrage, the U.S., British, and other national Olympic teams refrained from any contractual arrangements with athletes, instead organizing seminars on sportsmanship and complying with the spirit of the Olympic Charter, which specifies that athletes should not use the Games for purposes of political statements or racial discrimination. In support of "Rule 51" of the charter, the IOC also sent a letter to all of the national Olympic committees urging the discouragement of any political statements by the athletes, which clearly had limited impact.

With every issue that arose in which Chinese behavior could be implicated, the drumbeat of protest and pressure grew stronger. Olympic pressures on Beijing from around the world mounted after the Burmese military cracked down on peaceful protests by Buddhist monks against price hikes, killing thousands of demonstrators in September 2007. Virtually every internationally read newspaper and blog expressed outrage at China's inaction, deriding Beijing's cherished Games as the "Saffron Olympics" and declaring that "Burma's saffron-robed monks will join Darfur's refugees in haunting the Beijing Olympics—which are on their way to becoming a monument to an emerging superpower's immorality."[36] They implored Beijing to act in a case where the difference between good and evil was indisputable. As one columnist put it, "There's little to debate in young monks being gunned down, and everything to deplore. For a Buddhist, killing monks is like killing kin. Nine months from the Beijing Olympics, that's bad."[37] The columnist Fred Hiatt put it more bluntly: "Tell China that, as far as the United States is concerned, it can have its Olympic Games or it can have its regime in Burma. It can't have both."[38]

POLITICAL CHANGE, ALBEIT SELECTIVE AND TACTICAL?

As one might expect, Beijing strongly resisted any attempts to link the issues raised by NGO activists, politicians, and media celebrities with the Olympics. BOCOG spokespeople accused all who called for boycotts as afflicted with an anachronistic "Cold War" mentality that harks back to the 1980 Moscow and 1984 Los Angeles Games. Beijing advocated a purist view of sport, asserting that the Olympics should be played without politics. Organizers sought out sympathetic international voices to support the appeal for sport purism, including former Olympians, IOC members, and current and former heads of state, such as President George H. W. Bush. Standing next to former foreign minister Li Zhaoxing at an annual banquet dinner on U.S.-China relations in Washington, D.C., in October 2007, Bush stated that he was going to the Olympics and was not going to keep a scorecard on anything except sports.

Beijing did effect changes to both its human rights policy and its policies in Sudan and Burma in response to all the pressure, however. One would hardly consider these changes to constitute the type of watershed political transformations that gripped Korea in 1988. On the contrary, the changes were very calculated on the part of Beijing to gain maximum publicity without allowing fundamental change.

Regarding human rights, China adopted a calculated but unspoken strategy that focused on selective liberalization in certain cases or on issues that Beijing knew would garner international attention. But in other cases, particularly with regard to domestic human rights and activists, the regime continued to maintain draconian control and oversight. In the run-up to the Games, for example, Beijing made a pledge to the IOC that it would expand individual freedoms in the country. In March 2004, the Tenth National People's Congress adopted an amendment to the constitution stipulating that the state will respect and safeguard human rights. Chinese described this as a major milestone in China's development of democratic constitutional-ism, marking the first time the concept of human rights was codified in the constitution. [39] On January 1, 2007, the PRC relaxed restrictions on the foreign press. The government allowed foreign reporters to travel around the country for interviews without requiring prior permission. Given that China has detained more reporters than any other country in the world and has blocked Web sites and television and radio broadcasts, this was a posi-tive step. Beijing knew it would garner international attention and might even win them some positive press coverage.[40]

China also made token concessions on some other high-profile human rights cases. On September 15, 2007, the Chinese released Zhao Yan, a forty-five-year-old Chinese research assistant for the *New York Times* who was de-tained for three years on charges of fraud and disclosing state secrets linked to an article about the inner workings of the top leadership in China. A Beijing court convicted him of fraud in June 2006 without permitting him the right to cross-examine state witnesses. The case drew international at-tention and quickly assumed a high profile when President George W. Bush and Secretary of State Condoleezza Rice raised it with President Hu Jin-tao.[41] The same month, China released an American citizen, Steve Kim, who had been detained for four years for working through Christian churches in New York City to provide food and shelter to North Korean defectors hiding in China. In June 2007, Chinese authorities permitted the mother of a man killed in the Tiananmen Square massacre to publicly mark the an-niversary of his death on the square before television cameras.[42] In January 2008, with the unveiling of some of its new iconic Olympic facilities, Beijing organizers finally admitted that at least six migrant workers had died in the construction. In February 2008, Ching Cheong, a Hong Kong reporter for the Singapore *Straits Times*, was released after having been detained since 2005 on charges of spying for Taiwan.[43] That same month, Foreign Minister Yang Jeichi of the PRC announced Beijing's intention to restart a bilateral human rights dialogue (suspended since 2004) with the United States. As per Beijing's calculations, these cases gained a great deal of media attention, lending some credence to the view that the regime was liberalizing in the run-up to the Games.[44]

Beijing also reacted immediately to any media stories linking human rights abuses and the Olympics. In 2007, the NGO advocacy group Play Fair claimed that manufacturers of official Beijing Olympic merchandise were using child labor. The Chinese responded immediately; they claimed that an investigation found one company (Lekit Stationary in Dongguan) guilty of using eight underage children and promptly stripped the company of its

Olympic license. They also claimed that three other companies were stripped of their Olympic licenses for other labor violations.[45] In response to media reports that some 14,900 people were relocated since 2001 by the Olympic venue preparations, in some cases forcibly, BOCOG members hastily called a press briefing to state that all residents have been given compensation, vocational training, and replacement residences that were better than their previous homes.[46]

While any liberalization of China's human rights policies should be seen in a positive light, there should be no false sense of optimism that the political change wrought by the pressure of the Olympics in this particular area is long lasting. Beijing adopted a conscious strategy of selecting key, high-profile cases, usually involving foreigners, to demonstrate token liberalization. But even in these cases, the permanence of these changes is hardly assured. A ban on the printing of foreign newspapers and magazines in China was lifted in the run-up to the Games (these were previously available only to foreigners at hotels and certain other venues), but Liu Binjie, the minister of the General Administration of Press and Publication, made clear that this relaxation was only for the Olympics. The widely publicized lifting of restrictions against the foreign press, for example, was scheduled to end on October 18, 2008—one day after the conclusion of the last event of the Beijing Paralympics. Moreover, the Foreign Correspondents Club of China released a statement in August 2007 saying that 95 percent of foreign reporters still believe that even with the expanded freedoms, reporting standards in the PRC are far below the international norm.[47]

DOMESTIC CRACKDOWN

While China showed some leniency in particular internationally known human rights cases, they cracked down against all domestic dissent in the run-up to the Games. The "red line" in terms of Chinese leniency or accommodation of outside pressures was clear: When it came to domestic human rights cases or any separatist elements, Beijing would continue to deal with these swiftly, decisively, and with the subtlety of an iron fist. It was reported in the press in fall 2007 that the PRC Ministry for Public Security had issued an internal secret black list of individuals—including falun gong activists, domestic media, Xinjiang activists, and others who were considered "antagonistic elements"—to be banned from the Games.[48] To avoid publicity, officials increasingly used house arrest and detention without trial to silence dissidents, and Chinese intelligence operatives worked to prevent any organizations, foreign and domestic, from staging protests in Beijing.[49] Using the pretext of the Lunar New Year holidays about five months before the Games, the government instituted new inspections at train and bus stations, airports, and major roadways of all migrant populations traveling into Beijing in order to monitor and control the potential for domestic activists infiltrating the city. All Beijing residents were also required to apply for provisional residence permits. It was reported that Chinese authorities usurped the passports of all Uighurs in advance of the Olympics and restricted access to the Tibetan side of Mount Everest as part of a clampdown on any protests during the torch relay.[50] The government went after all Chinese activists who might be suspected of using the Games to embarrass Beijing. In July 2007, Yang Chunlin was arrested and tortured for gathering 10,000 signatures on a petition opposing the Olympics and demanding redress for citizens who had lost their land to make way for construction of Olympic facilities. He was sentenced to five years in prison in March 2008.[51] On December 27, 2007, Hu Jia, an advocate for AIDS victims and an active blogger on Chinese human rights violations, was detained by Chinese authorities and formally arrested for "inciting subversion." Liu Gengsong, a democracy activist and writer, was sentenced to four years in prison. Another victim of detention was Jiang Yanyong, a military surgeon who first revealed the scale of the SARS outbreak in 2003. Jiang was banned from leaving the country to accept a human rights award. Gao Zhisheng, a Chinese human rights lawyer, was arrested and tortured after writing an open letter to the U.S. Senate in October 2007 detailing Chinese human rights abuses. British minister Lord Mark Malloch Brown raised with Foreign Minister Yang Jeichi in August 2007 the case of Chen Guangcheng, a Chinese citizen who, his attorneys say, was also jailed in retaliation for his activism.[52] Just as the government temporarily reduced restrictions against foreign reporters, it implemented tighter restrictions on domestic reporters, restricting Web access and continuing to jam radiowaves.[53] According to Reporters Without Borders, Zhang Jianhong remained under arrest for his powerful writings about human rights abuses and press censorship. In the summer of 2007 there were also reports that more than one hundred foreign missionaries were expelled from the country to prevent Christian activity in Beijing, Xinjiang, Tibet, and Shandong ahead of the Olympics.[54] To reduce the number of house church activities in the run-up to the Games, the Beijing Municipal Public Security Bureau issued guidelines in October 2007 to landlords to deny rentals to "unregistered religious activities" and has arrested several Chinese citizens involved in organizing these informal prayer activities, according to Christian Web sites.[55]

Chinese authorities continue to show little patience for domestic human rights activists even as they selectively demonstrate flexibility on cases that gain notoriety in the international spotlight. Any separatist protests have been and will be put down ruthlessly, regardless of whether the regime needs to quash these acts of defiance in the public spotlight. Beijing's response to the demonstrations in Lhasa, Tibet, in the spring of 2008 provided clear evidence of Chinese decisiveness. Peaceful protests against Chinese rule grew violent as Chinese police closed down the city and rioters, expressing opposition to the influx of Chinese immigrants since 2006 (after a railroad was built to Lhasa) and the gradual usurping of Tibetan grasslands by the Chinese, destroyed many Chinese-owned shop fronts. Beijing accused the Dalai Lama of inciting these protests, and police cracked down ruthlessly—without any regard for world opinion. Jiang Xiaoyu, executive vice president of the BOCOG, declared unapologetically that the antigovernment riots in Lhasa and the government's stern response would not disrupt plans for the Games.

Human rights groups have adjusted to Chinese tactics, trying to draw international attention to the plight of persecuted Chinese activists, but a vicious circle characterized the Olympics—the more activists tried to leverage the Games to embarrass Beijing, the more Beijing cracked down as the protests threatened to disrupt the Games. This, in turn, whipped up virulent national ism among Chinese at home and among the expatriate communities around the world in reaction to attempts to ruin China's Olympic celebrations.

AFRICA POLICY: A METRIC OF CHANGE?

China has long held a policy of noninterference in the domestic affairs of African nations while maintaining robust energy and military relationships with many of the illiberal regimes in power there. It has provided fighter jets to Zimbabwe, helicopters to Angola and Mali, and light arms to Namibia and Sierra Leone. During the war between Ethiopia and Eritrean (1998–2000), China sold $1 billion worth of arms to both sides. In Sudan, China has gone against the climate of international opinion and been the largest supplier of arms, including munitions and antipersonnel mines, all of which the Khartoum regime has used against the Sudanese people. The West has maintained sanctions on Sudan since the 1990s for the government's use of Arab militias to prosecute genocide in Darfur. Yet China remains Sudan's top customer for oil, purchasing two-thirds of all Sudanese oil exports, and the PRC invests in the country's infrastructure as a base for broader petroleum interests in Africa. Beijing has supported trophy and construction projects in Sudan and Africa more generally, including stadiums, government ministry buildings, pipeline construction, supertanker terminals, and hydropower dams. When asked about China's human rights concerns and their relationship with Sudan, President Hu Jintao responded during a 2004 state visit to Gabon that Chinese aid is "free of political conditionality and serving the interests of Africa and China." A Chinese Trade Ministry official put PRC motives more bluntly: "We import from every oil source we can."[56]

China's resistance to any efforts at putting international pressure on the Sudanese regime was clear. China did not support U.N. Resolution 1556 in July 2004, which called for Sudan to disarm the militias, and it abstained from the final vote. Resolution 1564 in September 2004 considered imposing sanctions against Sudan for noncompliance with Resolution 1556. China threatened to veto this resolution then demanded its watering down and again refused to support it, abstaining in the end. In response to subsequent resolutions in 2005 by the U.N. that called for an embargo and referred the situation in Darfur to the International Criminal Court, Beijing again threatened vetoes. In each instance, China defended its actions by stating that Darfur was not China's responsibility and that the causes for Sudan's problems were not politics but poverty—in which case Chinese investments in the country were part of the solution, not part of the problem. Zhou Wenzhong, then deputy foreign minister and now the PRC's ambassador in Washington, summed up China's defense: "Business in business. We try to separate politics from business . . . the internal situation in the Sudan is an internal affair, and we are not in a position to impose upon them."[57]

As the pre-Olympics pressure mounted on Beijing, the regime quietly started to effect changes in Sudan policy to bring itself more in line with the international community. During the China-Africa summit in November 2006, Hu pressed President Omar al-Bashir of Sudan to accept a proposed hybrid U.N.–African Union peacekeeping force in the country. In February 2007, Hu traveled to Sudan and again pressed al-Bashir to comply with the hybrid PKO plan offered by the former U.N. secretary-general Kofi Annan. Upon his return, he sent a letter to the secretary-general expressing China's disappointment at Sudan's intransigence, and Wang Qun, the PRC ambassador to the U.N., conveyed China's support of a U.S.-sponsored resolution calling for sanctions on the Sudan Oil Company. In March 2007, China quietly removed Sudan from the list of countries with preferred trade status, effectively taking away government incentives for Chinese companies doing business in Sudan.[58] The following month Zhai Jun, an assistant minister for foreign affairs, traveled to the region to push again for acceptance of the peacekeeping force, and, in an extraordinary gesture for China, he visited three refugee camps and publicly called for the Sudanese government to show some "flexibility" with regard to the U.N. calls.[59] In the most explicit acknowledgment of the responsibility imputed to China for Sudan, Beijing appointed a special envoy for Darfur, Liu Guijin, in May 2007. Liu became the public face of China's efforts to explain to the world about the turn in China's policies. He made several trips to the region for the purpose of pressing the Khartoum regime to accept its obligations under the U.N. plan.

These actions on Beijing's part might appear small, but they are nonetheless evidence of a clear policy shift away from its principle of noninterference in the domestic affairs of African countries. Hu's trip to Sudan in February 2007 was reportedly marked by strong personal interventions to press for acceptance of the hybrid PKO plan, and was described by press coverage as a "quiet revolution in Chinese attitudes to sovereignty and noninterference, and position[ed] China as the protector of the repressed citizens of the region."[60] When the United Nations made the July 2007 decision to deploy a 26,000-strong peacekeeping operation to Sudan the following December, the largest such force ever used, it was widely accepted that China's efforts were critical to Sudan's acceptance of the plan. Even China's harshest critics acknowledged that their behind-the-scenes diplomacy with the Khartoum regime was decisive in gaining its consent to the Annan Plan. The U.S. special envoy for Darfur, Andrew Natsios, in congressional testimony openly credited Beijing's critical role and their use of considerable leverage to get U.N. peacekeepers into the country.[61] Beijing then participated for the first time in the African Union–U.N. force by contributing a 315-member peacekeeping unit of construction workers, medical units, and a force protection unit to be deployed in October 2007.[62] This commitment made China the first non-African country to contribute to the effort.

There is no question that the pressure in advance of the Olympics played a role in the shift in China's policy. Beijing had demonstrated little if no interest in the killings in Darfur, but as NGOs, entertainers, and athletes linked the situation to something the Chinese held very dear—their own prestige—the situation in Sudan grew in importance to Beijing. Mia Farrow's op-ed pieces and Spielberg's resignation as artistic advisor, in the words of one British official, "made China sit up and take notice. It certainly had the effect of concentrating minds in Beijing and elsewhere."[63] Chinese actions were clearly strategic, not motivated by some sense of moral outrage at the atrocities in Darfur, and were designed to relieve some of the pressure. The outcome, however, was one in which sport effected political change that might not otherwise have been possible. Extreme pressure at a vulnerable time for Beijing's quest for Olympic Gold was able to accomplish more in shaping Chinese behavior than years of diplomacy.

BURMA: ANOTHER METRIC OF CHANGE?

China's collusive relationship with the Burmese military junta garnered little attention among the general public before the Olympics. As Burma's largest trading partner (since 2005), leading investor, and diplomatic protector, Beijing enjoyed access to Burmese timber, gems, and other raw materials. It has sold $2 billion worth of arms to the country, including aircraft, patrol boats, tanks, missiles, antiaircraft guns, and armored personnel carriers and has enjoyed the use of naval bases along the Burmese coastline. Scores of Chinese multinationals operate in the country on large projects, including the construction of oil and gas pipelines stretching some 1,500 miles from Burma's Araksan coast to China's Yunnan province in order to facilitate China's oil and gas imports from the Middle East, Africa, and South America. Beijing consistently opposed any attempts by the United States or other countries to bring the issue of human rights in Burma to the U.N. Security Council.

After the Burmese junta's September 2007 crackdown on dissent, China was caught in a storm of public-opinion pressure from all over the world to stop the bloodshed in Burma. Beijing initially defended its inaction based on its principle of noninterference in the domestic affairs of other countries. The PRC also sought to stop any attempts to link Burma with the Olympics. In a hastily arranged press conference (on a Chinese national holiday, no less) in Washington, the Chinese embassy spokesman Wang Baodang claimed that it was totally irresponsible to make such linkages and that the Olympics should not be politicized. The PRC blocked a U.N. Security Council resolution condemning the Burmese regime's actions. Liu Jianchao, a PRC foreign ministry spokesperson, rationalized Beijing's position, saying, "What happens in Myanmar, in essence, is an internal matter of itself."[64]

As the pressure mounted and the Burma issue shaped up to become another rallying cry for those seeking to embarrass Beijing at the Olympics, however, the Chinese started to make quiet changes in the policy. PRC foreign ministry officials grew concerned that blame for the situation in Burma would be pinned on China and would tarnish the Olympics when there were other colluding parties (such as Japan and India) that could be the focus of international opprobrium. In June 2007, Beijing hosted two days of talks between representatives of the Burmese junta and Deputy Assistant Secretary of State Eric John of the United States to discuss relaxing house arrest for Nobel Peace Prize laureate Aung San Suu Kyi, leader of the Burmese democratic opposition. PRC foreign ministry and party officials began making guarded statements about the need to restore internal stability in the country. In the aftermath of the military crackdown, State Councilor Tang Jiaxuan of the PRC pressed Foreign Minister U Nyan Win of Burma to restore stability and, more significantly, told him to "push forward a *democracy* process that [is] appropriate for the country" (emphasis added).[65] News reports from the region surmised that Chinese officials were working behind the scenes to persuade the regime to reduce the use of violent force against unarmed demonstrators.[66] In the most marked sign of change, Beijing dropped its longstanding position and did not oppose the October 18, 2007, U.N. Security Council resolution condemning Yangon for the crackdown.

Some of the biggest shifts in China's policy were not readily evident to the public. While Beijing publicly stated that pressure would not work to stem the bloodshed, Chinese arms sales to the Burmese regime decreased in the months after the September crackdown. China also played an important role in the first effort to get U.N. representation on the ground in the aftermath of the crackdown. The United Nations initially could not get the Burmese regime's consent to send the U.N. special envoy, Ibrahim Gambari, into the country to survey the situation. After numerous attempts, Secretary-General Ban Ki Moon asked for U.S. assistance. State Department and White House officials made direct contact with their Chinese counterparts and demanded that China pressure Burma to allow the United Nations into the country. Within a couple days, China reported that Gambari would be allowed into Burma. Moreover, in another sign of Chinese assistance, Gambari was escorted around the country by the Chinese ambassador to Yangon.[67]

BEIJING'S SPORTING CHANGE

As in the case of Sudan, China's policy in Burma underwent subtle but important changes, bringing the PRC more in line with the norms of the international community. The point of enumerating these changes in Chinese policy toward Sudan and Burma is not to sing the praises of the regime in Beijing: far from it. The point is that sport has a way of prompting changes in longstanding policy that years of diplomacy are unable to achieve. These political changes by Beijing are not nearly of the scale we saw with the Seoul Olympics in 1988, and for every positive action that

Beijing took, the regime took equally negative actions against other groups (e.g., domestic activists and separatists). Moreover, the question of how long-lasting the changes in Darfur and Burma policy will be remains to be answered. However, faced with mounting pressure and the prospect of an Olympics haunted by demonstrations about human rights, Darfur, and Burma, the Chinese authorities relented as a means of relieving some of the pressure and trying to keep the international focus on sport and the message of China's greatness through the Games. Sport created more than just physical change in China.

7

THE SLIPPERY SLOPE OF CHANGE

Just after Beijing won its bid to host the 2008 Olympics, a U.S. government official with years of experience dealing with China predicted that China might have bitten off more than it could chew by hosting this event. She predicted that the Chinese leadership would find itself in the glare of the international spotlight; that thousands of journalists from around the world would be scrutinizing all aspects of life in China, including human rights practices; that Chinese leaders would not be able to hide from this scrutiny; and that if they did so, China would sacrifice a historic opportunity to bolster its reputation and place in the world.[1]

These were prophetic words; they amplify the connections between sport and politics that constitute the themes of this book. The 2008 Beijing Olympics was arguably the most important event for China since the 1949 revolution in terms of its identity, diplomacy, and development. Beijing sought to use the Games as a diplomatic tool to reach out to the world and to bolster China's status as a great power. In this book, I have shown how sport is a prism through which national identity and images are refracted. For the Chinese, the Olympics became a means to create a new identity and narrative for a China that is no longer the sick man of Asia. The Olympics showed how China is now a powerful and prosperous nation steeped in an ancient and great civilization. The ultramodern Bird's Nest and Water Cube stand in tandem with the Great Wall. The Chinese astronaut carried the Beijing Olympic banner on the country's first orbital mission. The Chinese Communist Party found it important to convey these messages of China's blend of modernity, tradition, and nationalism to a domestic audience as the Party continues its struggle for legitimacy. For the rest of the world, the images of the iconic Olympic complexes and the extravagant opening ceremonies were meant to wash away images of the brutality of Tiananmen Square and provide something else by which to remember Beijing.

But in the run-up to the Games and during their prosecution, groups mobilized to ensure that not one bedazzled spectator would lose sight of the human rights abuses and irresponsible foreign policies of the Chinese regime. This chorus was an entire universe of voices—entertainers, politicians, students, athletes, and even Nobel laureates. Illiberal regimes that host the Olympics must face the catch-22: they seek the Games for the limelight, but they must pay the price in terms of public pressure for political change.

CHINESE PRIDE

The Chinese were undeniably determined to be proud of their Olympics. This was their moment in the sun, finally, after centuries of perceived exploitation by the West and Japan. Olympic organizers ignored the cacophonous protests, focusing instead on hosting a great Olympiad as the backdrop to China's gold-medal performances. Just as the Chinese gymnasts and swimmers had to hit their marks, China had to hit four key marks to demonstrate success: the highest medal tally; a well-organized two weeks of games; good air quality; and marginalized protests. The four marks for failure were the opposite: a poor showing in the medal count; logistics difficulties; bad air; massive protests. At any point in the Games or in the run-up to them when it looked as though failure might be possible in any of these areas, the Chinese authorities tried their best to hide that from the domestic audience even as foreign journalists broadcast the story around the world. Chinese newspapers chose not to bother themselves with giving major coverage to protests because the main story of the Games was about China's greatness (unlike in Western coverage). The Chinese strove to censor international broadcasts and blogs in order to keep the focus on sport and to rob protestors of the global stage they sought to use to embarrass Beijing. This led to a sometimes yawningly wide gap between domestic and international coverage of the Games. But this was not embarrassing at all for the Chinese. This was not limited to officialdom. Regular Chinese citizens, for the most part, were equally proud of their nation's hosting the world. They were not supportive of the demonstrations in Tibet or other displays during the Games. On the contrary, they took umbrage at the persistent abuse of great Olympic moments by the protestors to try to embarrass their country. Rather than dissent, there was a rally-around-the-flag effect among the Chinese. After the huge embarrassments to China at the Olympic torch processions in London, Paris, and San Francisco, the Chinese government encouraged its citizens abroad to come out to defend the country's honor. In Seoul, Tokyo, and Canberra, thousands of Chinese students, clad in patriotic red and yellow, came out to protect the torch from demonstrators. In Tokyo and Canberra, they outnumbered the demonstrators. While it was clear that the local embassy encouraged this outpouring of China pride by providing shirts and flags, there were also rumors that, in Tokyo at least, citizens were being paid by the government to "counterprotest."[2] As Korea's experiences in 1988 also showed, when a nation tries so hard to use the Olympics to demonstrate its arrival to the world, any elements that seek to disrupt this show feed the inherent insecurity that drives much of the Olympic energy. For this reason, Chinese complaints about unfair media coverage and critical commentary were not uncommon; many Chinese citizens saw them as yet more attempts by the outside world to keep China down.

The result was one of two reactions by the Chinese body politic. While the world saw both the glory and the gaffes of China during the Games, the Chinese people responded nationalistically. Negative events such as pro-

FIGURE 17. PARALYMPIC TORCHBEARER JIN JING SHIELDING THE OLYMPIC TORCH DURING DEMONSTRATIONS IN PARIS, APRIL 7, 2008

SOURCE: © YOAN VALAT / EPA

tests, or negative coverage of Chinese society, politics, and people by the international media, had a cohering effect on the Chinese, particularly on young people, who saw the negativity as yet another sign of the centuries-old effort by the outside world to keep China down. While the rest of the world saw images of protestors ostensibly standing up for the downtrodden in Tibet and jailed democracy and AIDS activists in China, during the Olympic torch procession in Paris, London, and San Francisco, the image deeply seared in the Chinese mind is that of a young Chinese female paralympic fencer, Jin Jing, being accosted in her wheelchair by pro-Tibet demonstrators in Paris as she pridefully clenched the Olympic torch in both arms and sought to complete her route as torchbearer.[3] Even in its moment of glory, the West was trying to prevent China from shedding its image as the sick man of Asia. In response to public criticism of China's handling of the demonstrations in Tibet and the attempts by NGO demonstrators to foil the Olympic torch relays in London, Paris, and San Francisco in April 2008, widespread protests broke out across China beginning in the spring 2008 at perceived Western media biases. Protestors rallied at branches of the French chain Carrefours calling for a boycott of its products because of alleged support of Tibetan independence. In a related event, the Chinese government made an unusually terse public statement against remarks made by the CNN commentator Jack Cafferty when he referred to Chinese products as "junk" and the leadership as "the same bunch of goons and thugs they've been for the last fifty years" and attacked the country for exporting unsafe products to the United States:

> We are shocked to hear the malicious attacks of CNN commentator Cafferty against the Chinese people and express our strong condemnation. Taking the advantage of the microphone in his hand, Cafferty vilified China and the Chinese people, seriously violated the ethics of journalism and human conscience. His arrogance, ignorance and hatred to the Chinese people have aroused indignation of the Chinese people at home and abroad, and will definitely be denounced by righteous people all over the world. We solemnly request CNN and Cafferty to take back the malicious remarks and apologize to all the Chinese people.[4]

Insulting as some cable news commentators can be, Cafferty's remarks were hardly worthy of a government-level response (think about what world media says about the United States on any given day), yet this level of anger and the protests throughout China, while not directly sponsored by the government, were clearly allowed to go unimpeded in Beijing, Qingdao, Wuhan, Hefei, Kunming, and Xian, among other cities, as a way to rally public sentiment against any separatism and against the attempts by outsiders to ruin Beijing's cherished Olympic ceremonies. After thousands of Chinese students studying in South Korea beat up on Korean NGO demonstrators during the Olympic torch relay in Seoul in April 2008, the foreign ministry was unapologetic in characterizing the incident as "righteous [Chinese] students" standing up to safeguard the dignity of the Olympic torch and the country's honor.[5] On the other hand, hitting any of the four positive marks during the Games further reinforced Chinese pride and their belief that their country was now strong and prosperous and offered a model of development to the world based on semiopen markets and political control in juxtaposition to the West.

SLIPPERY SLOPE

What are the implications of Chinese pride and nationalism for political change? Skeptics might argue that the types on display after the Games—the reactive "us-against-the world" nationalism and the active "prideful arrogance"—regardless of how misplaced they might be, augur poorly for more political change. Because of this nationalism, skeptics would argue against those who wrote about the potentialities of a fruitful dialogue between twenty-first-century China and twenty-first-century Olympism.[6] They would deny any elective affinity between the ideals of market capitalism and liberal democracy and reject the idea that the Olympics would be the catalyzing event that could bring the two into alignment.[7]

It became clear in 2008 that a political transformation on the scale of Korea's in 1988 was not possible. Although both regimes faced the same dilemma, the cases in other critical respects were very different. While both China and South Korea possessed late-developing Asian economies, rapid urbanization, and a burgeoning middle class, the CCP in China, despite its flaws, was infinitely more stable than the Chun Doo Hwan regime in the ROK. As I described earlier, Beijing sought to make tactical concessions in certain aspects of its human rights and foreign policies. These were designed to gain maximum international credit while minimizing any fundamental change. The tactical nature of these political changes were evident in the expiration of the liberties granted to foreign reporters and the detention of dissidents, which were timed to coincide with the end of the Olympics period. Meanwhile, Beijing continued to crack down ruthlessly on domestic activists and separatists. The Chinese did make noticeable and notable changes in policies toward Sudan and Burma. This was not because of a new found belief in justice and democracy but because the pre-Olympics pressure was worst on these issues. Critics would argue that these changes hardly constitute lasting political change in China. I seek not to praise the policies but only to make the point that however small the changes were, they would not have been possible if not for sport. Pressing China so visibly at such a vulnerable moment under the international spotlight arguably accomplished more in terms of cooperative Chinese policies in Africa than years of diplomacy and demarches had done.

Contrary to the skeptics, I hold out more hope for change in China beyond the tactical and temporary. All states, whether liberal or illiberal, are on their best behavior when they host the Olympics. Yet there is still in my view some hope that the changes in aspects of Beijing's foreign policy and human rights policy will be more than temporary. This is largely because change, of any kind, made so obviously under the glare of the Olympics spotlight, cannot be easily reversed without severe damage to the reputational capital and legitimacy that illiberal regimes like Beijing so dearly crave. Moreover, political change sets the regime on a slippery slope—once it occurs, it is not only difficult to reverse, but the expectations grow for even further change. In this sense, I believe the Olympics can set trends in society rather than merely reflecting it.

Some permanent change is inherent in the preparations for the Games. Although the Games saw their difficult moments regarding the environment and air quality, they created new infrastructure, new practices, and a new appreciation for the environment in China. Domestic advocates now have a multi-billion-dollar springboard (in the environmental cleanup preparations for the Games) from which to advance their agenda. The international community will also be able to encourage China toward more environmentally friendly policies, now that many of the start-up costs have been borne by the preparations for the Olympics.

China's policies in Africa are also likely to undergo permanent and more comprehensive change. Beijing's actions on Darfur are an example. When China took steps in response to the international outcry for action, they presumed that this would relieve the pressure. They went on a public relations campaign, trumpeting the steps they had taken to gain Khartoum's acceptance of the U.N. plan and gave training demonstrations for the international media of the 315-member engineering unit that they planned to contribute to the peacekeeping operation. They even drew attention to the fact the Sudanese government criticized Beijing for siding with those in favor of the Annan plan.

But what Beijing did not account for is that change begets demands for more change. When Beijing helped to get the Khartoum regime to accept the hybrid African Union–U.N. force and then contributed a small number personnel, it probably thought it was done. Far from it. Stephen Spielberg still resigned from his role as artistic advisor to the Games because, he said, China had not yet done enough to stop the bloodshed in Darfur. Other foreign directors hired by the BOCOG (Beijing Organizing Committee for the Olympic Games) to make promotional films were spurred by Spielberg's actions to reconsider their role. The British film director Daryl Goodrich made a short promotional film, *Belief*, that premiered at a red-carpet event in Beijing in February 2008 with Goodrich sitting uncomfortably amid starched Chinese party officials. Goodrich and his producer's uneasiness with their newfound role was clear: "I think that both of us acknowledge a bit of naivety now that we've been involved in the situation here, and been confronted with the kinds of questions we've had in the last few days."[8] The day after Spielberg's resignation, Archbishop Desmond Tutu warned that Chinese inaction could lead many more to boycott the Games. While he gave China credit for taking some action, the South African cleric's well-publicized remarks made clear the heightened expectations: "We believe that they could use *a great deal more of their leverage* to help to change the situation drastically" (emphasis added).[9] When the Khartoum regime slowed the timetable for allowing the hybrid peacekeeping force into the country, the international community looked to Beijing to exercise more leverage. PRC foreign ministry officials became extremely defensive, saying that China had done enough.

Why was the world asking Beijing to do more, Chinese officials asked? China's actions—which many judged to be a quiet but revolutionary move away from China's strict noninterference policies in Africa—only created expectations for further change. In spite of Chinese efforts, international pressure mounted on corporate sponsors of the Olympics to withdraw from the Games over Darfur. Chinese Olympic officials complained publicly: "If you respect the truth, you will see that China has been doing a lot towards the resolution of the Darfur issue."[10] Premier Wen Jiabao enumerated a long list of new Chinese efforts to establish peace in Darfur to Prime Minister Gordon Brown of the United Kingdom after Spielberg's resignation, emphasizing Beijing's role in the peace negotiations and its being the first non-African country to contribute to the peacekeeping contingent. Liu Guijin, China's special envoy for the Darfur region (a position created in direct response to the international pressure), before another planned trip to the region, maintained that China would not continue to be "blackmailed" in this manner.[11] Yet when he was in Sudan in February 2008, Liu was actively trying to persuade the

Khartoum government to accept the non-African U.N. peacekeeping troops and working to encourage competing rebel groups to enter into peace talks. This is a far cry from earlier Chinese statements that they would stick to their principle of nonintervention in Africa and would simply import oil. The fact that the public discussion has now moved to Chinese officials' citing what they have done in Darfur to deflect pressure is a sign of how much change has already taken place.

China now contends with the slippery slope of political change—every change it made under the Olympic spotlight brings heightened pressure for changes in other areas. During a February 2008 trip to Beijing by Secretary of State Condoleezza Rice of the United States, Foreign Minister Yang Jeichi announced that China agreed to restart a bilateral dialogue on human rights that had been suspended since 2004, when the United States had sponsored a resolution in the U.N. Human Rights Commission condemning China. Yang's action was designed as a response to international criticism that China was an unfit host for the Olympics because of rights abuses. Again, the Chinese action was tactical, designed to relieve pressure, but the cumulative effect of these actions add up to a changing Chinese foreign and domestic policy.

In another atypical Chinese action, rumors surfaced that Beijing was going to move some of its best diplomats from their normal posts to public relations during the Games, trying to manage the public message. These included He Yafei, who was slated to be China's chief representative at the Six Party Talks—arguably the most important multilateral diplomatic effort that China has been involved in. The fact that Beijing would shift its best resources to the Games is even further indication of how a sporting event of this nature causes even the most rigid regimes to break out of their old molds.[12]

In perhaps in the most telling change on Beijing's slippery slope, Xi Jinping, a rising star in the Communist Party and the likely successor to President Hu Jintao, was put in charge of Olympic preparations shortly after Spielberg announced his resignation as artistic advisor. Xi, in his new post, internalized all that was at stake for China's international standing during the Olympics—not unlike what Roh Tae woo experienced when he was head of Seoul's Olympic effort before becoming president and overseeing democratization in 1987. Like Roh, Xi had to face the catch-22 of political change and international prestige. This does not promise, by any means, the sweeping political liberalization that came to Korea in the aftermath of the Games. But it does provide the future leadership of Beijing with a very unique understanding of the pressures that sport can bring for change in illiberal systems.

The biggest variable affecting political change in China, however, is nationalism. The China emerging after the Olympics will be undeniably more prideful and nationalist. This nationalism, as I noted earlier, will have a proactive element growing out of China's performance in the Games and its newfound place as a major power in the international system. It will also be reactionary, fueled by perceived attempts by outsiders to spoil China's moment in the sun through their support of separatist movements and their desire to embarrass China during the Games. But for an illiberal regime, nationalism, even if it is intended to cohere the system, can be a very dangerous element of change. Chinese leaders may have stoked the fires of nationalism to legitimize their actions in Tibet and allowed for the "spontaneous" demonstrations to take place against CNN and foreign companies seen as part of the so-called Western conspiracy, but that energy could easily become directed against the government once the Games have passed. Indeed, the government, after encouraging these expressions of nationalism, also called for calm amind fear of the different directions in which the energy could be vented. This is a variable in the Chinese system that will not pass with the end of the Games in large part because it is a byproduct of them. For the Chinese Communist Party leadership seeking to legitimize its place in the eyes of a younger generation of capitalist-oriented Chinese, "Olympic pride" is clearly a double-edged sword.

While economic growth in China is fast, political change is slow. But some change, even Beijing's tactical measures, is better than no change at all—which would almost certainly have been the outcome had Beijing lost its bid to host the Olympics. The IOC's legal advisor Francois Carrard summed up the sentiment: "If the Games were not awarded to China, the situation would not have progressed. . . . The issue of human rights is not satisfactory in many countries around the world today, not only in China. . . . But I'm convinced that when we look at this with the perspective of history we will see that the Olympic Games will have been an opportunity for considerable progress."[13]

FINAL THOUGHTS

Admittedly, the argument for more permanent change in China is an optimistic one—perhaps too much so given the events that transpired during the Games. However, there is no denying that China is in a different place in terms of its identity, diplomacy, and politics after the 2008 Olympics. This basic fact underlines the larger message of how sport—a variable we normally do not think about in world affairs—is more than just a game. Whether it is soccer and the unification of Yemen, or Japan's importation of American baseball in the nineteenth century, sport shapes and reshapes how nations and their citizens think of themselves. Just as a ping-pong ball contributed to a breakthrough in relations between the two most important countries in Asia at the height of the Cold War, Asian countries like South Korea were able to use sport as a tool of diplomacy to break through Cold War barriers and establish diplomatic relations with China and the Soviet Union. Sport has transformed the physical space of cities that have hosted global events: just as today's Seoul grew out of the 1988 Olympics, tomorrow's Asian cities will all be greatly shaped by the events that they host. Indeed, sport is part of the growth and modernization paths of Asian nations. Sometimes, sport creates change in nations that goes beyond the physical to the political. In the case of South Korea, sport was a tremendously underestimated agent of political change. Though sport purists detest the dynamic, sport is not just a spectacle; it is a powerful political agent that generates internal and external pressures for change that are difficult to ignore. And if the most populous country in the world could not ignore these pressures, all future hosts of the Games will know that sport matters politically—far beyond the final score.

POSTSCRIPT

LONDON 2012 AND SOCHI 2014:
THE NEXT POTEMKIN VILLAGE?

What will be the link between sport and politics in the future? When London hosts the 2012 Summer Games or when Sochi, Russia, hosts the Winter Games two years later, what might we expect to see? On day seventeen of the Beijing Olympics, the Chinese breathed a huge sigh of relief. Exhausted but gleeful officials congratulated one another on a job well done. Though not without its share of embarrassing moments, the Beijing Games concluded as many Chinese had hoped. They portrayed China as a great power, in Hu Jintao's words now "open" to the world. Their athletes performed well, topping the gold medal count, personifying China's swift rise to the top of global prestige. The Games were, according to most accounts, beautifully hosted, and staged in about as grandiose a fashion as Olympic historians have ever witnessed.

Will politics and sport intersect in parallel fashion in 2012 or 2014? For London, the return of the Olympics will be used to celebrate the renewal of the city and to welcome the Games home to its European roots in a place where it had been hosted many times since 1896. While there is political significance to this British message, it will not rival the political stakes for Russia. The Sochi Winter Games will parallel Beijing in its significance for nation building and national identity. As then-president Vladmir Putin explained, the IOC's decision to award him the 2014 Games symbolized Russia's "return" to the international system as a major power. After the collapse of communism and decades of Russian economic malaise, defaulted debt, and other problems, the Sochi Games will become the platform from which to demonstrate a new Russia to the world, newly prosperous from energy resource revenues and more confident (and, some would argue, more aggressive) in international relations. Moscow will pour huge sums of money into creating the iconic Olympics facilities—its own versions of the Bird's Nest and the Water Cube—in this sleepy resort on the Black Sea to exemplify Russia's place at the top.

As was the case with the Beijing Games, political activists, NGOs, and other personalities will endeavor to use the Olympic spotlight to embarrass Russia and draw international attention to its deficient practices at home and abroad. Calls for boycotts will undoubtedly emerge from global citizens and from governments. People will coin a new phrases for the Games that will be meant to denigrate Moscow's foreign policy or its authoritarian turn in domestic politics.

However, will political activists who seek to use the Games to highlight Russia's deficient human rights practices find sport to be their biggest adversary, as some did in China in 2008? Despite all of the attention to protests in the run-up to the 2008 Beijing Games, once the Olympic torch was lit atop the Bird's Nest, the world was completely and totally captivated by the sports. Few if any athletes used the world stage to make political statements despite much speculation that some would. And stories about the detainment of applicants for China's designated "demonstration areas" were buried under news about Michael Phelps, Usain Bolt, Shawn Johnson, and the "Redeem Team." For the Chinese organizers, the purist love of sport eclipsed the attention to politics, much to their relief. But for the activists, the leverage of the Olympics was greatest in advance of the Games. Dissidents undeniably learned important lessons from the Beijing experience and will seek new ways to press the Russian leadership into the catch-22 dilemma of political reform faced by the Chinese in the run-up to the Games.

It is safe to say that London's Olympics in 2012 will not be nearly as spectacular as its predecessor. Eighty-six heads of state are unlikely to show up for the opening ceremonies. The opening ceremonies will be artful and chic but not nearly as majestic and gargantuan as those in Beijing.

This is not a bad thing.

What the London Games will have is an organic quality that was missing from the Beijing Games. In retrospect, the nagging question about the 2008 Games was whether they were the greatest games ever or just too perfect. The Games turned out not to be the "genocide Olympics" as pre-Games protestors termed the validation of a regime that treads over human rights, but perhaps they were the "Potemkin Olympics." The picture-perfect staging of a seventeen-day performance, down to the graphically enhanced opening ceremony fireworks over the Bird's Nest, or the dubbing of children's singing voices, left everyone mesmerized and marveling at the spectacle. But beneath this, some would argue, was an emptiness; an organic quality of the Olympic spirit was missing. The Olympic Green was beautiful, according to many accounts, but it was also deafeningly quiet and barren as access was restricted. Arenas were half-empty and then filled with "phony fans" (people who were bused in security screened) to ensure good camera shots of spectator enthusiasm. The village-like atmosphere of a global festival that was so evident in places like Atlanta in 1996, Barcelona in 1992, and Sydney in 2000 was strangely absent in Beijing. While London is likely to have its logistics difficulties (traffic will be a nightmare), the spirit of Olympism is sure to be present. A little less order and little more party is not necessarily bad.

For China, the biggest political story about the Olympics will continue to be written long after 2008: the extent to which China's authorities will meet the world's expectations, which they raised with the Games. The Olympics was China's announcement to the world that it is a global power. But as I have said, with this prestige come global responsibilities in foreign policy and in domestic human rights. The expectations of the international community as well as the Chinese people is that the Chinese authorities do better. Let's see if they can hit that mark—which would bring the country far more international acceptance than any Olympics could.

NOTES

1. PURISM VERSUS POLITICS

1. Lincoln Allison, "Sport and Politics," in *The Politics of Sports*, ed. Allison (Manchester: Manchester University Press, 1986), 7.
2. Peter Beck, "The Most Effective Means of Communication in the Modern World? British Sport and National Prestige," in *Sport and International Relations*, ed. Roger Levermore and Adrian Budd (London: Routledge, 2004), 80.
3. "An Athlete's Voice of Protest Could Become a Roar at Beijing Games," Associated Press, 17 February 2008.
4. Simon Lee, "Moving the Goalpost: The Governance and Political Economy of World Football," in *Sport and International Relations*, ed. Roger Levermore and Adrian Budd (London: Routledge, 2004), 112–28.
5. Paul Close, David Askew, and Xin Xu, *The Beijing Olympiad: The Political Economy of a Sporting Mega-Event* (London: Routledge, 2006), 19.
6. Edward Iwata, "U.S. Companies Carry a Touch for Olympics," *USA Today*, 14 November 2007.
7. Sarah Skidmore and Joe McDonald, "Sneaker Cos. Go for China's Olympic Gold," Associated Press, 3 October 2007.
8. Iwata, "U.S. Companies."
9. Close, Askew, and Xu, *The Beijing Olympiad*, 22.
10. IOC, "Fact Sheet: Olympic Truce" (February 2007), http://multimedia.olympic .org/pdf/en-report.839.pdf, accessed 1 April 2008.
11. Allen Guttmann, *From Ritual to Record: The Nature of Modern Sports* (New York: Columbia University Press, 1978); B. Peiser, "Western Origins of Sport in Ancient China," *The Sports Historian*, 16 May 1996; and Aaron Beacom, "A Changing Discourse? British Diplomacy and the Olympic Movement," in *Sport and International Relations*, ed. Roger Levermore and Adrian Budd (London: Routledge, 2004), 94.
12. Roger Levermore, "Sport's Role in Constructing the 'Inter-state' Worldview," in *Sport and International Relations*, ed. Roger Levermore and Adrian Budd (London: Routledge, 2004), 22–23.
13. Allison, "Sport and Politics," 14–15.

14. George Orwell, "The Sporting Spirit," in *The Penguin Essays of George Orwell* (New York: Penguin, 1994), 321; originally published in *Tribune*, 14 December 1945.

15. Interview with Japanese diplomats, Washington D.C., 9 May 2007; also see Frank Ching, "Removing the Thorn from Japan-China Ties," *Japan Times*, 19 September 2004.

16. John Nauright, *Sports, Cultures, and Identities in South Africa* (London: Leceister, 1997); and Trevor Richards, *Dancing on Our Bones: New Zealand, South Africa, Rugby, and Racism* (Wellington, N.Z.: Bridget Williams, 1999).

17. Christopher Hill, "Keeping Politics in Sport," *The World Today* 52, no. 7 (July 1996).

18. R. D. Mandell, *The Nazi Olympics* (New York: Macmillan, 1971).

19. "Munich Massacre Remembered," CBS News, http://www.cbsnews.com/stories/2002/09/05/world/main520865.shtml, accessed 2 November 2007.

20. Cited in Close, Askew, and Xu, *The Beijing Olympiad*, 55–56; also see Barrie Houlihan, *Sport and International Politics* (New York: Harvester Wheatsheaf, 1994), 2.

21. Kate Clark, "Soccer Stretches Taleban Rules," 12 August 2000; http://news.bbc.co.uk/2/hi/programmes/from_our_own_correspondent/876238.stm, accessed June 25, 2007.

22. James Riordan, *Sports, Politics, and Communism* (New York: Manchester University Press, 1991), 127.

23. James Riordan, "The Impact of Communism on Sport," in *The International Politics of Sport in the Twentieth Century*, ed. James Riordan and Arnd Kruger (London: Taylor and Francis, 1999), 57.

24. James Riordan, "Elite Sport Policy in East and West," in *The Politics of Sport*, ed. Lincoln Allison (Manchester 1986), 78.

25. Close, Askew and Xu, *The Beijing Olympiad*, 11.

26. Robert Jervis, "The Future of World Politics: Will It Resemble the Past?" *International Security* 16, no. 3 (Winter 1991–1992): 39–73, esp. 53; and Aaron Friedberg, "Ripe for Rivalry: Prospects for Peace in Multipolar Asia," *International Security* 18, no. 3 (Winter 1993–1994): 5–33, esp. 16.

27. James Larson and Park Heung-Soo, *Global Television and the Politics of the Seoul Olympics* (Boulder, Colo.: Westview Press, 1993), 158.

28. Larson and Heung-Soo, *Global Television*, 158.

29. "Chinese Footballers Fined as Japan Protest 'Dangerous' Play," Agence France Press, 22 February 2008.

30. Paul Close and David Askew, "Globalization and Football in East Asia," in *Football Goes East*, ed. Wolfren Manzenreiter and John Horne (New York: Routledge, 2004), 250.

31. Opening dinner remarks by George H. W. Bush at the Texas A&M University conference on U.S.-China Relations, October 24, 2007.

32. Aaron Beacom, "A Changing Discourse? British Diplomacy and the Olympic Movement," in *Sport and International Relations*, ed. Roger Levermore and Adrian Budd (London: Routledge, 2004), 95.

33. Close, Askew, and Xu, *The Beijing Olympiad*, 80–81.

34. Susan Brownell, *Beijing's Games: What the Olympics Means to China* (Lanham, Md.: Rowman and Littlefield, 2008), 8–9.

35. "IOC Member: Sports Should Not Be Mixed Up with Politics," Xinhua News Agency, 25 February 2008.

36. "Activists Warn China's Olympic PR Woes set to Deepen," Agence France Press, 15 February 2008.

2. THE ARGUMENT

1. Two of the better early looks at the topic are Lincoln Allison, "Sport and Politics," and Trevor Taylor, "Sport and International Relations," both in *The Politics of Sport*, ed. Lincoln Allison (Manchester: Manchester University Press, 1986).
2. Taylor, "Sport and International Relations," 28.
3. Roger Levermore and Adrian Budd, "Sport and International Relations: Continued Neglect?" in *Sport and International Relations: An Emerging Relationship*, ed. Levermore and Budd (London: Routledge, 2004), 9.
4. While not discounting the insightful work on sport of Levermore and Budd, their work does contain this rather daunting phrase; see Levermore and Budd, "Sports and International Relations," 8. Other works in this vein include, Paul Close, David Askew, and Xin Xu, *The Beijing Olympiad: The Political Economy of a Sporting Mega-Event* (London: Routledge, 2006), chapter 1; Close and Askew, "Globalisation and Football in East Asia," in *Football Goes East: Business, Culture, and the People's Game in China, Japan, and South Korea*, ed. Wolfram Manzenreiter and John Horne (London: Routledge, 2004); and J. Short, "Going for the Gold: Globalizing the Olympics, Localizing the Games," *Globalization and World Cities Research Bulletin* 10 (2003).
5. Roger Levermore, "Sport's Role in Constructing the Interstate Worldview," in *Sport and International Relations: An Emerging Relationship*, ed. Levermore and Adrian Budd (London: Routledge, 2004), 21.
6. Lincoln Allison and Terry Monnington, "Sport, Prestige, and International Relations," *Government and Opposition* (July 2002): 129–30.
7. Quoted in Jonathan Watts, "China Takes Tough Line on Olympics Protests," *Guardian*, 2 November 2007, http://www.guardian.co.uk/world/2007/nov/02/china.international, accessed 28 February 2008.
8. "2014 Winter Olympics: The Decision," Associated Press, 1 July 2007.
9. "Sochi Win Hailed as sign of Russia's Revival," Reuters, 5 July 2007.
10. "Pyeongchang Victory Would Awaken Asian Winter Sports Tiger," Agence France Press, 2 July 2 2007, http://fe15.news.spl.yahoo.com/s/afp/20070702, accessed 3 July 2007.
11. "Pyeongchang Win Would Add to Korean Peace, Roh Says," Reuters, 1 July 2007, http://sport.guardian.co.uk/breakingnews/feedstory, accessed 3 July 2007.
12. "North Korea's Support Boosts Pyeongchang's 2014 Bid," Gamesbid.com, 3 July 2007, http://www.gamesbid.com/cgi-bin/news, accessed 3 July 2007.

3. MORE THAN JUST NATIONAL PRIDE

1. John Hargreaves, "Globalisation: Sport, Nations, Nationalism," in *Power Games: A Critical Sociology of Sport*, ed. J. Sugden and A. Tomlinson (London: Routlege, 2002), 25–43.

2. Thomas Stevenson and Abdul Karim Alaug, "Football in Newly United Yemen," *Journal of Anthropological Research* 56, no. 4 (Winter 2000): 466.

3. "Korean Teams Cross Sticks, Not Swords at Asian Games," *New York Times*, 4 February 2003.

4. This dilemma surfaces largely with the fielding of athletes for team sports. Individual athletes are eligible to compete at sporting events for the Games based on criteria set by the IOC and international sporting federations. See Brian Bridges, "Olympic Clock Ticks for Unified Korean Team," *Asia Times*, 20 March 2008, http://www.atimes.com/atimes/Korea/JC20Dg01.htm, accessed 20 March 2008.

5. Personal Interview, ROK Unification Ministry official, Washington D.C., 9 July 2007.

6. "Korean Fans to Travel Safely – if Slowly – to Olympics," *Macau Daily Times*, 6 February 2008, http://www.macaudailytimes.com, accessed 6 February 2008.

7. Some believe the DPRK should not be accorded the equality and respect that comes through sport diplomacy. The *New Republic* offered the following observation on the joint Korean presence at the 2000 Games: "The joint march (in which some North Korean athletes wore pins bearing the visage of Kim Il Sung) didn't promote world peace; it promoted more the equality of states—the notion that there is no important distinction between a liberal democracy like South Korea and the primitive despotism to its north. North Korea shouldn't even have an Olympic team. . . . For the Olympics to help the Stalinists in Pyongyang—whose only deserved international exposure would be in front of a human rights tribunal—place propaganda above food is bad enough" ("Games Over," *New Republic*, 2 October 2000, 13).

8. Barrie Houlihan, *Sports and International Politics* (New York: Harvest, 1994), 191; and Susan Brownell, *Beijing's Games: What the Olympics Mean to China* (Lanham, Md.: Rowman and Littlefield, 2008), 129.

9. Houlihan, *Sports and International Politics*, 197–99; Robert Whiting, *You Gotta Have Wa* (New York: Vintage, 1990); and Robert Whiting, *The Meaning of Ichiro: The New Wave from Japan and the Transformation of Our National Pastime* (New York: Warner Books, 2004).

10. Houlihan, *Sports and International Politics*, 197–99.

11. "Promising 'Toilet Revolution,' New Worldwide Toilet Organization Launches in South Korea," Associated Press, 22 November 2007.

12. There was clearly a business rationale for the toilet campaign as well. The Koreans understood that becoming Asia's leader in this industry would stand them in good stead as Beijing prepared to host the 2008 Olympics and would probably go through the mother of all toilet revolutions.

13. An effort was made to get a tree from the president's ranch in Crawford, Texas, for the Australian ambassador, but we found that no tree in Texas could fare well in Washington given the climate differences.

14. It should be noted that in the 1998 IOC corruption scandal, it was revealed that the president of the Australian Olympic Committee offered 50,000 Australian dollars to the Kenyan and Ugandan members of the IOC on the eve of the final vote, although it is unclear whether this alleged bribe made the difference in the final IOC vote. See Brownell, *Beijing's Games*, 142.

15. Actual attendance at the Tokyo Games amounted to only 70,000.

16. Ian Buruma, *Inventing Japan: From Empire to Economic Miracle, 1853–1964* (London: Weidenfeld and Nicolson, 2003), ix; and William Horsley and Roger Buckley, *Nippon: New Superpower* (London: BBC Books, 1999), 72.

17. "Japanese Throwing off Cloak of Isolation," *New York Times*, 11 October 1964.

18. Personal interview with Japanese diplomat, Washington, D.C., 18 July 2007.

19. Rio Otomo, "Narratives, the Body, and the 1964 Tokyo Olympics," *Asian Studies Review* 31 (June 2007): 120.

20. Article 8 status for a country means it forgoes the right to restrict its imports for balance of payments purposes. See Hans Baerwald, "Japan: The Politics of Transition," *Asian Survey* 5, no. 1 (January 1965): 33–42; and Kazuhiko Togo, *Japan's Foreign Policy: The Quest for a Proactive Policy* (Brill, Leiden: Boston, 2005), 347.

21. Robert Trumbell, "City Gay, Excited with Week to Go," *New York Times*, 4 October 1964.

22. Trumbell, "City Gay."

23. James Larson and Park Heung-Soo, *Global Television and the Politics of the Seoul Olympics* (Boulder, Colo.: Westview Press, 1993), 16–17.

24. Sung-joo Han, "Seoul in 1988: A Revolution in the Making," *Asian Survey* 29, no. 1 (January 1989): 34.

25. Don Obderforfer, *The Two Koreas: A Contemporary History* (Reading, Mass.: Addison-Wesley, 1997), 180–81.

26. Ian Buruma, *The Missionary and the Libertine* (New York: Random House, 2000), 166.

27. Buruma, *The Missionary and the Libertine*, 157.

28. See Jeffrey Wasserstrom, "Using History to Think About the Beijing Olympics: The Use and Abuse of the Seoul 1988 Analogy," *Harvard Journal of Press and Politics* 7, no. 1 (2002): 126–29.

29. Larson and Park, *Global Television and the Politics of the Seoul Olympics*, 158.

30. Oberdorfer, *The Two Koreas*, 182–83.

31. Oberdorfer, *The Two Koreas*, 185.

32. Qin Xiaoying, "Harmonious Confluence of ideas at Olympics," *China Daily*, 17 August 2007.

33. Brownell, *Beijing's Games*, p. 34.

34. Nick Mulvenney, "Pollution Intrudes on Beijing Countdown," Reuters, 8 August 2007.

35. Michael Collins, "China's Olympics," *Contemporary Review* (March 2002): 135.

36. "Playing Games with Human Rights," *Economist*, 18 September 1993, 37–38.

37. This section is based on the discussion in Brownell, *Beijing's Games*, chapter 6. The quote is from NBC sports commentator Bob Costas, cited on 166–67.

38. On this debate, see the interview transcript between Brownell and Bob Costas in Brownell, *Beijing's Games*, chapter 6.

39. Steve Ranger, "The Tech Behind the Beijing Olympics: The World's Largest Sports IT Contract, Running from Salt Lake City to London, Was Won by Atos Origin," *BusinessWeek*, 8 May 2008.

40. "Drive to Make Beijing Taxis Smoke-free," *China Daily*, http://www.chinadaily. com.cn/olympics/2007-09/21/content_6124300.htm, accessed 27 February 2008.

41. "Beijing Policy Work to Polish Image in Run-Up to Olympics," 30 December 2007 http://news.xinhuanet.com/english/2007-12/30, accessed December 31, 2007.

42. Sam Beattie, "Beijing Puts on Friendly Face for Olympics," VOA.com, January 30, 2008 http://www.voanews.com/english/archive/2008-01/2008-01-23, accessed 26 February 2008.

4. GREASING THE WHEELS OF DIPLOMACY

1. Karen Marcus, "Ping Pong Melts Cold War," 27 September 2007, U.S.-China Institute, University of Southern California, http://china.usc.edu/ShowArticle. aspx?articleID=814, accessed 25 October 2007.
2. Henry Kissinger's memoirs offer a slightly different story, although the thrust is similar. He recounts that Cowan on a day of rest in the competition got on a bus with Zhuang and other players to go to a pearl farm. The next day, Cowan gave Zhuang the tie-dyed t-shirt and Zhuang gave him the printed scene picture. Henry Kissinger, *White House Years* (Boston: Little, Brown, 1979), 708–10.
3. *Wall Street Journal*, 14 April 1971.
4. Paul Close, David Askew, and Xin Xu, *The Beijing Olympiad: The Political Economy of a Sporting Mega-Event* (London: Routledge, 2006), 155.
5. "The Ping Heard Round the World," *Time*, 26 April 1971.
6. In 1979 when the U.S. and China formally normalized relations, sport diplomacy was again employed, though in a less sensationalistic way. In remembrance of ping-pong diplomacy, the U.S. initiated "basketball diplomacy": exhibition games between the 1979 NBA champion Washington Bullets and the Chinese national team. The idea was that in the competition eight years earlier, ping-pong was China's game, so in a reciprocal contest in an American game, there would be no embarrassment to either side for losing. See Barrie Houlihan, *Sport and International Politics* (New York: Harvester, 1994), 10.
7. Richard Nixon, "Asia After Vietnam," *Foreign Affairs* 46, no. 1 (October 1967): 11–25.
8. Lifting the embargo allowed for trade on a limited basis, including tourism and nonstrategic goods. It abolished currency restrictions for businessmen going to China; allowed U.S. companies to provide fuel for ships and planes going to China; and authorized U.S. ships and planes to carry Chinese cargo and call at Chinese ports. See Robert Keatley, "US Announces Five More Steps to Spur Commerce with Red China," *Wall Street Journal*, 15 April 15, 1971.
9. Kissinger, *The White House Years*, 702.
10. James Mann, *About Face: A History of America's Curious Relationship with China, from Nixon to Clinton* (New York: Knopf, 1999), 27–29.
11. Mann, *About Face*, 29
12. Kissinger believes the Chinese choreographed these "impromptu" ping-pong meetings as a signal that then-secret messages being sent from Nixon's White House were being received. He believes the Chinese also wanted to invite U.S. team to China before Dobrynin came to Washington DC to announce an impending U.S.-Soviet summit. Kissinger, *White House Years*, pp. 708–710.
13. "The Ping Heard Round the World," *Time*, 26 April 1971.
14. Yasuhiro Izumikawa, "South Korea's Nordpolitik and the Efficacy of Asymmetric Positive Sanctions," *Korea Observer* 37, no. 4 (2006): 605–42.

15. Soviet opposition was even more important to overcome than Chinese opposition since achievement of South Korea's U.N. seat came in 1991, a year before Sino–South Korean normalization.

16. Izumikawa, "South Korea's Nordpolitik," 622–23.

17. Portions of this section are based on Victor Cha, "Engaging China: The View from Korea," in *Engaging China*, ed. Alastair Johnston and Robert Ross (New York: Routledge, 1999), 32–56.

18. Chae-jin Lee, *China and Korea* (Stanford, Calif.: Hoover Press, 1996), 145–46.

19. Lee, *China and Korea*, 112.

20. Izumikawa, "South Korea's Nordpolitik," 629.

21. Lee, *China and Korea*, 150.

22. Jae-hoon Shim, "Diplomatic Games: South Korea Uses Asian Sports to Boost China Ties," *Far Eastern Economic Review*, 4 October 1990.

23. *Los Angeles Times*, 21 September 1990, cited in Lee, *China and Korea*, 150.

24. Shim, "Diplomatic Games," 26.

25. Robert Trumbell, "Brundage Condemns Political Interference," *New York Times*, 8 October 1964.

26. I deal with the issue of boycotts of the 2008 Beijing Olympics in the next chapter.

27. "Beijing 2008: 72% of British Public say no to Beijing Olympic Games Boycott," *Guardian*, 21 February 2008, http://sport/guardian.co.uk/athletics/story, accessed 24 February 2008.

28. This section draws from Gerald Chan, "The 'Two-Chinas' Problem and the Olympic Formula," *Pacific Affairs* 58, no. 3 (Autumn 1985): 473–90, esp. 474; and from Susan Brownell, *Beijing's Games: What the Olympics Mean to China* (Lanham, Md.: Rowman and Littlefield, 2008), 131–44.

29. Cited in Brownell, *Beijing's Games*, 133–34.

30. Chan, "The 'Two-Chinas' Problem," 476.

31. Richard Espy, *The Politics of the Olympic Games* (Berkeley: University of California Press, 1979), 153–54; and Chan "The 'Two-Chinas' Problem," 478.

32. Chan, "The "Two-Chinas" Problem," 476; and Espy, *The Politics of the Olympic Games*. Also see Lord Killanin and John Rodda eds., *The Olympic Games, 1984* (London: Willow Books, 1983); and Jonathan Kolatch, *Sports, Politics, and Ideology in China* (New York: Jonathan David, 1972).

33. Charles Hutzler, "China Blames Taiwan for Scuttling Olympic Torch Relay through Taipei," Associated Press, 21 September 2007.

34. Ronan Farrow and Mia Farrow, "The Genocide Olympics," *Wall Street Journal*, 28 March 2007.

35. Fred Hiatt, "What We Owe the Burmese," *Washington Post*, 1 October 2007.

5. THE OLYMPIC FACELIFT

1. Weiming Wang and Eleni Heodoraki, "Mass Sport Policy Development in the Olympic City," *Journal of the Royal Society for the Promotion of Health* 127, no. 3 (May 2007): 126.

2. Greg Andranaovich, Matthew Burbank, and Charles Heying, "Olympic Cities: Lessons Learned from Mega-Event Politics," *Journal of Urban Affairs* 23, no. 2 (2001): 122.
3. Andranaovich, Burbank, and Heying, "Olympic Cities," 124.
4. Wang and Heodoraki, "Mass Sport Policy Development," 126.
5. Andranaovich, Burbank, and Heying, "Olympic Cities," 114.
6. Paul Close, David Askew, and Xin Xu, *The Beijing Olympiad: The Political Economy of a Sporting Mega-Event* (London: Routledge, 2006), 14.
7. See John Horne, "The 2002 Global Game of Football: The 2002 World Cup and Regional Development in Japan," *Third World Quarterly* 25, no. 7 (2004); J. Crompton, "Public Subsidies to Professional Team Sports in the USA," in *Sports in the City*, ed. Grattong and I. Henry (London: Routledge, 2001), 15–34; A. Jennings and C. Sambrook, *The Great Olympic Swindle* (London: Simon and Schuster, 2000); and H. Nogawa and T. Mamiya, "Building Mega Events: Critical Reflections on the 2002 Infrastructure," in *Japan, Korea, and the 2002 World Cup*, ed. John Horne and Wolfram Manzenreiter (London: Routledge, 2002), 177–94.
8. These figures are from Horne, "The 2002 Global Game of Football," 1240.
9. For example, Niigata Big Swan Stadium was built at a cost of $250 million, of which 82.5 percent of the cost of floating public bonds was borne by the prefectural government and 17.5 percent by the city. See Horne, "The 2002 Global Game of Football," 1241.
10. Close, Askew, and Xu, *The Beijing Olympiad*, 12.
11. Andranaovich, Burbank, and Heying, "Olympic Cities," 119.
12. Horne, "The 2002 Global Game of Football," 1241.
13. Emerson Chapin, "Tokyo All Set for Olympics," *New York Times*, 13 September 1964.
14. Chapin, "Tokyo All Set."
15. Norman Sklarewitz, "Tokyo Races to Finish Preparations by October 10 Opening," *Wall Street Journal*, 23 July 1964.
16. James Matray, *Japan's Emergence as a Global Power* (Westport, Conn.: Greenwood Press, 2001), 150.
17. Robert Trumbell, "Gay City, Excited with Week to Go," *New York Times*, 4 October 1964.
18. Much of the material below draws from James Larson and Park Heung-Soo, *Global Television and the Politics of the Seoul Olympics* (Boulder, Colo.: Westview, 1993), chap. 6, which is the best account in English.
19. David Armstrong, "China, Air Travel, and the 2008 Beijing Olympics," MSNBC, 30 January 2008, http://www.msnbc.msn.com/id/22803912/, accessed 26 February 2008.
20. Brownell, *Beijing's Games*, 81–83.
21. Rene Henry, "Beijing Cleaning the Air for the Olympic Games," HuntingtonNews.net, 31 August 2007 http://www.huntingtonnews.net/columns/070831-henry-columnsbeijing.html, accessed 31 August 2007.
22. Simon Scott Plummer, "Olympic Games in Beijing will Expose China," *Daily Telegraph*, 14 February 2008.
23. "Olympic Athletes Choose Japan for Training Ahead of Olympic Games," Associated Press, 7 February 2008; and *Chosun Ilbo*, 5 September 2007.

24. Laurie Garrett and Jane C. S. Long, "2008 Beijing Olympic Games: Cutting Through China's Smoke," *Los Angeles Times*, 7 October 2007.

25. "Key Polluters Closed to Ensure Air Quality for Beijing Olympics," *CSR Review*, http://www.chinacsr.com/2008/02/21/2110, accessed 21 February 2008.

26. Michael Collins, "China's Olympics," *Contemporary Review* (March 2002): 138–39.

27. Barbara Demick, "China Plans to Halt Rain for Olympics," *Los Angeles Times*, 31 January 2008.

28. Maureen Fan, "Beijing's Pollution Rises in 4-Day Restricted Driving," *Washington Post*, August 21, 2007.

29. Henry, "Beijing Cleaning the Air."

30. Fan, "Beijing's Pollution Rises."

31. Philip Hersh, "Airing Out (Cough, Wheeze) Beijing's Olympic," *Chicago Tribune*, 24 September 2007, http://newsblogs.chicagotribune.com/sports_globetrotting/2007/09/airing-out-coug.html, accessed 27 February 2008.

32. *New York Times* reporter Jim Yardley quoted by Medindia.com, http://www.medindia.net/news/, accessed 27 February 2008.

33. "Beijing Unveils New Olympics Aquatics Venue, Admits Workers' Deaths," Agence France Press, 28 January 2008.

34. Ariana Eunjung Cha, "In China, A Green Awakening," *Washington Post*, 6 October 2007.

35. "Better Environmental Practices Pushed For," *CSR Review*, http://www.chinacsr.com/2007/10/29/1799, accessed October 29, 2007.

36. Collins, "China's Olympics," 138–39.

37. "Chinese City Tries to Come back from Ecological Brink," *Washington Post*, 6 October 2007, quoting Council on Foreign Relations China expert Elizabeth Economy.

6 . CATCH-22

1. Bruce Cumings, "China Goes for the Gold," *The Nation*, 13 August 2001, 7.

2. Paul Close, David Askew, and Xin Xu, *The Beijing Olympiad: The Political Economy of a Sporting Mega-Event* (London: Routledge, 2006), 42

3. Allen Guttmann, *The Games Must Go On: Avery Brundage and the Olympic Movement* (New York: Columbia University Press, 1984), 27. Also see David R. Black and Shona Bezanson, "The Olympic Games, Human Rights and Democratization," *Third World Quarterly* 25, no. 7 (2004): 1245–46.

4. See Arnd Kruger, "The Unfinished Symphony: A History of the Olympic Games from Coubertin to Samaranch," in *The International Politics of Sport in the Twentieth Century*, ed. James Riordan and Arnd Kruger (London: Taylor and Francis, 1999), 3–27.

5. IOC, *Olympic Charter in Force*, July 7, 2007, http://multimedia.olympic.org/pdf/en_report_122.pdf, p. 11, accessed 1 April 2008.

6. James Larson and Park Heung-Soo, *Global Television and the Politics of the Seoul Olympics* (Boulder, Colo.: Westview, 1993), 200.

7. Sung-joo Han, "Seoul in 1988: A Revolution in the Making," *Asian Survey* 29, no. 1 (January 1989): 34; also see Alice Amsden, *Asia's Next Giant: South Korea and Late Industrialization* (New York: Oxford University Press, 1989), 237.

8. Nancy Cooper, "High Stakes Games: Are the Olympics at Risk?" *Newsweek* 29 June 1987, 32.

9. Larson and Park, *Global Television and the Politics of the Seoul Olympics*, 161.

10. Interview, former U.S. government official with personal knowledge of Roh's role, Washington, D.C., 12 July 2007.

11. Larson and Park, *Global Television and the Politics of the Soeul Olympics*, 161.

12. Mark Fineman, "Future of Olympics Called 'Great Factor" in Regime's New Policy," *Los Angeles Times*, 2 July 1987; and Sam Jameson, "US Reportedly Had Little Influence in South Korean Policy Turnabout," *Los Angeles Times*, 3 July 1987; and Black and Bezanson, "The Olympic Games, Human Rights, and Democratization," 1245–46.

13. "Excerpts from President Roh Tae Woo's First Press Conference, Seoul, April 21, 1988," and "Address by President Roh Tae Woo at the Opening of the 13th ROK National Assembly, Seoul, May 30, 1988," in *Source Materials, Korea and World Affairs* 12, no. 2 (Summer 1988): 428.

14. "Darfur Activists Push Spielberg to Pressure China," http://www.npr.org/templates /story/story.php?storyId=12204096, accessed 25 July 2007.

15. Tom Leonard, Richard Spencer, and Matthew Moore. "Beijing Olympics: Nobel Winners Accuse China Amid Boycott Calls," *Daily Telegraph*, 14 February 2008.

16. "Gere Urges Beijing Olympics Boycott", *Film Monday*, 3 September 2007.

17. Leonard, Spencer, and Moore, "Beijing Olympics."

18. Comment by Chinese official, Washington D.C., 22 October 2007.

19. Close, Askew, and Xu, *The Beijing Olympiad*, 170.

20. Human Rights Watch, "China: Issue Moratorium on Executions Before Olympics," http://hrw.org/english/docs/2007/10/07/china17046.htm.

21. Sun Ruoyu, a fifty-five-year old woman, lived in a two-story house in an area designated for Olympic construction. She did not respond to notices to telling her to abandon her home before the bulldozers arrived on August 6, 2007, to tear down her neighborhood in order to make way for the marathon course. Jim Yardley, "Little Building Defies Beijing's Olympic Ambitions," *New York Times*, 9 August 2007.

22. Patrick Goodenough, "Olympic Chief Plays Down Idea of Beijing Boycott," CNSnews. com, http://www.cnsnews.com/ViewForeignBureaus.asp?Page=/ForeignBureaus/ archive/200802/FOR20080222b.html, accessed 21 April 2008.

23. Ellen Bork, "While in Beijing . . . ," *Washington Post*, 7 January 2008.

24. "Pre-Olympic Games," *Washington Post*, 1 February 2008.

25. John Ruggie, "Globalization, the Global Compact, and Corporate Social Responsibility," *Transnational Associations* 52, no. 6 (2000): 291–94; and Black and Bezanson, "The Olympic Games, Human Rights and Democratization," 1256.

26. "Expressing the sense of the House of Representatives that the United States Government should take immediate steps to boycott the Summer Olympic Games in Beijing . . ." 110th Cong., 1st sess., H.R. 608 (2 August 2007); "Expressing the sense of the House of Representatives that the President should take immediate action to boycott the Summer Olympic Games in Beijing in August 2008 unless . . ." 110th Cong., 1st sess., H.R. 610 (3 August 2007); "Expressing the sense of the House of Representatives that the President should take immediate action to boycott the Summer Olympic Games of 2008 in Beijing, China," 110th Cong., 1st sess., H.R. 628 (4

August 2007). The text of the resolutions is available at http://thomas.loc.gov/home/gpoxmlc110/hr608_ih.xml and http://thomas.loc.gov/home/gpoxmlc110/hr628_ih.xml.

27. James Butty, "U.S. Congressman Calls for China Olympics Boycott," VOAnews.com, July 31, 2007, http://www.voanews.com/english/archive/2007-07/2007-07-31-voa11.cfm, accessed 15 August 2007

28. "British Minister Presses China on Human Rights, Darfur," Associated Press, 30 August 2007.

29. "Dutch Party Seeks Boycott of Olympics Opening," *Guardian*, 18 February 2008.

30. Cited in Stephen Wade, Chinese Media Ignores Olympic Protests," Associated Press, 25 March 2008.

31. "Press Arrests Fuel Fears Over Beijing Olympics," *Financial Times*, 7 August 2007.

32. David Clay Large, *Nazi Games: The Olympics of 1936* (New York: Norton, 2007).

33. "Activists Warn China's Olympic PR Woes Set to Deepen, " Agence France Press, 16 February 2008.

34. Justin Pritchard, "Olympics Highlight Human Rights in China," Associated Press, 5 July 2007.

35. "An Athlete's Voice of Protest Could Become a Roar at Beijing Games," Associated Press, 17 February 2008.

36. For example, see "The Saffron Olympics," *Washington Post*, 29 September 2007.

37. Roger Cohen, "Beijing May Hedge Its Burmese Bets," *International Herald Tribune*, 10 October 2007, http://www.iht.com/articles/2007/10/10/news/edcohen.php, accessed 7 November 2007.

38. Fred Hiatt, "What We Owe the Burmese," *Washington Post*, 1 October 2007.

39. Close, Askew, and Xu, *The Beijing Olympiad*, 109. In 2000 and 2001, China also signed the International Covenant on Economic, Social, and Cultural Rights and the U.N. Convention on Civil and Political Rights, which guarantee freedom of expression, fair trials, and protection against torture and arbitrary arrest (Michael Collins, "China's Olympics," *Contemporary Review* [March 2002]: 141).

40. Xiaogang Zhang, "The Market Versus the State: The Chinese Press Since Tiananmen," *Journal of International Affairs* 47 (1993): 196.

41. Maureen Fan, "Chinese Journalist Freed from Prison," *Washington Post*, 15 September 2007.

42. Pritchard, "Olympics Highlight Human Rights."

43. John Ruwitch, "Freed Journalist Calls for China Olympics Amnesty," *Reuters*, 21 February 2008.

44. In a similar vein, in September 1993 only ten days before the IOC was to decide on the venue for the 2000 Olympics between Beijing and Sydney, the Chinese released Wei Jingshing, a Chinese dissident who had been sentenced to fifteen years in prison ostensibly for criticizing Den Xiaoping. It was a transparent effort to win the IOC's favor. See "Playing Games with Human Rights," *Economist*, 18 September 1993, 37–38.

45. Pritchard, "Olympics Highlight Human Rights"; and "Olympics Ban for China Firm," BBC News, 31 July 2007, http://news.bbc.co.uk/2/hi/asia-pacific/6924116.stm, accessed 15 August 2007.

46. Goodenough, "Olympic Chief Plays Down Idea."

47. Foreign Correspondents Club of China, *FCCC 2007 Survey on Reporting Conditions, August 2007,* http://www.fccchina.org/when/FCCCSURVEYAUG2007.pdf, 1.

48. Anita Chang, "Report: China Issues Broad Olympic Ban," Associated Press 9 November 2007.

49. Arch Puddington, "China Games," *Commentary* 124, no. 4 (November 2007): 58.

50. Interview with Uighur expert, Washington, D.C., 17 February 2008.

51. China Arrests Activist Who Hit Out at Olympics," Agence France Press, 4 September 2007.

52. "British Minister Presses China on Human Rights, Darfur," Associated Press, 30 August 2007.

53. "Press Arrests Fuel Fears Over Beijing Olympics," *Financial Times,* 7 August 2007.

54. "Christian Group Says China Kicking Out Foreign Missionaries Ahead of Olympics," *Canadian Press,* 19 July 2007.

55. "China Police Impose New Restrictions On Religious Activities," *Christian Today,* 4 October 2007, http://www.christiantoday.com/article/china.police.impose.new .restrictions.on.religious.activities/13639.htm, accessed 27 February 2008.

56. Chris Alden, "China in Africa," *Survival* 47, no. 3 (Autumn 2005): 155. The only condition for Chinese aid to Africa is Taiwan. When Chad recognized Taiwan (after a $125 million loan from Taiwan), Beijing cut off diplomatic relations and assistance. China ended assistance to Liberia in the mid-1990s for similar reasons.

57. Quoted in Howard French, "China in Africa: All Trade and No Political Baggage," *New York Times,* 8 August 2004.

58. Bates Gill, Chin-Hao Huang, and J. Stephen Morrison, "Assessing China's Growing Influence in Africa," *China Security* (Summer 2007): 3–21.

59. Helene Cooper, "Darfur Conflict Collides with Olympics and China Yields," *New York Times,* 13 April 2007.

60. "Chinese President tells Sudan Counterpart to Give UN Bigger Role in Resolving Darfur Conflict," *International Herald Tribune,* 2 February 2007; Gill, Huang, and Morrison, "Assessing China's Growing Influence in Africa," 3–21; Andrew Small, "China, the Unlikely Human Rights Champion," *Policy Innovations,* German Marshall Fund, 14 February 2007.

61. Lydia Polgreen, "China, in New Role, Press Sudan on Darfur," *International Herald Tribune,* 23 February 2008; and "Sudan: Showcase for New Assertiveness," Inter Press Service, 21 September 2007.

62. "Chinese Troops Prepare for Mission to Darfur," *Washington Post,* 16 September 2007.

63. Lord Mark Malloch Brown, British minister for Africa, quoted in Nigel Morris, "Malloch-Brown to Pressure Chinese Envoy on Darfur," *Independent,* 18 February 2008.

64. "Foreign Ministry Spokesperson Liu Jianchao's Regular Press Conference on 13 November 2007," available at http://www.china-embassy.org/eng/fyrth/t380945 .htm, accessed 2 May 2008.

65. Cohen, "Beijing May Hedge Its Burmese Bets."

66. "China Puts Pressure on Burma Not to Use Force," BBC, 26 September 2007.

67. Information based on interviews, White House and State Department officials, Washington, D.C., 17 October 2007.

7. THE SLIPPERY SLOPE OF CHANGE

1. Laura D'Andrea Tyson, "China: Under the Glare of the Olympic Torch," *Business-Week*, 13 August 2001.
2. Interview, senior Japanese newspaper editor, Washington D.C., 8 May 2008.
3. James Millward, "China's Story: Putting the PR into the PRC," openDemocracy.net, 18 April 2008, http://www.opendemocracy.net/article/governments/how_china _should_rebrand_0, accessed 18 April 2008.
4. Embassy of the People's Republic of China in the United States of America, "Foreign Ministry Spokeswoman Jiang Wu's Remarks on CNN Commentator Cafferty's Insulting Remark," not dated, http://www.china-embassy.org/eng/fyrth/t425459 .htm, accessed 3 May 2008.
5. Embassy of the People's Republic of China in the United States of America, "Foreign Ministry Spokesperson Jiang Wu's Regular Press Conference on April 29, 2008," http://www.china-embassy.org/eng/fyrth/t430491.htm, accessed 5 May 2008.
6. Paul Close, David Askew, and Xin Xu, *The Beijing Olympiad: The Political Economy of a Sporting Mega-Event* (London: Routledge, 2006), 40; and Donald Black and Shona Bezanson, "The Olympic Games, Human Rights and Democratization: Lessons from Seoul and Implications for Beijing," *Third World Quarterly* 25, no. 7 (2004): 1245–61; and Stephen Sullivan, "Beijing Olympics: Opportunity or Mockery?" *Media Monitors Network*, http://usa.mediamonitors.net/headlines/beijing_ olympics_opportunity_or_mockery, 26 February 2004.
7. Close, Askew, and Xu, *The Beijing Olympiad*, 117–18.
8. Comments by producer Caroline Rowland and British film director Daryl Goodrich in James Reynolds, "UK Director's Olympic Role Unease," BBC News, 25 February 2008, http://news.bbc.co.uk/2/hi/asia-pacific/7262942.stm, accessed 25 February 2008.
9. "Now Archbishop Desmond Tutu Urges Boycott of Beijing Olympics Over China's Failure to Act in Darfur," *Daily Mail*, 14 February 2008.
10. Quote by Yuan Bin, Olympics official cited in *International Herald Tribune*, February 20, 2008 ("Beijing Olympic Officials Urge Darfur activists not to pressure sponsors").
11. Adrian Croft, "Spielberg Never Took on Beijing Olympic Role—China" Reuters, 21 February 2008
12. Personal interview, PRC official, Washington, D.C., 27 February 2008.
13. "IOC Backs China Human Rights Push," BBC News, 26 February 2008, http:// news.bbc.co.uk/sport2/hi/olympics/7265593.stm, accessed 28 February 2008.

INDEX

humiliation as concern: China, 129; South Korea, 126–28

Hungary, 8, 97

Hyundai, 95

identity, national, 2, 33–34, 37, 40, 96; China, 63–65; Tokyo Olympics and, 50–54. *See also* nationalism

image consultants, 36

imagination, national, 40

independence, assertion of, 42–45

Indonesia, 97, 99–100

International Criminal Court, 142

International Monetary Fund Article 8 countries, 53

International Olympic Committee (IOC), 6, 53; China-Taiwan relations and, 98–102; membership in, 23, 24, 25; opposes boycotts, 132; South Korea and, 126–27; two-China policy, 10; Winter Olympics 2014 decision, 38

international relations, 2; schools of thought, 30–32

International Rugby Board, 11

international sport federations, 31, 100

Iphistos of Elis, 7

Iran, 16, 35, 73, 97, 100

Iraq, 7, 9

Irish sport, 43–44

Israel, 16, 97

Jang Ung, 38

Japan: 2004 Asian Football Cup, 8, 25; baseball, 44–45; bid for 1988 Olympics, 56; bid to host 1960 Games, 51; coming-out idea refuted, 52, 54; as major power, 52–53; medals, 51, 67–69; negative stereotypes of, 34; ping-pong diplomacy and, 78; women's volleyball team, 51–52. *See also* Tokyo Olympics

Japan Airlines, 22

Japanese-Korean relations, 24–25

Jiang Xiaoyu, 141

Jiang Yanyong, 140

Jiang Zemin, 66, 95

Jin Jing, 150

John, Eric, 145

Jones, Quincy, 131, 133

journalists, 130; detainment of, in China, 132, 135, 138, 140; restrictions lifted, 138, 139

Juan Carlos I, 71

June Declaration (South Korea), 125, 127

Junichiro Koizumi, 24, 44

Kahn, Yahya, 79, 81

Keino, Kip, 29

Keita Suzuki, 26

Kennedy, Edward, 82

Khatami regime (Iran), 35, 73

Killanin, Lord Michael Morris, 100

Kim, Nelli, 89

Kim, Steve, 138

Kim Dae Jung, 42, 48, 59, 123, 125

Kim Il-sung, 60

Kim Jong-Il, 13

Kimpo airport (Seoul), 110

Kim Woo Chung, 88

Kissinger, Henry, 3, 35, 79, 82

Korean Air flight 007, 84, 89

Korean Air flight 858, 13, 60–61

Korea National Olympic Committee, 123

Korean War, 91

Koreas, 33–34, 38; Beijing Olympics negotiations, 42; inter-Korean relations, 59–60; Sydney Olympics and, 7

Korea Trade Promotion Association (KOTRA), 85

Kuhn, Bowie, 35

Lake Placid Olympics (1980), 102

Leach, Jim, 74

League of Nations, 28

Lebanon, 9

Lee, Ang, 133

Lewald, Theodor, 34

Lho Shin-yong, 56

liberalism, 121–22

Li Lanqing, 91

Liu Binjie, 139

Liu Gengsong, 140

Liu Guijin, 143, 153–54

Liu Qi, 135

Li Weifeng, 26